Children, Deafness, and Deaf Cultures in Popular Media

Susan Honeyman, Series Editor

Children, Deafness, and Deaf Cultures in Popular Media

Edited by

John Stephens and
Vivian Yenika-Agbaw

University Press of Mississippi / Jackson

The University Press of Mississippi is the scholarly publishing agency of
the Mississippi Institutions of Higher Learning: Alcorn State University,
Delta State University, Jackson State University, Mississippi State University,
Mississippi University for Women, Mississippi Valley State University,
University of Mississippi, and University of Southern Mississippi.

www.upress.state.ms.us

The University Press of Mississippi is a member
of the Association of University Presses.

Chapter 2 is reprinted from *Multicultural Perspectives* 4.4 (2002):
3–9 by permission of Cynthia Neese Bailes and Taylor & Francis Ltd.

Chapter 7 is reprinted by permission from Springer Nature: Springer Nature.
It originally appeared in *Children's Literature in Education*, "'We are Just as
Confused and Lost as She is': The Primacy of the Graphic Novel Form in
Exploring Conversations Around Deafness" by Sara Kersten, volume 49.3, 2018.

First printing 2023
∞

Library of Congress Cataloging-in-Publication Data

Names: Stephens, John, 1972– editor. | Yenika-Agbaw, Vivian S., editor.
Title: Children, deafness, and deaf cultures in popular media / edited by John
Stephens and Vivian Yenika-Agbaw.
Other titles: Children's Literature Association series.
Description: Jackson : University Press of Mississippi, 2023. | Series: Children's
Literature Association series | Includes bibliographical references and index.
Identifiers: LCCN 2022032891 (print) | LCCN 2022032892 (ebook) |
ISBN 9781496842046 (hardback) | ISBN 9781496842053 (trade paperback)|
ISBN 9781496842060 (epub) | ISBN 9781496842077 (epub) |
ISBN 9781496842084 (pdf) | ISBN 9781496842091 (pdf)
Subjects: LCSH: People with disabilities in literature. | Children with disabilities
in literature. | Deaf culture. | Popular culture. | Childre's literature.
Classification: LCC PN56.D553 C48 2023 (print) | LCC PN56.D553 (ebook) |
DDC 809/.892820872—dc23/eng/20220928
LC record available at https://lccn.loc.gov/2022032891
LC ebook record available at https://lccn.loc.gov/2022032892

British Library Cataloging-in-Publication Data available

Contents

PART 1: NARRATIVES OF D/DEAFNESS

PART 2: DEAF CULTURES IN VISUAL TEXTS

PART 3: DEAFNESS AND CULTURAL DIFFERENCE

Acknowledgments

Vivian Yenika-Agbaw, coeditor of this collection, died on September 30, 2021, following a brief illness. It is sad that she will not see the final version, although at the time of her death the manuscript was complete apart from minor corrections and revisions, so she had that satisfaction. I remain forever grateful to her for initiating this project, working with me to bring it to completion, and drafting its introduction.

Vivian had some personal acknowledgments she wished to make:

This project has a deep place in my heart, as I watch my mother cope with gradually losing hearing in one of her ears but neglect to tell her children about it. This loss is of great significance to her as a professional midwife, who took delight in listening to baby sounds in pregnant women's wombs. She never complains but simply lives her life to the fullest!

I want to thank the Children's Literature Association Diversity Committee that accepted my abstract on this topic and thus created a platform for me to tease out my initial ideas.

Together, we owe thanks to Sharon Pajka, of Gallaudet University, for sharing with us her blog in which she introduces so many of the creative works that have been published in the area. We are grateful to Cynthia Neese Bailes and Sara Kersten-Parrish for their warm assent to our request to reprint their work, thus enhancing our collection with two highly significant studies written from the perspective of deaf scholars. Cece Bell graciously gave permission for us to reproduce some panels from her unique, groundbreaking graphic novel *El Deafo*. Audiologist Lyndall Carter gave us generous advice when we really needed it, for which we are most grateful.

The intersections of children's literature and deafness have not been extensively or systematically researched, so the existing scholarship is quite scattered. The interlibrary loan unit of Pennsylvania State University and the interlibrary loan service of Macquarie University Library have both been fast and efficient in securing some of the resources needed for this project, for which we are very grateful. Finally, we wish to thank our contributors for the quality of their contributions, their attentiveness to our editorial suggestions, and their patience, as well as the editorial team at the University Press of Mississippi, who have ensured we maintained an impeccable standard. Special thanks are due to the anonymous reviewer of the manuscript, who made many apposite suggestions now implemented in the final version.

Deaf Characters and Deaf Cultures in Texts for Children

—John Stephens and Vivian Yenika-Agbaw

Historically, deafness has been regarded as a subcategory of disability, and in relation to children's literature and culture, scholarly writing has mostly fallen under that umbrella, although the nexus is often challenged. The general field of disability studies scholarship has had a long history in the social sciences, entered the humanities around forty years ago, but has had a shorter existence in children's literature. While portrayals of deafness and deaf characters in adult literature have been extensively studied,[1] only a handful of scholars have devoted attention to the depictions in children's or young adult literature. Landmark twenty-first-century events have been themed issues in *Disability Studies Quarterly* in 2004 (issue 24.1), in *ChLAQ* in 2013 (issue 38.3), and in *interjuli* in 2017, although only Brittain's article (in DSQ) focused on deafness. While considerable interest has been shown in children and deafness and children in Deaf Culture in creative literature and film, scholarship has been somewhat sporadic. A common focus of attention has been the problem of representation: is there an emphasis on the "otherness" of deaf characters? Is representation from a hearing perspective? Do deaf characters occupy a central role and function, or are they subordinated to hearing characters? Does representation explain specific characteristics of a character's deafness, and is this grounded in an informed understanding of deafness?

This book attempts to address these questions. But first, what do we understand "deafness" to mean? According to disability studies expert Douglas C. Baynton, "Deafness . . . refers to those who cannot understand speech through hearing alone, with or without amplification" (2015, 48). He notes further, however, that "within the deaf community . . . the term 'deaf,' as well as its signed equivalent, usually refers to people who identify culturally as deaf, and is sometimes capitalized ('Deaf') to distinguish the culture from the audiological condition" (48). This latter usage poses some problems, which we will return to, but remains current in North America and to some extent in the United Kingdom (Napier, 141). It is employed by several contributors to this collection. The practice emerged in the USA from various attempts to formulate a concept of Deaf Culture, encapsulated in Carol Padden and Tom Humphries's (1988) definition: "We use the lowercase deaf when referring to the audiological condition of not hearing, and the uppercase Deaf when referring to a particular group of deaf people who share a language—American Sign Language (ASL)—and a culture" (2). A component essential to the definition is communication through sign language, and this is also the case in the United Kingdom (British Sign Language) and in Australia, where definitions of Deaf culture pivot on the use of Auslan (Australian Sign Language). Narrative fictions discussed in the following chapters are often concerned with the status of a sign language and its relation to the d/Deafness distinction.

Both outsiders to Deaf Cultures and deaf communities, the coeditors of this volume have sought to situate contributions to our project within the current conversations in children's literature and deaf studies. Vivian, whose interest in disability studies was also personal as she grew up within a home that continued to grapple with her sister's disability and societal attitude toward persons with disability within that context, developed a more recent interest in d/Deafness when her mother lost hearing in one of her ears. What she found worrisome was the idea of her mother not wanting even her children to know that she had lost hearing in one ear. Why was she hiding this? So, she started researching d/Deaf communities and their representations in the West and in Africa, her continent of origin, and was appalled at the silence about the subject. A children's literature scholar, she then wondered about the representations of d/ Deaf children, cultures, and communities in stories that target youth.

We sent out a general "call for papers" through the children's literature list-servs, and we invited scholars who are affiliated with the deaf community in some capacity and those actively doing research in disability and/or deaf studies to be part of the project. Unfortunately, some with an active research agenda in deaf studies had other commitments and were not available to contribute. However, we have been able to include two excellent previously published essays that approach children's literature from Deaf/deaf perspectives. We were also fortunate to receive a personal narrative from an Australian deaf scholar in

which she traces her experiences growing up deaf and her passionate commit-
ment to research into the high incidence of hearing disability within Australian
Aboriginal communities.

Although we include essays in this collection that highlight children and
deafness as a strand of multiculturalism,[2] we are mindful that, like disability
studies, deaf studies is not simply "the new multicultural kid on the block"
(Davis, 502). It is cultural and more, for as Davis posits, "Even within the disability rights movement itself, notions about who falls into the category 'disabled'
are unclear [because] many deaf activists do not consider themselves disabled.
Rather, the Deaf think of themselves as a linguistic minority" (503).

Awareness of deafness and deaf studies varies from culture to culture within
the Global North and South. According to a World Health Organization report
(April 2021), over 5 percent of the world's population—or 466 million people—
has "disabling hearing loss," of which 34 million are children. The figures are
expected to double over the next thirty years.[3] The majority of people who are
deaf or hard of hearing live in low- and middle-income countries. An example
of the discrepancy between incidence of and awareness about deafness was
brought home to Vivian when she attended an international book fair in
Accra, Ghana. Of the no less than twenty book publishers represented at the
fair—several of whom published for children—none carried a book on deaf
African children. This gave Vivian pause as to why that was so, and she was
advised to visit the website of the Ghanaian National Association of the Deaf
(GNAD), a not-for-profit NGO (http://gnadgh.org/). Here it is possible to learn
about Ghanaian Sign Language and find other pertinent information about
the organization. We draw attention to this to explain one of the gaps in our
collection—the lack of analyses of books with deaf African child characters. In
contrast, Baynton speculates that "the phenomenon of deaf communities was
born of a particular moment in history that may be coming to an end" (51).
Multiple factors underlie a perceived shrinking of sign-language-using communities: the ever-increasing efficacy of hearing aids and their use at earlier
ages; the majority of deaf children no longer attending separate schools; and,
as genetic screening for identifiable heritable causes of deafness become more
prevalent, a sizable minority of hearing parents (at least 40 percent) considering
termination (Johnston, 365). Baynton particularly links a shrinking of sign-
language-using communities to an increase in cochlear implants, and there
has indeed been a substantial shift in attitude from the deep hostility toward
implants articulated by Harlen Lane and Benjamin Bahan in 1998, when they
argued that the effect of routine implantation would be the genocide of Deaf
world culture (305), and the observation by Kusters et al. that implants have
become normalized (4). However, Baynton's speculation is grounded in anecdotal

evidence from the Global North, where, he asserts, "among wealthier countries implantation rates now range from 50 to 90 percent of deaf children" (51).

While the number of people who use cochlear implants has increased steadily over the past thirty years, the worldwide number in 2017 was around 324,200 people, or less than 1 percent of 466 million. Deaf cultures may shrink in some areas of the Global North but will be with us for the foreseeable future.

Our primary aim in this collection is to explore some popular representations of deafness and Deaf Culture in children's texts to understand how authors, movie producers, and researchers envision the phenomenon across various modes, historical periods, regions of the world, and cultural settings. Deaf studies has been dominated by the United States, but it doesn't represent deafness universally. Shirley Shultz Myers and Jane F. Fernandes identify a specific point of origin, when "Deaf Studies in the United States was born out of a movement in the 1960s and 1970s when linguistic scholars were struggling to prove that American Sign Language (ASL) is a language and that Deaf people have a culture, a history and educational practices that are important to learn about" (30), but it is also important to consider how deaf studies is perceived in other regions of the world, as well as how it has matured through the decades.

Annelies Kusters, Maartje De Meulder, and Dai O'Brien, coeditors of a groundbreaking book, *Innovations in Deaf Studies: The Role of Deaf Scholars* (2017), draw attention to some major concerns they have uncovered within their field of study. In the introductory chapter, "Innovations in Deaf Studies: Critically Mapping the Field," they outline specific concerns that have consistently plagued the discipline, ranging from who is doing research in deaf studies to what methodologies are privileged. The coeditors explain why the field was dominated by hearing scholars and researchers, but assure readers that all chapters in their book were contributed by Deaf scholars, with contributions "concentrating in areas around Deaf people's ontologies (deaf ways of being) and epistemologies (deaf ways of knowing), communities, networks, ideologies, literature, histories, religion, language practices, political practices, and aspirations" (3). Throughout the chapter, they discuss the innovations in the field pointing out gaps where more work needs to be done. While they remark that deaf studies "is geospatially predominantly located in the Anglophone west, mostly the United States and United Kingdom, where English is used as the academic lingua franca" (4), we are extremely pleased that contributions to our edited collection span beyond these two dominant Western spaces to include analyses of children's books in Asia and Australia as well.

In this book, we accepted that contributors might use the d/Deaf distinction, even though Kusters, de Meulder, and O'Brien (2017) contend that this distinction creates a "*dichotomy* between deaf and Deaf people" (14) and thus fails to be inclusive. Exclusivity is not our aim. Rather, the d/Deaf dichotomy is an attempt to respect continuing practices within the community itself and within scholarship of the past three decades, even though Kusters et al. also remark that, "This dichotomy is, in fact, an oversimplification of what is an increasingly complex set of identities and language practices, and the multiple positionalities/multimodal language use shown is impossible to represent with a simplified binary" (14). We are aware of this trap of oversimplification and so also encouraged contributors to eschew language choices that essentialized deaf people and their cultures. The essays in this collection reflect this heightened sense of awareness as they tease out some of the tensions evident in the representations of the child characters in the various texts analyzed. In this way, we believe our book is timely and fills a gap in cultural studies that locates children at the center of the discourse on disability and particularly deafness, children, and culture. We embrace the shift in trends in deaf studies research for how they may enable us to deepen our understanding of deaf people and their cultures.

In working on this project, we demonstrate how deaf studies is impacting the field of children's literature through its pairing with other theoretical frameworks commonly associated with our discipline such as childhood studies, queer theory, and cognitive theory of the mind. The combination of these theories enabled contributors to effectively analyze the texts under discussion in order to understand how deafness and Deaf cultures are represented.

While our focus is on children's literature and other modalities, creative writers exist in the Deaf community whose adult works would be of interest to literary scholars regardless of the age group targeted. Of great interest are, for instance, John Lee Clark's story "The Vibrating Mouth" in Christopher Jon Heuer's *Tripping the Tale Fantastic: Weird Fiction by Deaf and Hard of Hearing Writers* (2017); Jennifer L. Nelson and Kristin Harmon's miscellany *Deaf American Prose, 1830–1930* (2013); and the prolific artist/theorist Raymond Luczak, who shifts the conversation to an intersectionality of Deafness, gayness, and artistic creation through such works as *Assembly Required: Notes from a Deaf Gay Life* (2009) and *The Last Deaf Club in America* (2018).

REPRESENTATIONS

Representations of deaf characters range from texts that continue to construct deaf children through a medical and thus a pathological perspective to those that leverage a balanced perspective that takes into consideration the complete child as a complex human being. For the most part, the narratives center the child characters' experiences regardless of how positive or negative that may be. Some texts accord deaf characters agency, and others simply objectify them, especially texts that reflect a particular historical or cultural context. The narratives are preoccupied with these characters' struggle to self-actualize, to belong within a particular community of interest, and to be recognized for the human beings they are regardless of their status as children who happen to be deaf. The characters are located within both domestic, private settings such as the home and public settings such as the school or the larger society, where they are more prone to encounter the prevailing, often negative, societal attitudes toward deaf people. Intersectionality is highlighted in some cases in order to render visible the multifaceted nature of a character's struggle. Chapters in some cases also broach tenets of disability studies theory including the medical and social models.

Contributors (some of whom are familiar with the sign language of the respective communities of the texts under study) explore, from a global perspective, various representations of deafness and Deaf Culture in children's texts, in which the phenomenon of deafness (and sometimes Deafness) is depicted within specific cultural settings. A surprising number of people (and an occasional nonsigning author) assume that the world has one universal sign language, so an obvious piece of information to take away from the collection of essays is that sign languages have evolved and are rooted within specific regions where the stories are set or events unfold. There are more than two hundred sign languages in the world, but in most of the texts discussed in this collection the sign language employed happens to be ASL. Within the population of American Deaf people who use ASL there is great diversity, but all have in common the use of some variety of ASL (Padden and Humphries 1988, 4). The complex history of many sign languages and the general absence of standardizing forces has led to a diversification of regional variants: Auslan, for example, has distinctive northern and southern dialects, and became another distinct language when introduced into Papua New Guinea. Stories that involve sign languages do not reflect such differences, however, and present sign language as a reified and singular entity.

Contributors to this collection have explored a wide range of texts and genres—picture books, graphic novels, young-adult fiction, and film (anime and live performance)—so they offer a symptomatic example of what has been produced. While the corpus of available primary texts is not huge, a collection such as this cannot be exhaustive, and there are many books and multimodal fictions of considerable interest that have not been included. Some of these could be gathered for specific studies: for example, it is well known that pets play complex roles in picture books and junior fiction, whether as helper-companions, metonyms, or narrators, and so the extensive representation of dogs within stories about deafness is itself a possible area for research. We think of such books as Ben M. Baglio, *Doggy Dare*; Mary L. Motley, Timy Sullivan, and Jenny Campbell, *Deafinitely Awesome: The Story of Acorn*; Gloria Roth Lowell, *Elana's Ears, or, How I Became the Best Big Sister in the World*; and Lynn Plourde, *Maxi's Secrets: (or, What You Can Learn from a Dog)*.

Multimodal texts, especially film and graphic novel, have a rich potential for representing visual elements of deaf worlds, and there is much scope for further work here. Taiwanese film director Fen-fen Cheng depicted characters communicating through sign for much of *Hear Me* (Taiwan 2009). Graphic novels have also exploited their blending of semiotic codes and narrative styles to produce simulacra of elements of deaf experience. In issue #14 of Alex de Campi and Carla Speed McNeil's serial *No Mercy*, the narrative wraps up the story strand about Anthony Uluski, a prominent character who is deaf. While the issue is not specifically about deafness, it thematizes it to a greater extent than in earlier issues. Only seven of its twenty-eight pages do not include some representation of deaf experience. Anthony is depicted signing, but because the hearing friends he is with do not sign, he implicitly speechreads throughout (he is oral). Speechreading is pointed to explicitly on several occasions, especially early in the story, so that readers are cued to the fact that Anthony is constantly speechreading. On most pages some speech bubbles are blank or are faded (often unevenly) so that they are barely legible, which indicates that Anthony does not fully pick up what is being said. In the same bubbles, words are often shown with phoneme alternatives, such as p/b or f/v—that is, readers are reminded or made aware that a speechreader cannot distinguish visually within voiced and voiceless pairs and so has to work to determine meaning from context. Similarly, issue #19 of the best-selling graphic series *Hawkeye*, by Matt Fraction and David Aja, includes blank and illegible speech bubbles but also includes ASL finger-spelling charts and cartoon figures such as are used to demonstrate ASL signs. Readers are thus given enough information to enable them to determine most of the meaning of signed communications within the narrative. As Oliver Sava remarks in a perceptive online discussion of issue #19, the creators found in the representation of deafness "an avenue for visual experimentation while making a bold statement about making your voice heard" (2014).

ORGANIZATION OF THE BOOK

The chapters are arranged in three parts with each discussing representations of d/Deafness within a particular genre of texts. Part 1, "Narratives of d/Deafness," analyzes forms of representations that appear mainly in print. Part 2, "Deaf Cultures in Visual Texts," examines representations that are constructed through multimodal systems that fuse various sign systems to convey perspectives on deaf characters and Deaf Cultures. Part 3, "Deafness and Cultural Difference," addresses the intersectional nature of what it means to be deaf and a child or youth within a sociocultural context, while teasing out the idea of deafness as a cultural phenomenon.

There are fifteen chapters including an introduction, plus a glossary of key words that are often encountered in deaf studies. We expect that readers new to the area will find the glossary useful in helping them become more familiar with such concepts and terms (and a few others of a technical nature) that are not explained whenever they appear. As aptly observed by Kusters et al. (2017), who have worked long in the field and are members of the deaf studies community, it is a field of studies that is still maturing and, as we remarked earlier, it has been an emerging concern for children's literature scholarship only within the past fifteen years. Through this project we ourselves found that we grew in our awareness of the field and its affordances and in particular in relation to children's literature.

Part 1 opens with Jessica Kirkness's beautifully written and moving analysis and sample of the process of writing a creative nonfiction narrative about the lives of her Deaf grandparents. She analyzes and demonstrates the potential of creative nonfiction to present writers with fresh approaches to their material and readers with new ways to see the world, but also laments that, "I cannot tell this story in Auslan. The language, with its own distinct grammar and syntax, has no written form." This chapter is followed by Deaf scholar Cynthia Neese Bailes's forceful discussion of how the representation of a deaf character in children's literature may be rooted in Hearing-ness as its dominant referent. She points to the dearth of, and need for, children's literature capable of rich multiple perspectives of children situated within Deaf cultural groups.

In chapter 3, Nerida Wayland explores how humor raises social awareness, generates empathy, and interrogates ableist, normative ideologies that marginalize, trivialize, or misrepresent deaf culture. In a range of multimodal texts that includes graphic novels, a movie, and young adult fiction, she demonstrates how the blend of the comedic mode with narrative and filmic strategies interrogates both principal ideologies that shape the context of deafness and the impact these have on representations of child subjectivity.

There is a long history in Western discourses of deafness functioning as a pejorative metaphor: deaf to reason, deaf to history, arguments that fall upon deaf ears, and so on (see Grigely 2006 for numerous examples). In chapter 4, Hélène Charderon focuses on a corpus of nineteenth-century French *bil-*

dungsromans and tales for children by Sophie de Ségur and examines the representations of adult characters who metaphorically "turn a deaf ear to children." As Hélène Charderon demonstrates, Ségur's stories for children seem to be populated by hearing characters who "turn a deaf ear" and *choose* not to hear, bringing the idea of deafness to the fore as a metaphorical means to undermine the authority of others or to deny a voice to others. A habit of linking disability with moral lack entails that metaphorical deafness becomes inextricably linked with transgression: adult characters who turn a deaf ear transgress the codes of their educating roles and society's morals in order to wield power, while child characters who ignore adult authority transgress the social norms regulating the power relations between child and adult. The positioning of deafness in relationship to culture, whether it be Deaf Culture or hearing society, is often an issue in fiction writing as it reflects or seeks to model social practice. The next two chapters explore fictive texts in which ideological and practical conflicts between oralism and sign language (manualism) are at the center. The historical context for such conflicts is the "Milan Conference" of 1880, at which educators of deaf children resolved that as a mode of education oralism was superior to manualism, and sign language should be banned. The ban was generally implemented in Europe and the United States and was not repudiated for a century (at the 15th International Congress, 1980), when it was affirmed that "all deaf children have the right to flexible communication in the mode or combination of modes which best meets their individual needs" (Brill 1984, 385). In chapter 5, John Stephens explores how d/Deaf characters are represented in two books of very different kinds; one that is narratively, epistemologically, and ideologically positioned within Deaf Culture and the other that is a coming-of-age novel in which the deaf protagonist has a hearing family and has been mainstream schooled. Piper communicates through a combination of modes—speech, residual hearing supported by hearing aids, speechreading (lip reading), and sign language— so the novel is able to canvass a wide range of deafness issues, including the challenge to depict a deaf first-person narrator.

The controversies that revolve around oral and sign language-based education are also examined in chapter 6, in which Helene Ehriander investigates how the discourses that define the protagonist's deafness in the novel *Hurt Go Happy* are constructed in ways that marginalize her in many contexts and define her in terms of her deafness. The main narrative arc draws upon successful attempts to teach a sign language to chimpanzees (and gorillas), but a key element for protagonist Joey Wilson is her eventually successful struggle to learn sign language in face of the hostility of her mother, who regards sign language as "stunted language," wishes to conceal the fact of Joey's deafness, and will therefore not even consider a hearing aid. *Hurt Go Happy* is a strong advocate of sign language.

Part 2 of the collection—"Deaf Cultures in Visual Texts"—consists of five chapters devoted to representations of deafness in multimodal texts. This section opens with Sara Kersten-Parrish's analysis of how the multimodality of a graphic novel—Cece Bell's *El Deafo*—expressively conveys experiences of deafness and the challenges involved in engaging with a hearing community. A deaf scholar herself, she sensitively explores the insights developed by her hearing students from reading and discussing *El Deafo*. Vivian Yenika-Agbaw (chapter 8) examines secret spaces and places where childhood and Deaf Cultures intersect in a graphic novel and a movie. She argues that in both cases the deaf child protagonist is constructed as a child flâneur and/or flâneuse who wanders through urban and rural spaces navigating and creating secret spaces that allow them to imagine a world of possibilities. Neither Selznick's unusual graphic novel *Wonderstruck* nor Krasinski's movie *A Quiet Place* adopts the direct-advocacy approach to deaf children and Deaf Culture discussed in some other chapters. Rather, each centers the deaf character as a child with a rebellious spirit—children who are not willing to accept the perceived "limitations" of deafness within their fictional society. Their characterization thus affords them with ample opportunities to self-actualize. Self-actualization is also important for Helen Kilpatrick's analysis (chapter 9) of the coming-of-age anime *A Silent Voice*. She argues that the movie challenges the implicit habit of portraying Deaf culture in modern Japanese film and television dramas from a dominant hearing perspective and demonstrates that fictional films can promote audience mental and affective activity and foster understanding about less visible social groups. Her discussion focuses on the links among issues of deafness, marginalization, and gender in a narrative about a romance between a deaf girl and a hearing boy and shows how narrative processes operate to counteract dominant perspectives and foster communicative skills between hard of hearing and hearing people.

Media representations of deafness are even more constrained in South Korea, where there are individual campaigners but no organized Deaf Culture. In chapter 10, Sung-Ae Lee considers four films that in different ways challenge conventional media representations of deafness grounded in unexamined assumptions about normality, the legitimacy of a patriarchal Confucian society that tolerates the abuse of women and the disabled, and a legal system that privileges the rich and powerful and habitually prevents the abused from finding justice. The standout film in this group is arguably *Dogani* (*The Crucible*), which, as a work of activism and advocacy, seized the public imagination and inspired legislation to protect deaf children growing up in institutions.

A thematically different topic is addressed in chapter 11 by Nina Benegas, Stuart Ching, and Jann Pataray-Ching, who discuss the state of Hawaiʻi Sign Language (HSL) noting that current revitalization efforts by linguists to prevent HSL's extinction have neglected to include local Hawaiʻi children's literature. The chapter traces this history of exclusion, analyzing how local Hawaiʻi children's literature might reconnect HSL to a local identity that translates especially well to a deaf audience. The authors also theorize how sign, picture, and cultural context when integrated become even more culturally and politically empowering.

In our final grouping—"Deafness and Cultural Difference"—chapters deal with a range of interactions in fiction between deaf characters and d/Deaf and hearing communities. The deaf community is a very diverse group, comprising several major subgroups. We mention some here that are pertinent to these chapters; for a more extensive account see Janet L. Pray and I. King Jordan (2010). First, people who identify with Deaf Culture and employ a sign language (for example, American Sign Language or British Sign Language) as their first or primary language and might be members of Deaf families. This is a cohesive group, but by no means the largest (Pray and Jordan, 168). Second is a prelingually deaf group who do not use a sign language and are not affiliated with a Deaf culture. Third, there are people who have become deaf or hard of hearing postlingually, who mainly communicate using speech, hearing aids, and/or speechreading. Chapter 12 opens this section with Josh Simpson's study of how narrative fictions depict the intersections of compulsory heterosexuality and compulsory able-bodiedness and their impact on characters who are both deaf and queer and thus prone to double marginalization. Given that social ideology is apt to assume that dominant identities—here heterosexuality and compulsory able-bodiedness—are not "identities" but represent the natural order of things, it seems easy for novels to render beauty, youth, and ability as compulsory and even as compensatory for perceived weakness and imperfections. Overcoming imperfection is also a theme in chapter 13, in which Lijun Bi and Xiangshu Fang examine disabilities, especially deafness, as an emerging theme in contemporary Chinese children's literature. They argue that the dominant trend in the emerging group of Chinese children's stories dealing with disabilities follows closely the traditional Confucian notion that literature is primarily informative and didactic, a tool serving social and moral purposes. In the case of the two stories analyzed, the assumption therefore is that children with disabilities should strive to improve themselves for the overall good of the society. In chapter 14 Angela Schill works within a multicultural framework to analyze depictions of Deaf Culture in coming-of-age young adult novels to illustrate deafness as a cultural phenomenon. The primary corpus of this chapter is two novels that are unusual in their intricate depiction of "strong

Deaf" characters, a term used within Deaf Culture to refer to people who fully embody the values embraced and advocated by the culture that constitute it as a distinct minority culture. As in other multicultural-themed works, the adolescent protagonists of these novels are depicted in their struggles to negotiate the complexities entailed in living in and between two cultures.

The collection concludes with a coda, a personal reflection from Corinne Walsh, who was identified as profoundly deaf at age four. As an eloquent counterpoint to the many fictive accounts of deaf experience elsewhere in this collection, Corinne maps her trajectory from early schooling through her recent research on hearing loss in a remote Australian Aboriginal community, for which she was awarded a doctoral degree in 2021. Her work is grounded in health and wellbeing, holistic healing, medical anthropology, and community-led development.

CONCLUDING THOUGHTS

This book is one of a few theoretical writings and empirical research that exist on deaf studies and children's texts. In selecting proposals for the chapters, we took a global perspective to demonstrate that while the phenomenon is global in nature and urgently warrants further research, the practices as depicted in the different texts are local. We are disappointed that we did not receive submissions from Africa or Latin America in order to further understand how creators of children's texts might imagine deaf child characters and people in story worlds set in those regions of the world.

In "Representations of Deaf Characters in Picturebooks," Debbie Golos and Annie Moses (2011) members of the Deaf community, conclude on the basis of a content analysis of twenty picturebooks published in the United States that depictions of deaf characters were purely from a medical perspective and not necessarily from a cultural perspective. They note further that while there is an "increase in the number of books incorporating minority characters . . . it did not parallel the percentage of minority individuals in the U.S population" (272). Chapters in our book reveal similar findings with several also indicating that portrayals have transcended these binary models of deafness. In this way, we believe that this book has succeeded in expanding the discourse on deafness, Deaf culture, and children's texts. Representations from a variety of texts across the globe give readers a sense of what progress has been made in the discipline as well.

A future project to sustain the dialogue may entail a partnership between children's literature and Deaf scholars to investigate new representations of deaf characters in texts produced or written by members of the deaf community, including deaf children. This book has made such a partnership possible and invites more conversation from varied perspectives, and of course, analysis using various methodologies that may help tease out the nuanced nature of identity, literary, and cultural representations in texts and their possible implications.

NOTES

1. Notable examples are Lennard J. Davis, *Enforcing Normalcy* (1995); Jennifer Esmail, *Reading Victorian Deafness* (2013); Christopher Krentz, *Writing Deafness* (2007); Cynthia Peters, *Deaf American Literature* (2013); and Rebecca Sanchez, *Deafening Modernism, Embodied Language and Visual Poetics in American Literature* (2015).

2. That is, in the US sense in which multiculturalism embraces "all minority groups, regardless of the particular demographic characteristics that define them" (Agosto, Hughes-Hassell, and Gilmore-Clough 2003, 260).

3. https://www.who.int/news-room/fact-sheets/detail/deafness-and-hearing-loss.

PART 1

Narratives of d/Deafness

CHAPTER 1

Writing the Hearing Line

Representing Childhood, Deafness, and Hearing through Creative Nonfiction

—Jessica Kirkness

DEAFNESS, INVISIBILITY, AND SCARCITY: RESPONDING TO THE NEED FOR (RE)PRESENTATION

In "Why Study People's Stories," Arthur Frank writes of the value of narrative in making particular lives visible. He contends that, "narratability means that events and lives are affirmed as being worth telling and thus worth living. Being narratable implies value and attributes reality" (111). In the light of Frank's statement, it is concerning and somewhat problematic that so few stories of deafness exist.

In a literary sense, authentic stories of deafness are rare, almost "exotic" entities that are limited in number and exist in relative obscurity from the reading public. When I began my research I could scarcely recall a single story of deafness in all the stories I had read and loved over the years. I had stumbled across one or two autobiographies that my grandparents had lying around the house; but in bookstores and libraries such texts were scarce and required lengthy searches to uncover.

The paucity of texts about deafness leads some, such as deaf memoirist and scholar Donna McDonald, to declare that "the lives of deaf people seem to be invisible to the general population, and . . . the field of literary studies is largely

silent about representations of deafness and deaf lives in all genres of literature" (*Hearsay*, 64). A study she undertook in 2011 found that even Gallaudet
University Press—the primary distributor of deaf studies work—had a catalog
of only nine memoirs in their "Deaf Lives Series." Certainly, this speaks to a
need for more stories to be told. Moreover, it is frequently acknowledged that
stories about deaf lives have typically fallen prey to a range of representational
pitfalls and tropes that act to reify hegemonic scripts and assumptions about
deafness that are at best problematic and at worst plainly offensive (Couser,
Signifying, 34; McDonald, "Not Silent," 464).

As the field of deaf studies helps us to understand, deafness as a discursive
construction is marked by suggestions of muteness, dumbness, infirmity, and
lack, resulting in the pathologizing of the deaf individual (Thoutenhoofd, 261;
Sengas and Monaghan, 70; Bauman, "Listening," 4). As a condition subjected to
the clinical gaze, deafness has been implicated in a long history of misguided
philanthropy and paternalism that manifests itself particularly in the practices
of deaf education and restrictions on (sign) language. Frequently deafness is
invoked as a condition to be pitied and has historically been conflated with
muteness or dumbness (Davis, 118). Since the nineteenth century, the pathological perspective of deafness has pervaded western thought, and as such,
conversations that swirl around the lexicon of deafness, disability, and deaf
lives continue to grapple with the notions of difference and heterogeneity. As
Brenda Jo Brueggemann writes, "The very subject of . . . deafness has almost
always been read socially, educationally, linguistically, culturally, philosophi-
cally as a trauma, both expected and repeated, both mitigated and amplified
in the history of 'reason'" (*Deaf Subjects*, 2).

How then, can we respond meaningfully to the task of representation without caricature or reliance upon pathological understandings of deafness that
pervade much existing literature?

This chapter reflects on my own practice in undertaking the task of writing
pieces of creative nonfiction/hybrid memoir about my relationship with my
Deaf grandparents as I was growing up. As a hearing researcher and writer, my
focus here has not been to make truth claims on behalf of my grandparents,
but rather to thematize and tease out the ways in which the hearing line—the
invisible boundary between the deaf and the hearing (Krentz, 2)—is implicated
and negotiated in our interactions. To this end, my writing experiments attempt
to realize the potential of creative nonfiction to animate a child's lived experience of hearing and deafness. It further suggests its value in giving legibility to
embodied, lived experiences of and with the Deaf world. As Christopher Krentz
points out, "Literature has the power not only to buttress and affirm the hearing
line, but also to offer opportunities for its effacement. . . . [Reading and writ-

ing] offer a meeting ground of sorts between deaf and hearing people, a place where differences may recede and binaries may be transcended" (Krentz, 16).

As I show in subsequent sections, much of this writing hinges on a dual sense of intimacy and distance, acknowledging the complexities and nuances of my relationship with my grandparents and the hearing line. As a hearing grandchild to two deaf adults, I am placed as a simultaneous insider and outsider, and as such I am writing from a type of "contact zone" in which I attempt to negotiate this often confounding "between space."

In attempting to articulate, as well as enact, the potential of creative nonfiction for representing d/Deaf lives, I hope to create a space in which to discuss deafness in a nonreductive and nonessentialist manner. Writing is discussed and employed in this chapter in the spirit of Frank's claims about narrative—as a powerful mechanism that attributes value and gives coherence to particular experiences. In recognizing that the stories we tell make particular lives visible, it is crucial that new ways of imagining and engaging with d/Deaf literature are sought out. In contributing an intimate account of deafness, I hope to make the lives and issues at stake matter. It is not my desire to produce or play into any totalizing narratives about deafness but rather to provide insights into the deaf/hearing divide *and* to locate this tension in the lives of real people. In doing so, I draw on deaf studies scholarship in order to provide a critical framework and guiding sensibility for my study. With due care and consideration, I hope to produce new literary work that resists the medical model and helps to give visibility to cultural understandings of deafness and d/Deaf lives.

LITERARY REPRESENTATIONS OF DEAFNESS

Writing about deafness, in various forms and across a range of literary genres, has historically been beset with a range of problems still to be negotiated by critics and writers alike. Since the 1980s, a range of deaf studies and literary disability studies scholars have entered into a critical discourse about the way that deafness is represented in both fictional and nonfictional literary texts. Despite an increasingly rich academic culture around the representation of deafness in western works of prose fiction, and more recently, children's literature, there is little work that offers creative practice as a methodology for alleviating or writing against the structures of phonocentrism and audism, defined by deaf studies scholar Tom Humphries as the "notion that one is superior based on one's ability to hear or behave in the manner of those who hear" (Humphries in Bauman, 4).

In fiction, deafness has been romanticized, demonized, and portrayed as innocence and even as a threatening savagery (Krentz, 17). Lennard Davis argues that deafness is rarely centrally represented in the novel (41). Literature that does include deaf characters is often problematic and relies heavily on essentialism or a paternalizing style of humor (Davis, 113, Golos and Moses, 270, Pajka West, 1). In nonfiction, deafness tends to be depicted as a subject of caricature, a melancholy condition, or a problem to be "overcome" (McDonald, *Hearsay*, 11). McDonald identifies the dominant tropes of deaf narratives to be those of grief, trauma, and triumphalism (*Hearsay*, 14). Couser too, highlights a key issue regarding access to diverse and counterdiscursive stories of deafness. The literary marketplace, he contends, can function to limit the dynamism and range of stories that discuss disability (and indeed deafness) through the imposition of hegemonic scripts upon disempowered groups (Couser, *Signifying*, 32). People with disabilities, he argues, may be granted access to the literary marketplace on the condition that their stories conform to preferred plots and rhetorical schemes—rhetorics that reinforce conventional attitudes and adhere to tropes of triumph, horror, spiritual compensation, and nostalgia (Couser, *Signifying*, 34).

In contemplating the ways that writing might serve to complicate or even interrupt the hegemony of the normal, Couser offers an invaluable insight that could be applicable to deaf narratives. He argues for the value of what he terms "auto/somatography" and the opportunity it brings for enhancing disability literacy in the body politic. He states,

> auto/somatography . . . can play a crucial role by providing the reading public with mediated access to lives that would otherwise remain opaque and exotic to them. In a culture such as ours, which is at once fixated on and dismissive of bodies, narratives of anomalous somatic conditions offer an important, if not unique, point of entry for inquiry into the responsibilities of contemporary citizenship. (*Signifying*, 15)

Fundamental to the project of deaf studies, and indeed, my own work, is the desire to challenge mainstream societal views of deaf people as disabled, in need of cure or patronage (Sutton-Spence and West, 422). Numerous deaf studies resources illuminate a desire within the Deaf community to overturn the dominant audist and phonocentric discourses that have failed to acknowledge deaf people as part of a linguistic and cultural minority (Davis, 109; Thoutenhoofd, 261; Sengas and Monaghan, 70; Bauman, 241; Sutton-Spence and West, 422). In my own writing, I want to reveal deafness as an experience rather than an absence, as a presence rather than a lack. I want to capture my grandparents' "condition" as a unique way of being and engaging with the world.

Both Donna McDonald and Brenda Jo Brueggemann draw attention to the need for deaf studies to begin to realize the productive and countercultural capacity of telling "deaf narratives." McDonald asserts the value of the role that literary works can play in enhancing literacy regarding deafness in the body politic. She states,

> We can learn about the diversity of deaf experiences and the nuances of deaf identity by reading memoirs of deaf people and novels with deaf characters. Whether they are written by hearing or deaf writers, by providing different perspectives on deafness, they have something useful to say, demonstrate and illustrate about deafness and deaf people. (89)

It is important to note the political value McDonald envisions for writing about deafness. The illustrative potential she articulates here offers a way of conceptualizing narratives that contribute to destabilizing existing rhetorical tropes. Brueggemann too is particularly optimistic about the potential offered in the telling of deaf stories that would have otherwise remained "silent" or unheard. She suggests a shift is upon us, altering our willingness—even in the academy—to consider hybrid texts. She states,

> Heteroglossia is here. . . . Our ability . . . to go actively seeking the both/and of "utterance," the double (or more) stance, and the nearly infinite possibilities of multilingual, multicultural, multisensorial experience, all these, I think, will make space for deaf writing and deaf autobiography. (318)

I see my own creative-writing work as a participant in what Brueggemann calls "heteroglossic space": where textual hybridity, multiple voices, styles of writing, and ways of engaging sensorially with the world are represented in their deserved fullness. Creative nonfiction texts, based on lived experience and personal narrative, can thus open up a space from which to discuss deafness and the hearing line more effectively.

My choice to employ creative nonfiction writing as a vehicle for such inquiry is fitting too, given its flexibility and resistance to simplistic truth telling (Alasuutari et al., 607). Margot Singer and Nicole Walker suggest the inherent fluidity of creative nonfiction, stating, "Creative nonfiction does not simply borrow elements from fiction and poetry, but bends and recombines them to make a hybrid that perpetually troubles and transcends generic bounds" (4). They argue that much creative nonfiction actively produces "unconventions." That is, it is a fundamentally innovative form, which presents writers with fresh approaches to their material and new ways for the reader to see the world (4).

Similarly, Whiteman and Phillips suggest that creative nonfiction can function as a "useful qualitative method for exploring empirical reality and pulling
together fragments from fieldwork" (296). Certainly, the unique empirical
knowledge(s) gleaned through spending time with others and rendered through
creative nonfiction can be of great value in exploring and representing the issues
and lives at stake. Of particular worth is the degree of intimacy enabled through
depicting the embodied quotidian "everydayness" of deafness, hearingness,
and the deaf/hearing divide within a specific life-world. In writing from and
about this "between" space—i.e., the hearing line—a greater understanding of
(and perhaps narrowing of) the interstitial space between deaf and hearing
people can be produced. As ethnographer Kirsten Hastrup writes, the emphasis
should be on dealing with the world between ourselves and the others (116–33).

A LITERARY EXPERIMENT: "OUR PLACE"

I turn now to discuss my own creative work as an offering that moves towards
the task of representing deafness without reducing it to pathological scripts
and tropes that pervade collective consciousness. I quote at length from my
work here, providing an excerpt that appeared in *Meanjin Quarterly: A Literary
Journal*, in 2018. I include this work not because I see it as an exemplary piece,
nor that it altogether avoids issues around depicting deafness, but because it is
the product of thinking through and responding to some of the issues raised in
critical scholarship on deafness and its manifestation of the page. As I discuss
in subsequent sections, there are a number of rhetorical strategies employed
in this excerpt in order to destabilize existing knowledge(s) of deafness and
d/Deaf lives, all of which will be explicated shortly. But first, the story.

Our Place

If I were to tell you our story in sign language—the story of my grandparents
and me—I'd begin with a single finger touching my chest. My hands would
form the signs for "grew up" and then "next door": a flattened palm rising from
my torso to eye level; followed by my index finger hooked over my thumb
and turned over at the wrist like a key in an ignition. I'd use the signs for "my
grandparents": a clenched fist over my heart, and the letter signs "G, M, F" to
represent "grand–mother-father." Then, placing two fingers over my right ear, I'd
use the sign for "Deaf" to refer to them, and to describe myself, I'd use "hearing":
a single digit moved from beside the ear to rest below the mouth. I'd stress the
closeness of our relationship by interlocking my index fingers in the sign that

doubles for "link" or "connection" depending on context. By puffing air from my lips, squinting my eyes slightly, and rocking my looped fingers back and forth, I'd place emphasis on the sign—the duration, direction, and intensity of its delivery giving tone and shape to the meaning made.

Like an opening montage to a film, I would set up the space before my body, carving a visual representation of the dual occupancy home where I lived beside Nanny and Grandpa for most of my life. With my hands poised as though ready to play a piano, I'd sculpt a diagram of our long, narrow house, showing its shared roof and the single wall that separated my place from theirs. By turning my hands with the thumbs facing upwards, I'd slice through the air, two-thirds of the way through the structure, to mark out the four-bedroom residence that belonged to my parents, my sister, my brother, and me. By repositioning my hands to the left and pointing to the remaining third, I'd show you the semi-detached granny flat where my grandparents live to this day.

In Auslan, or Australian Sign Language, stories unfold like moving pictures, with images sewn together in an art similar to cinematography.[1] Narratives are rendered through a sequence of different frames, shots, and angles conveyed by the signing body. A signer can zoom in or zoom out of aspects of the action by employing different visual and spatial tactics. Within seconds, a fluent signer might weave between a "birds-eye-view" perspective: giving topographical information about the place depicted, and then, through shifting the body, will become the character in the scene as they open a door, for example, or rifle through a filing cabinet. Much like a panning or tracking shot, movement functions in these frames by directing the viewer's attention. Particular types of movement can also indicate shifts in character and point of view: where the body inhabits and takes on a new set of idiosyncrasies including stance, gaze, and range of facial expressions.

But I cannot tell this story in Auslan. The language, with its own distinct grammar and syntax, has no written form. There is no accurate way to represent it on the page. In fact, it's only in recent years I've known how to sign some of its parts at all. I am not a native signer. English is my first language and dominant tongue.

Before we moved to the long, narrow house with the shared roof, my extended maternal family lived within walking distance from one another. If you look on a map you can draw a straight line that intersects each house: Nanny and Grandpa's place in the middle, Uncle Ray and Auntie Ruth to one side, and my Mum and Dad on the other. We got together every weekend for barbecues or curry nights, taking it in turns to host the gatherings. Sometimes I saw my cousins multiple times a week, when our grandparents would mind us while our parents went to work. We had our own set of toys in the playroom, with books and videos that were collected for our visits. The six of us kids regularly had sleepovers, cramming ourselves into the spare room where we screamed and squealed until the wee hours, unbeknownst to Nanny and Grandpa, who slept on soundly unless we made the mistake of turning a light on.

I was three when I first realised my grandparents were deaf. Before then, I'd sensed that they were somehow different from me, that there was a line that separated us. They didn't use the telephone; their doorbell had a flashing light and not a bell; and maybe Mum and Dad had told me that Nanny and Grandpa couldn't hear. But it was when I was three that I decided to experiment on my Grandma. She was stooped over the sink, washing the dishes. I stood behind her and screamed with all the force my little frame could muster. She didn't flinch. I howled, cried for help, thinking surely she'd respond to that. Nothing. In my indignation, my temper rose. I stomped on the ground, at which point Nanny turned around. "I hate you," I snarled, and watched as the color drained from her face. I knew then that she hadn't heard me, but she'd understood. Afterwards, when I found my grandmother sobbing in the bedroom, I patted her hands and stroked her back, like Mum would do for me when I was sad. "I'm sorry," I mouthed, making sure this time that she'd seen my lips.

As a child, I spent a lot of time in the company of Deaf people. Nanny and Grandpa's Deaf friends often dropped by for a chat and stayed for several hours. They spoiled and flattered me, pinched my cheeks affectionately. Whenever my grandparents held parties, I was drawn to the liveliness of signed conversations. Information was delivered with such verve and gusto, I wanted badly to be involved. But mostly, I was an observer. To me, Auslan looked operatic and grand. There was something artful, perhaps even musical about its prosody. It felt like an elaborate secret code that sometimes I could penetrate, but otherwise remained obscure and unknown. The adults signed so quickly, and my skills were limited. I'd soon reach that inevitable juncture, the point where I could no longer follow or contribute to discussions. Then, I would gaze at the crowd before me, mesmerized by the uniqueness of individual signing styles. Everyone had their own flair and panache, their signature tone and energy. There were those who signed with utilitarian brevity, some were slower and drawling, and then there were others who possessed a cascading gestural intonation, with a seamlessness to the flow of their prose. Looking on as they chatted, I'd hum quietly to myself, composing accompanying soundtracks to the motion pictures before me: tunes that rose and fell with the dynamics of their movements.

Other times I listened intently, enjoying the murmurs and sounds that punctuated Deaf interactions: the soft clicks and clacks of jaws, lips, and teeth.

I loved the raw, breathy notes of my grandparents' vocalizations: the expulsions of air, the throaty gurgles of excitement, and their raucous laughter that soared in pitch and volume. I liked to hear the swish of skin against skin as their hands brushed together in motion. Even the clunk of bone meeting bone, or the thump of a hand against a chest cavity felt to me like a kind of percussive refrain. When I was small, Nanny would often rock me to sleep while humming her own sort of lullaby. "Tee tee tee," she'd croon over and over on a single note. I'd doze off to the steady monotony of that repeated sound, and wake to the hushed, sibilant rasp of my grandfather's voice: the one he uses when he signs to my grandma. As I'd stir from my slumber, groggy and dazed on their couch, I'd see Grandpa's hands in rapid motion: a series of clipped "shhs" and "pahs" interspersed between his movements despite his efforts to be quiet.

Somewhere in the juncture between knowing and not knowing, in the space between these homes, and between Deaf and hearing cultures, I grew up.

RHETORICAL DEVICES: THE CHILD AS SYMBOL

In the excerpt above, much of the narrated material is focalized by my child-self, particularly in the latter half of the excerpt. From paragraph six onwards, the information given is seen through the eyes of the child as they/I attempt to understand the implications of somatic and cultural difference. Here, my intent is to employ the figure of the child as a rhetorical device: a symbol of hearingness, embodying the confusion, misunderstanding, and potential harm that can arise from interactions across the hearing line. While children are often romanticized figures in literature—symbols of innocence and purity—my purpose here is to highlight the child as a subject betwixt and between knowledges. In doing so, I'm aiming to bring to light the liminality of my subject position, but also the deeper cultural issues present in interactions between deaf and hearing people, that, on the whole, hearing people are generally ignorant (however well-intentioned) about deafness, and such ignorance can produce harms to d/Deaf people.

In the scene in which I describe the ways I "tested" my grandmother's deafness, standing behind her and screaming as she stood washing the dishes, I'm attempting to animate the potential misunderstandings that occur at the juncture of deaf and hearing cultures, and the interface of deaf and hearing people in the everyday. This domestic incident illuminates the particular difficulty I had in comprehending and responding to difference in my youth, but resonates more broadly with the dominant hearing position of indignation and entitlement when it comes to communicative exchange. I have witnessed countless occasions where strangers have spoken to my grandparents in public places, and when they've failed to respond, the hearing person has erupted into anger, sometimes swearing and hurling insults. Such experiences speak perhaps to uncomfortable truths about the ways audism functions in the interstice between deaf and hearing subjectivities. The narrated incident of my childhood memory of this type of anger, particularly in the severity of the utterance "I hate you," acts to dramatize such cultural tensions and generate a moment's pause in readers as they contemplate the ways in which misunderstanding can manifest in rage, even within the bounds of otherwise loving relationships.

In my writing, I document a combination of lived and observed experiences. In another chapter of the memoir, for example, I discuss my grandmother's speech pathology and the legacy of oralism in the way she told it to me. There her voice is thrust to the foreground, with dialogue intercutting my first-person narration. Of course, my narrative voice is still the guiding consciousness that steers the reader through the material, but there are certain times at which my grandparents come forward, and I am in the background. Other times, such as in "Our Place," it was disingenuous not to acknowledge the ways in which I saw and understood their lives.

For a long time, I struggled to take ownership of my story, and found myself muting my voice in what then felt like a kind of political act. I wanted my grandparents' stories to be heard—for their experiences to be acknowledged and elevated over my own. In the writing process, I frequently found myself immobilized by anxiety about my decision to write about their lives, reprimanding myself for my audacity despite having their wholehearted permission and encouragement (in fact, they read and often collaborate with me in the drafts of my writing). I worried that I was occupying a paternalizing role; that my position as a hearing person did not entitle me to speak, regardless of the fact I want to speak with, rather than for them. I have since come to see the story as neither mine nor theirs, but rather "ours"—that these narratives constitute a shared history whose telling toggles between multiple voices and points of view throughout. Moreover, I am conscious that writing in this context is an avenue to tell stories that would otherwise be lost or remain obscure and inaccessible to the reading public.

This is not to deny or minimize my executive role in shaping and organizing narrative material. However, in occupying a strong and unabashed first-person voice, I am acknowledging rather than shying from the constructedness of my own work. Throughout "Our Place," I have tried to foreground my insider/outside status. My descriptions of sign language in the excerpt also illustrate the ways in which I gazed upon a language that did not wholly belong to me and which I struggled to fully access until later in life.

Many of these narrated memories are deliberately political and inspired by deaf studies scholarship that discusses the oppression of Deaf people, their language, and their culture throughout history. In describing the way my body would engage in a signed representation of our story, I am attempting to highlight the cultural significance of sign language in order to assert its value within a hearing world. However, in referring to sign language as "musical," I am constructing a mode of understanding that illustrates my hearing subjectivity and tendency to relate to things in an auditory fashion.

I admit here that I cannot altogether exclude myself from a position that places deafness under a cultural microscope in a way that might avoid pathologizing scripts but might also be said to be objectifying. This is a common issue in filial narratives, which Couser brings to our attention in "Signs of Life" (*Recovering*, 249). He explains that memoirs written by children and grandchildren of deaf adults are less likely to pathologize deafness (249), but that such acts of representation, particularly by hearing persons, are increasingly subject to criticism on the grounds of exploitation or inadvertent objectification (252). It is exceedingly difficult to avoid such a problem—that in resisting the medical model, and attempting to champion the cultural, my descriptions of signing, which are full of whimsy and adoration, might be read as objectifying Deaf culture.

Worth considering here too is Rosemarie Garland-Thompson's work on staring and disability, which illustrates significant issues in the ways that hearing subjects have traditionally gazed upon disability and deafness. In her paper "The Politics of Staring," she elaborates a taxonomy of four primary visual rhetorics of disability, including the wondrous, the sentimental, the exotic, and the realistic, which can be of use in thinking through ways of representing deafness (Garland-Thompson, 58). It could be argued that the child's fixation with sign, and my use of sonic-centric metaphors, border on Garland-Thompson's ideas of the wondrous, where my framing "capitalizes on physical differences in order to elicit amazement and admiration" (59).

However, to leave out the ways my child-self came to love and appreciate my grandparents is to ignore the ways that such scripts function in relation to deafness and our social and cultural readings of it. My descriptions of the sounds that accompany deaf interactions too might be considered problematic, but I include them in my story because it is dishonest not to; but also because these were the bodily and sensory realities of my lived experience, and are crucial in framing the ways I have negotiated the hearing line in these relationships. I include auditory references because I cannot escape the fact of my hearingness, and the only antidote is to write it on the page with full transparency and self-reflexivity.

In narrating from the position of the child, I am given access to a range of narrative possibility that is not constrained by the adult voice. By illuminating both the generous accepting elements of childlike thinking, as well as the limits to a child's knowledge, I can make social commentary about hearing culture at large. In framing childhood in this way, as a mode of betweenness, I can draw on my childhood experiences in a way that animates the hearing line and the ways in which I have negotiated it in the past. In employing the figure of the child, I can highlight cultural issues without subscribing or collapsing entirely into them. Because I am now an adult, the voice and the actions of that configured child-self do not necessarily represent my current views. As such, I can use the child-self to highlight the ways I am and have been implicated in inflicting harm or engaging in audist modes of thinking. But also, I can engage in a form of resistance by allowing the adult voice to serve as a counterpoint.

CONCLUSION: THE VALUE OF CRITICALLY INFORMED PERSONAL NARRATIVES?

In rising to the task of depicting nuanced d/Deaf lives and the intersubjective exchanges that occur at and across the hearing line, I have experimented with the affective qualities of the creative nonfiction genre in order to animate lived experiences of deafness and hearing. By attempting to contribute a story from my childhood experiences with my Deaf grandparents, I am seeking to address the persistent issue of invisibility and pathological conceptions of deafness that have traditionally characterized literary representations of deafness. This chapter suggests the value of an approach that utilizes the political and philosophical vigor of deaf studies scholarship as a guiding sensibility in narratives about d/Deaf lives. Moreover, in illuminating the ways in which I've employed the figure of the child as a rhetorical device, I hope to unpack the various strategies available to writers as they negotiate how best to tell stories from the d/Deaf world. By offering my own creative work as a case study, I hope to institute a dialogue about how best to approach difficult issues around representation and to consider how to assemble narratives that resist the tropes that have hitherto dominated depictions of deafness and hearingness on the page.

NOTES

1. For more information about Australian Sign Language (Auslan), see: https://deafchildrenaustralia.org.au/wp-content/uploads/2014/12/What-is-Auslan-2012.pdf or "Australian Sign Language–Auslan": https://www.youtube.com/watch?v=SI0168-N6Ho.

CHAPTER 2

Mandy

A Critical Look at the Portrayal of a
Deaf Character in Children's Literature

—Cynthia Neese Bailes

When any segment of society is excluded from its literature, the implication is
thereby conveyed that the group is without value.
—Masha Kabakow Rudman, 219

The emergence of multicultural children's literature since the 1960s has inargu-
ably been a boon to the lives of child-readers by promoting the "personal development of *all* children by effacing notions of race, class, or gender superiority"
(Stephens, 51). However, Deaf culture, the culture of deaf people who consider
themselves a member of a cultural minority,[1] is virtually absent from the critical literature about multicultural children's books. While mainstream society
generally views hearing loss as a disability, many deaf people see themselves
as "visual people" (Lane, Hoffmeister, and Bahan, 159) and reject this disability
ideology and accompanying pathological labels such as "hearing impaired."
Their self-identification as a cultural group is defined by the commonalities
brought about by their visual nature. Despite this, hearing and speaking have
historically been deemed superior to and have led to the suppression of signed
languages. The history of oppression of deaf people has revolved around the
attempt to assimilate them into hearing society.[2]

Deaf children and adults are rarely characters in picture books for children. When they are, they tend to be positioned as members of a disability
group rather than of a culturally affiliated group, and the books thus impose a

hearing worldview on Deaf lives.[3] This article critically examines a children's picture book, *Mandy* (1991), written by Barbara D. Booth and illustrated by Jim LaMarche—one of the handful of children's picture books with a deaf character published by a mainstream publisher. In a review of children's picture books with deaf characters published from 1970 through 1995, I found that, by and large, the writers of these books are hearing professionals who work with deaf children in some capacity (Bailes, *Deaf Characters in Children's Picture Books*), and a casual review since has confirmed the continuance of this trend. Indeed, Booth was a hearing teacher of deaf children and of sign language. A professional affiliation, however, does not necessarily position an author to portray a group in a culturally sensitive manner.

Writers of children's books are in a powerful position to influence children with their personal ideologies and their commonsense assumptions about the world, whether intentional or not (Fairclough 1989). These worldviews are explicitly present and implicitly embedded in the text and illustrations. Children's literature has historically been used for the purpose of implanting ideas to socialize children (Stephens 1992). Through text discourse, readers are positioned to see the world through the eyes of the writer, and this positioning informs the reader of the values and mores of a specific society (Fairclough 1989). Such positioning is not problematic if we accept that the values and mores of mainstream society (e.g., White, male, and *hearing*) are appropriate for all. However, a culturally diverse world requires literature as a "window" to multiple realities and a "mirror" in which to reflect on how these realities relate our own humanity, indeed our "shared humanity" (Style and McIntosh 1988). If Deaf children are not well-represented in children's literature, the literature that exists cannot serve as a window for hearing children into the lives of D/deaf children and a mirror for D/deaf children of their own lives.[4]

Mandy is portrayed as a young Deaf girl visiting her grandmother. They make cookies together, dance, and go for a walk. During their walk, her Grandma loses a treasured brooch, which they unsuccessfully try to find before returning home. Mandy later decides to go out on her own to find the brooch, despite her fear of the dark. By happenstance, she is successful. This retelling is what Stephens (1–2) terms the "story" or primary reading. Likely, most readers will agree with my brief summary. Arguable would be the secondary reading or the "significance," where interpretations of meaning made by readers are shaded by their background knowledge and experiences. Emotional reactions and worldviews emerge in this reading. Readers also acquire new knowledge that confirms, adds to, or revises existing worldviews (Fairclough 1989). I will address this secondary reading, offering contrasting windows through my eyes as a Deaf individual—my perceptions of the author's reading as well as my own. In doing so, I offer one contrasting perspective grounded in a strong cultural view of Deaf people (see Humphries 2001 for a discussion of competing views). My intent is not to present Deaf culture as monolithic or to offer my arguments as the only credible reading of this book. Deaf culture is multifaceted, encompassing a broad range of Deaf individuals who differ by gender, race, ethnicity, locality, socioeconomic status, family background, and other important variables (Brueggemann 1999; Fletcher-Carter and Paez, 2000; Parasnis, 1996; Welch, 2000). My perspectives draw on my experiences as a Deaf professional woman from a White, hearing, middle-class family background, a background similar in many respects to that of the character Mandy. In my deconstruction of this story, I purport to critically challenge how Deaf children are viewed within the sphere of "Hearing-ness" as a dominant referent and to underscore the importance of the reclamation of power and identity by Deaf peoples (Giroux 1997). In framing my critical reading, I impose general guidelines for culturally diverse children's literature (e.g., Council on Interracial Books for Children, 1994; Shioshita, 1997). Of crucial consideration is how the author's background positions her to represent this cultural group through her characterization of Mandy. As such, I will consider whether Mandy's behavior, thoughts, and conversations are culturally situated and authentic. I will also consider whether stereotypes about Deaf people are conveyed and reinforced through the author's characterization of this Deaf child. I also will consider whether this characterization portrays this cultural group as the group might depict itself (Sleeter and Grant 1999). Since the author of *Mandy* is hearing, as I analyze the ideologies embedded with the text, I pose the question: whose worldview is mirrored here?

The story begins,

> Grandma was standing near the sink, tapping her fingers on the counter, and moving her lips as she stared out the window. She's singing, thought Mandy, and she looked to see if the radio light was on. Grandma had told her that music and talk came out of the little black box on the windowsill, but Mandy's hearing aid couldn't be turned high enough to let her hear the sound. She had never heard anyone talk or sing, and she wondered about voices.
>
> Once, Grandma had said that her mother's voice sounded sweet and soft. Mandy had put a half-eaten marshmallow to her ear, hoping to feel the sweet softness of her mother's voice, but she'd only ended up with a sticky ear.[5]

This opening narration slips between narrator focalization and character focalization (Stephens 1992). Mandy as the main character is focalized through the eyes of the narrator, while the events of the story are focalized through Mandy's visual and mental perceptions ("thought," "looked"), which affirms the authenticity of those perceptions. But insights into Mandy's mind are primarily conveyed within the perceptual frame of an omnipresent narrator. Implicit in the opening paragraphs and throughout the story is a strong ideological base grounded in narrator focalization. This framing is not inappropriate, since the story is the author's to tell and every author inevitably conveys an ideology. However, since Booth is not D/deaf, the window (and mirror) she offers readers may not represent aspects "self-proposed" by this cultural group (Humphries 2001, 350).

In watching her grandmother, Mandy's visual self, that is, a culturally situated characterization of Mandy as a visual person, emerges. She *sees* Grandma tapping her fingers and moving her lips and *looks* to confirm the radio light is on. Yet Mandy's assimilated-self—a delineation of Mandy as striving to mesh with mainstream hearing values, mores, and expectations—is manifested more strongly. Mandy's portrayal as a Deaf child in a hearing world, with a radio and a singing grandmother in the background, is not problematic in itself—Deaf children do exist within the dichotomy of a Deaf and hearing world. However, portrayed as obsessed with how things sound, Mandy appears not only tragically trapped in a "deaf body" (Davis 1995), she also seems to miscomprehend much of the surrounding world. Her age is not clearly evident; from the illustrations she appears to be between six and ten years of age. Her memory of sticking a half-eaten marshmallow in her ear relates to an earlier age, and a six-year-old who has eaten half a marshmallow would know instinctively that the only result to come from that is a sticky ear. A younger child is more likely to be attracted by a marshmallow's softness, sweetness, and stickiness than to wonder if it is comparable to a soft, sweet voice. Such imagery of a deaf girl who cannot differentiate between a sound and a *feel* may implicitly serve to reinforce a hearing-world ideology of "deaf and dumb."[6]

In these opening paragraphs, the pull for assimilation into hearing society is intensified by the fact that Mandy wears a hearing aid despite receiving apparently little benefit from it. A naive reader might pass by this passage without pause. A critical reading requires questioning why a child who cannot hear amplified sounds would be depicted as wearing an aid. Certainly, some deaf people can and do derive benefit from wearing a hearing aid, and some choose to wear them. Those who cannot hear a radio when their hearing aids are turned up full volume, however, are less likely to wear them. Thus, a hearing worldview is presented here: The impact of not hearing is so substantial that any means to recapture this loss, even if an illusion, is crucial. Curiously enough, the illustrations are neutral; none of them depict Mandy wearing an aid, a contradiction to the text, and more in keeping with her visual self.

Mandy, as portrayed in this opening, likely appeals to the senses of a majority-hearing population. Hearing readers presumably are unable to imagine a world without sound and thus sympathize with Mandy's constant need to question how things sound. In prolonging the image of Mandy silently wondering how things sound, Booth positions readers to reflect on how sound is taken for granted and hence to pity Mandy. Yet, I do not assert that Deaf children do not wonder about sounds, and there may be some who even obsess. This, however, is only one view of the world of Deaf children, and a stereotypical representation of Deaf children as "disabled-beings-who-cannot-hear" rather than as "visual-beings" who exist in a differing reality—they perceive the world through their eyes.

The author hints at Mandy's visual-self:

> When Mandy was sure the chocolate chip cookies were well mixed in, she walked over to Grandma and touched her on her arm. She pointed to the bowl and Grandma handed her the cookie sheets.

Gaining the attention of others through touching and calling their attention to phenomena by pointing comes naturally to this cultural group. As visual beings, Deaf people value eye contact and use touching, tapping, and pointing to direct the eyes of others to themselves and other points of focus (Padden and Humphries 1988; Parasnis 1996). Booth embeds the visual nature of being deaf into her story in other ways: A timer, for example, is *watched*, not listened to. Yet, this visual-self is not foregrounded. Instead, it is relegated to the background, suggesting vision is an unsatisfactory substitute for sounds:

> Mandy could have used her voice to ask for them [the cookie sheets]—Grandma never winced when Mandy spoke—but she wasn't sure if she would interrupt the sounds on the radio.

Thus, Mandy's means of communicating with her grandmother are not manifested in terms of her visual-self but are ways she consciously evokes to keep her place as an ever-wary assimilated-self—one that appears careful not to encroach on a world that she can never fully share. As such, Mandy is portrayed as a doting granddaughter who is very careful not to intrude uninvited—an outsider looking in. Indeed, only one spoken and one signed utterance are attributed to Mandy in either the text or illustrations: she "nodded and signed yes" in response to a question and she spoke to a raccoon in the woods. This framing is comparable to Deaf artist Susan Dupor's painting titled "Family Dog." Many of Dupor's pieces reflect her experiences as a sole deaf child growing up in a hearing family. Her painting depicts a deaf child on all fours, panting under a glass-top coffee table. Legs of seated hearing people with blurred faces and huge "chatting" mouths are behind the prone girl. In a presentation about her work at Gallaudet University (January 2000), Dupor described how she frequently felt like the family dog—she was there, smiled at, and even petted, but never truly a part of the action.

Booth further emphasizes this lack of belonging through narration that reinforces negative stereotypes about Deaf people: They often do not sound good when they vocalize, a noticeable phenomenon in hearing society, but unimportant in Deaf culture (Lane 1992; Padden and Humphries 1988). This narration serves several purposes other than to remind readers of the phenomenon itself. It makes them explicitly aware that Mandy knows she doesn't sound "natural" when she speaks—people other than Grandma apparently wince. It implicitly suggests that, even though people wince, Mandy is under societal pressure to vocalize, and that, try as she might, she cannot speak "normally," and thus reach full assimilation. Finally, it emphasizes, however implicitly, Mandy's disadvantaged positioning in a hearing world. Indeed, in each depiction of the visual-self, the assimilated self emerges and dominates, emphasizing the tenet that sound (or voice) is power:

> She dropped the dough by spoonfuls onto a sheet. It shook as each mound landed. Mandy wondered if cookies made a noise as they dropped onto the metal.

And,

> On the path through the woods, Mandy felt the leaves crackle under her shoes. The branches seemed to wave a friendly hello, and Mandy wondered what they sounded like. Grandma had told Mandy that leaves made small noises when the wind blew them. Since branches were so much bigger, Mandy reasoned, they must make really loud noises.

And,

> The sun was low in the sky, almost in front of them. Mandy stood in a patch of sunlight. It felt warm and strong, and she wondered how it sounded as it passed through the trees. She thought all the noises outdoors must hurt Grandma's ears. That was probably why there were never any people in the woods with them. It was too noisy.

Most Deaf children and adults are not naive about sounds. Although they may not hear in the same sense a hearing person does—there are variations in each individual deaf person—they are typically much more aware of sound than Booth positions readers to believe. Most know that when metal shakes, it makes a vibration that can be *felt*. and they typically know vibrations represent sound of some kind. It is doubtful that many, if any, ponder over whether sunlight makes a sound. These portrayals of Mandy's obsession reach beyond childlike naiveté; they convey an assumption that deaf people must desperately *wish* to be hearing. This is a problematic reading when taking a cultural view, for many Deaf people, when given a choice, would not opt to become hearing, and, furthermore, they often wish for Deaf children (e.g., Searls and Johnson 1996).

Booth depicts Mandy's attempts to speechread and her awareness that she is only taking in fragments of what her grandmother says:

> "Mandy," she saw Grandma's lips say. "Grandpa . . . I . . . dance . . . song." She watched Grandma's lips form the words, knowing there were others in between that she didn't understand. Grandmother pointed to the radio and pulled Mandy to her feet.

Through visual and tactile cues she understands that Grandma is asking her to dance. The reader is thus positioned to see Mandy as admirable for under-standing this much and being able to interface with Grandma's world, albeit on a limited basis. This approval is strategically reinforced by the satisfaction any young reader feels with their own ability to retrieve the full utterance, "Grandpa and I used to dance to this song," from the fragments. That Mandy does not have full access to oral language does not seem a concern for her grandmother. Yet, after the song ends, "Grandma released her. 'Song finished,' she signed." Grandma signs to Mandy only twice throughout the text (and in one illustration). Here Booth again hints at Mandy's visual world, as well as her grandmother's apparent awareness of it. But, by limiting the signing depicted, Booth may be implicitly asserting a belief in the superiority of the assimilated-self, thus positioning the reader to perceive (or confirm) this as the desirable self for all deaf children. In this view, Mandy is better off on the receiving end of scattered parts of oral communication because signed lan-guages are deemed inferior.

Booth's depictions of Mandy and her grandmother are idyllic. Absent is the frustration and anger commonly communicated by Deaf children and adults who attempt or have little recourse but to assimilate into the hearing world. A feeling of not belonging brought on by this lack of ease in communication is a recurring theme in the life stories of Deaf people (e.g., Ballin 1998; Mow 1989). Mandy, in contrast, is portrayed as docile and accepting of her "place" in the hearing-world, in both text and illustrations. That she cannot fully understand her grandmother's speech appears a fact of life for her, easily accepted. Readers are thus positioned to see a black and white world and are led to cast a favorable eye on a Deaf child who tries to fit in the mold imposed by a hearing society. Grandma, who appears equally contented, represents this world.

Mandy's grandfather is an unexplored and unexplained component of the story. When looking through a picture album, Mandy finds her favorite picture of him, in which he is described as wearing a behind-the-ear hearing aid, visible because he has turned his head to look at "Amanda aged 2½." I refer to Mandy as Deaf, inferring a cultural membership because of the handful of references to her signing, especially with Deaf friends. In my reading, implicit in Mandy's noticing her grandfather's hearing aid is her strong identification with him because of their common bond. Just as many Deaf people wish for Deaf children, they also value and strongly identify with Deaf parents, siblings, and other relatives. Most Deaf people, indeed approximately 90 percent of them, do not have these blood bonds with other Deaf people. Many of these form close bonds with Deaf people with whom they come into contact (Lane et al. 1996). Such a bond is typical in Deaf culture, indeed any culture, for it is by making connections with those like us that we form our identity. Here Booth hints at this connection; however, a naive reader is likely to miss it.

These suggestions of Mandy's visual-self notwithstanding, Booth seems to confirm a mainstream view of being deaf as undesirable. Mandy's fear of the dark, a common childhood phenomenon, is directly attributed to the fact that she is deaf:

> Mandy hated the dark. It made her so alone. She remembered how frightened she'd been when she went camping last spring with her Brownie troop. At night she couldn't sign to her friends or see anyone's lips. It felt as if the world ended at the edge of her flashlight beam. She startled when people stepped into the light, or worse, tapped her on the shoulder from behind.

Here, being deaf is ideologically placed literally and figuratively as akin to being thrust into a world of darkness. When the lights are out, Mandy is alone, lost, and fearful. In darkness, cut off from the hearing world as well as her visual world, Mandy ceased to exist. Here Booth appears to portray a hearing person's dread of the very idea of being deaf—that deaf equals disempowerment.

The conflict of this story centers on Mandy's search for Grandma's brooch, which she undertakes, unbeknownst to her grandmother and despite her extreme fear of the dark. A primary reading would indicate that Booth aimed to show a D/deaf child in a positive light—a brave deaf child, out of love for her grandmother, can overcome her fear of the dark and save the day. Mandy gets the idea to look for the brooch when she closes her eyes and visualizes light reflecting off her grandmother's silver pin. In this visual remembering, her visual-self manifests itself; she is confident she can find it. She takes a flashlight, traces back through their path, and carefully looks for the brooch. In her search, the visual-self again takes command as she trains her eyes on the beam of the flashlight. Yet her visual-self does not resolve the conflict. Instead, Booth resolves the conflict through a mishap: Mandy trips and falls, and the flashlight flies from her hand, landing nearby. Mandy, ready to give up in despair, reaches for the flashlight as the lightning strikes.

> Then she saw it. From under the grass came a small twinkle, barely visible in the circle of light. For a moment Mandy didn't move or even breathe. Then she carefully separated the blades of grass with her fingers. It seemed that the pin shone more brightly than it ever had before. She lifted it tenderly and pushed it straight down to the bottom of her pocket.

Here the text is augmented with an illustration indicating that the flashlight, in falling from Mandy's hands, landed with its beam flashed directly on the brooch.

The conflict was thus resolved by coincidence, and with such a resolution my critical reading demands the question: why was this story written? What did the author wish to convey to the reader about this Deaf child, or about D/deaf children in general? One possible reading is that Booth's intention is to inform the reader about deaf children—her ideological vision of a D/deaf child—in a positive light. Using her authority as an experienced teacher of deaf children and of sign language, the author positions the reader to see a deaf child through her eyes. In assuming the power vested by this authority, however, she does not invite readers to stretch their perceptions of the lives of D/deaf people. Instead, she induces confirmation and acceptance of common stereotypes pervading this group of people. Rather than allowing Mandy as a Deaf child to "speak" to the reader through her Deaf eyes, Booth positions the reader to rely on her own professional authority to mediate a window to Mandy's world. While Booth's intentions may be well meaning, her depiction of this Deaf child places higher value on assimilated deaf people and cannot be viewed as an authentic cultural representation. Further, although this story may provide one representation of a Deaf child as seen through hearing eyes, it does not push the hearing reader to expect and seek out multiple realities of the lives of culturally diverse children (Sleeter and Grant 1999), in this case, Deaf children.

My reading of this picture book positions Mandy in an extreme contrast to that of Booth's. I do not intend to represent the views of all Deaf peoples.

Though not all Deaf individuals may share my views, many have and continue to object to attempts by hearing people to define them (e.g., Ballin 1998; Bienvenu 2001; Levesque 2001; Wing 2001). *Mandy* is yet another attempt, however well-meaning, to impose a hearing worldview on Deaf lives. My arguments are meant to bring forth a critical discussion about how Deaf children are characterized in literature, and to spur interest in the many competing views self-imposed by the very people portrayed. As Humphries (2001) asserts in his "theory of self proposed by others,"

> Deaf people were unknowable but not uncategorized and undefined. Theories of deaf people abound among people who hear. And in their failure to know, the impossibility to know, hearing people permitted no other theory that Deaf people might have had of themselves to compete. The first theories that Deaf people have had about themselves are those of others.
>
> Because hearing people could not know us, we could not know ourselves. Because the concept of the self was so much a variation of the hearing self, there could be no Deaf self that was any different. How could any Deaf person have a self different than what was imposed? It was unimaginable. There were no other possibilities. Deaf people were just what hearing people said they were (350).

On the surface, *Mandy* is a well-written story of a brave little Deaf girl and her grandmother; indeed, among such children's picture books *Mandy* possesses a literary quality found lacking in the majority. While each single depiction of this Deaf character may appear harmless, even endearing to the senses of the hearing reader, taken as a whole, these representations have a tremendous impact on perpetuating existing two-dimensional and stereotypical beliefs about Deaf people rooted in Hearing-ness as the dominant referent. Indeed, the body of literature portraying the lives of Deaf children in children's picture books reinforces this hearing worldview. *Mandy* is the story of a White, seemingly middle-class Deaf child, as is most of the existing children's literature with D/deaf characters. Yet, not only are these White, middle-class Deaf children not culturally situated in this body of literature, the fact that Deaf children spring from varying backgrounds, including other ethnic and racial cultures, is essentially ignored. Lukens (1995) states, "Information is not a person, spirit is" (2). The spirit of Deaf children is not information about what they can or cannot do with their ears and mouths. Deaf children are as diverse as the population at large, and to capture their spirit would require involving them in conflicts portraying them as visual people struggling with a variety of issues, some unique to them as visual people and some common to people everywhere. A literary work "grafting bits and pieces" (Sleeter and Grant 1999, 186) of the Deaf experience onto common hearing beliefs about what it means to be deaf does not provide rich multiple perspectives of this cultural group. Deaf children, like all children, are individuals with "complex personalities . . . they can be angry, pleasant, nasty, loving, irritable, in the same proportions as everybody else, and literature should portray them in this balanced way" (Rudman 1995, 307). They also need to be portrayed in literature by authors who can depict these children as members of cultural groups, rather than as people who are deficient, yet admirable. With past and current societal pressures to integrate deaf children into hearing society, and with the numbers of these children being small in proportion to the overall population, it is unlikely that publishers will see value in promoting books promoting this group as other than disabled, if at all. Yet, it is important that they do so. Literature is not only about economics. It is about representing people as they are and in reading about them, to experience their lives vicariously:

> Another person's words are the windows to his or her world, through which I see what it is like to be that person. When another speaks to me in truth, he or she becomes a transparent self, and releases in me an imaginative experience of his or her existence. If he or she cannot speak, if I do not listen, or if I cannot understand, then we must remain suspicious strangers to one another, uncognizant of our authentic similarities and differences. (Sidney Jourard, cited in Style 1988)

In this sense, the window into the lives of Deaf children, at least as far as children's literature is concerned, has not yet been framed, much less *seen*.

NOTES

1. I use *Deaf* to mean social and cultural collectiveness and *deaf* to mean an audiological condition; I use *D/deaf* as a term that includes both individuals who view themselves as culturally Deaf and those who do not (Woodward 1972).

2. To further investigate historical, cultural, educational, and oppression issues of deaf people, see Ballin 1998; Bayton 1998; Bragg 2001; Brueggemann 1999; Davis 1995; Lane 1992; Lane and Bahan 1998; Lane et al. 1996; Padden and Humphries 1988; Parasnis 1996; Van Cleve and Crouch 1989; and Wrigley 1996.

3. Representations of Deaf culture in picture books remain rare. Debbie Golos and Annie Moses together explored the incidence in overlapping articles in 2011 and 2012 and concluded that "children's books continue to portray deaf characters more from a medical than a cultural perspective" (2011, 279). The topic has not been researched more recently. Good examples from a cultural perspective are *Dad and Me in the Morning* (Lakin and Steele 1994/2019), *The Garden Wall* (Tildes 2006), *The Printer* (Uhlberg and Sørensen 2003), and the lifestyle picture book *Proud to Be Deaf* (Beese and Marti 2017). [JS]

4. Around eighty picture books that include one or more deaf characters were published between 2010 and 2020. The majority tend to focus on the technologies employed to combat "hearing loss," but include several books with storylines that aspire to engage both deaf and hearing children, for example, *Freddie and the Fairy* (Donaldson and George 2010), *Hands and Hearts* (Napoli and Bates 2014), and *My Happy Place* (Crockford and Butler 2018).[JS]

5. From *Mandy* by Barbara D. Booth, 1991, New York: Lothrop, Lee and Shepard. Copyright 1991 by Barbara D. Booth. Reprinted with permission.

6. Another possibility is that Booth aims to depict a deaf child who manifests delayed language acquisition. Mandy appears to be profoundly deaf since her hearing aids are ineffectual and she has rudimentary speech-reading ability and some knowledge of signing. One consequence of delayed language acquisition is typically thought to be an impaired comprehension of everyday figurative language such as the simile comparing soft, sweet confectionary and a soft, sweet voice. Such a deficit attribute would then form part of the basis for the "overcoming" script that frames the story. [JS]

CHAPTER 3

Caped Crusaders and Lip-Reading Pollyannas

The Narrative and Ideological Function of Humor
in Representations of Deaf Culture for Young People

—Nerida Wayland

It remains problematic in the twenty-first century that there are still limited examples in children's literature of diverse, genuinely agentic or empowered d/Deaf characters or distinct representations of d/Deaf experience.[1] Such a phenomenon suggests that children's literature has yet to achieve an inclusive, empathic, and broadminded discourse about diversity. A 1992 study conducted by Blaska and Lynch revealed the limited presence of persons with disabilities in literature for young people: only ten (2 percent) of five hundred award-winning and highly recommended books for children included persons with disabilities integral to the storyline or illustrations (Blaska, 1). A similar study in 2010 assessed the personal portrayal, exemplary practices, social interactions, and sibling relationships associated with characters with disabilities in Newbery Medal–winning books from 1975 to 2009 (Leininger, Dyches, Prater, and Heath, 594). This investigation highlighted problematic themes "such as elimination of the character with the disability or miraculous cures" (Leininger et al., 594). It noted few stories were told from the perspective of characters with a disability and that their experiences were instead used to "facilitate the emotional growth of characters without disabilities" (594). Rieger and McGrail detail the deleterious effects of misrepresentations of children with disabilities in books and media: (a) children with disabilities cannot "find" themselves or appropriate role models, and (b) abled students remain unaware of this absence, which amplifies their unfamiliarity with their differently abled classmates ("Exploring," 18–19).

These deleterious effects are pertinent to representations of deafness in children's literature because, typically, deafness is synonymous with disability in many literary and cultural depictions. Harlan L. Lane argues that deafness is associated with loss rather than gain "because the society that has elaborated the concept of *deaf* is largely hearing and conceptualizes *deaf* as a loss of hearing . . . although the Deaf person didn't lose anything" (366). Lane poses the question: "*Should* Deaf people seek this *disability* label assigned to them by the technologies of normalization or at least acquiesce in it, or should they actively resist it?" (368). Recent comedic texts for young people problematize the social assumptions highlighted by Lane and challenge the "implacable inadequacies found in representing disabled characters . . . caught between saccharine sentimentality and incarnate evil" (Pollard, 264).

Few researchers have explicitly examined the representation of d/Deaf characters in children's literature (see, for example, Brittain; Golos, and Moses; Golos, Moses, and Wolbers; and Pajka-West). Much of the research into depictions of disability does not explore the significance of illustration (Brittain, 4) or the function of humor in literary representations of Deaf culture. There are exceptions (see Reiger and McGrail, "Humor") but where Golos and Moses's research explores a content analysis of picture books and examines illustrations as a separate study (Golos, Moses, and Wolbers), I aim to focus on the power of the visual narrative space by exploring the interplay of words and pictures in the graphic novel format and film. Extending Golos and Moses's focus on the importance of examining children's literature for its messages and content regarding different people (272), this chapter will highlight the importance of the ideologies underpinning narrative and comedic choices.

A key framework for my investigation is the critical discourse of narratology. I employ narratology as a theoretical and analytic tool for legitimizing comedy as a subject of literary criticism, and for celebrating the social and educational signification of comedy in children's film and literature. I use this framework to examine key discoursal elements of narrative fiction and film, as outlined by John Stephens—narration and focalization, narrative structure and organization, and narrative beginnings and endings (2010, 55)—and how these strategies construct meaning. My research will explore how the blend of the comedic mode with narrative and filmic strategies interrogates the principal ideologies operating in a text and the impact these have on representations of child subjectivity.

Using this narratological approach, I analyze Cece Bell's graphic-novel memoir *El Deafo*; Troy Kotsur's feature film *No Ordinary Hero: The SuperDeafy*

Movie; and Libba Bray's satirical young adult fiction *Beauty Queens*. *El Deafo* is a graphic novel for junior readers about growing up with a hearing disability and, much to Cece's embarrassment, wearing a large phonic ear to school every day. *No Ordinary Hero: The SuperDeafy Movie* is a family movie that follows the popular Deaf television superhero, SuperDeafy, and parallels the obstacles he experiences with a d/Deaf boy in elementary school whose parents have opposing views regarding how he should navigate the world. *Beauty Queens* is a satirical young-adult novel where extreme, often absurd, settings, plot twists, and characterizations are consciously constructed and then parodied as a way to warn about the destructive power of capitalism in contemporary culture. The humor that characterizes these texts acts to expose and resist the limitations of social discourses that constrain diverse subjectivities, particularly pathological perspectives on deafness that pity and exclude. These comedic examples celebrate voices that have traditionally been sidelined or silenced. They use humor to experiment with innovative and transgressive ways to create fluid, distinct subject positions in order to challenge depictions that highlight "the ear rather than the person" (Golos and Moses, 271).

The texts use humor to pose ethical questions pertaining to viewing Deaf culture through an ableist lens. Questions that challenge socially constructed categories of "deafness" and "disability" interrogate binary depictions and attitudes to deafness as a deficit, weakness, or tragedy in need of a solution or cure. These texts highlight the importance of d/Deaf creative control in the production of stories for young people and multidimensional representations of d/Deaf characters in order to portray a spectrum of experiences that reflect the richness and diversity of Deaf culture. Such questions reinforce Dadlez's connection between humor and moral criticism: "the humor to be found . . . depends on the revelation of something that has been hitherto obscured, a revelation that often focuses on matters of ethical salience . . . on the exposure of a moral flaw" (2). The function of the humor in these texts complements Scott Pollard's discussion of the potent force of disability studies in the last two decades, particularly the development of a "complex theoretical and aesthetic lexicon for the study of disability in literature" (263). He describes this lexicon as moving beyond the categorization of representations of disability to "the very concept of representation—not only to challenge ableist hegemony but, more importantly to cripple representation and the perceptions and normative ideologies that have shaped and limited it . . . to *cripple* is a means of liberation, a universal gesture meant to impact everyone and change the world" (263). The potential for humor to be subversive and destabilize dominant ideologies can fulfill a similar function, "turning normative aesthetics and expectations on their heads" (Pollard, 265) and in turn, anticipate child readers as capable of altruism and activism.

(DIS)ABLING HUMOR

Changing attitudes and perceptions of disability have significantly affected disability humor in the last century. Haller and Ralph outline the three phases of disability humor evident in the twentieth century, and the recent fourth phase—an integrated approach rather than a disability-focused approach (12). Phase one is defined by freak shows and representing mentally disabled people as "fools"; phase two is defined by sick, inappropriate jokes that laugh at people with disabilities and their "limitations"; and phase three focuses on people with disabilities controlling the humor messages that ridicule social barriers and negative attitudes towards them (Haller and Ralph, 12). Haller and Ralph argue that, in the fourth phase, the person with a disability is simply another "character in the humor landscape," emphasizing that "disability is just part of the diverse humor panorama, not the reason for the comedy" (12). The texts in my corpus echo each of these phases, although phases one and two are exposed for the purpose of ridicule and critique. It follows, then, that humor operates as a powerful narratological and ideological strategy for endorsing and challenging cultural representations of deafness. Haller and Ralph's fourth phase of humor is categorized by "our shared human experiences, and [ensures that] having a disability is depicted as just another unique feature about human beings" (13). This type of humor can function to normalize disability experience for readers "in the sense that all characters are subject to humorous jabs, including characters with disabilities who make fun of themselves or initiate and create humor" (McGrail and Rieger, "Humor," 299). However, I would caution about the prospective dangers of this type of strategy. The depiction of sameness, as in "we are all the same," can act to simplify and generalize lived experience. Such a strategy can also function to efface difference—which, in effect, is another form of marginalization.

The narrative strategy of focalization in each text encourages readers to align with marginalized, d/Deaf characters; to privilege their points of view; and to empathize with their experiences as they negotiate hegemonic social spaces in the quest for subjective agency. The multiple focalizers in Bray's novel provide a range of voices, each one of them controlled and shaped by the pageant world. Repressive social and ideological spaces are satirized in relation to the way they function to marginalize minority groups. Preceding each chapter that focuses on a different narrator is the "Miss Teen Dream Fun Facts Page," where contestants are encouraged to make their profile "interesting and fun, but appropriate" (134). The fun facts page derides the tightly controlled nature of the pageant world, the importance of political correctness and the ever-present surveillance of female bodies. Sosie Simmons begins her "fun facts" list with,

"I am hearing impaired but that doesn't stop me!" (134). Her opening lines reflect Brittain's "pitfalls of disability fiction" (4) and are at odds with Blaska and Lynch's assertion of the importance for representations to use "language that stresses person first, disability second" (Blaska, 2).

Sosie's introduction defines her subjectivity by her impairment and follows with the kind of perky, condescending rhetoric that depicts her as an object of inspiration determined to endure despite her hearing loss. However, the shift in tone and register from "I hear with my heart" to "well not really. Because, as anybody who is not a complete and total moron knows, the heart does not have ears. This is the kind of s**t they make disabled people say all the time so everybody's all 'okay' with us" (134) alters the portrayal of Sosie from saccharine victim to disgruntled teen dissatisfied with the labels that bind her. The incongruous blend of the "saintly invalid" (Dowker, 1) with the sarcastic social commentary challenging the sentimental rhetoric often used to categorize deafness dismisses the pressure to placate society and conform to ableist ideologies. In her next dot point on the list, Sosie states that she performs with the "non-hearing dance troupe Helen Kellerbration!" (134) followed by the sentence, "And by 'non-hearing' I mean deaf. Again, people, get over yourself" (134). Sosie's defiance is evident in both dot points on her list. However, the opening sentence of each cumulative point echoes ableist rhetoric and because it precedes Sosie's retorts in the sentences that follow, it conveys the dominance of such attitudes in this society and the necessity for Sosie to constantly redefine her subjectivity beyond her "disability."

The humor in the pun "Helen Kellerbration" is an example of Haller and Ralph's first two phases of disability humor where the reference to one of the most well-known individuals with a disability—Helen Keller—displays the reductive view that all disability experience is interchangeable. The black comedy employed in the farcical and offensive nature of the troupe's name depicts a society whose oversimplified categorization of disability experience is worthy of ridicule. Troy Kotsur's feature film *No Ordinary Hero: The Super-Deafy Movie* reflects the same social assumptions and ignorance underpinning "Helen Kellerbration" when Tony, an actor who is Deaf, attends a casting call, only to realize they are auditioning everyone in the room—male, female, deaf, and hearing—"for the deaf role." The humor, however, stems from Haller and Ralph's fourth phase of disability humor when Tony encounters the actor next to him whose wildly gesticulating hand movements and tendency to yell in his face to admit she is "not really deaf" (but she does know how to sign "hi," "tree," and "ball") makes her ignorance and belittling views of deafness an object of derision. In her quest to "look authentic" Tony offers to teach her how to sign her name. To the viewer, his kindness feels extraordinary after her insensitive behavior, but as Tony teaches her sign language that the closed captions translates as "I'm a fool" (which she continues to recreate whilst giggling) Tony shifts the balance of power in his favor while teaching her a lesson.

Kotsur's feature film and Cece Bell's *El Deafo* utilize humor directed at d/Deaf people as both harmful and liberating depending on the type of comedy and the purpose of the humor by demonstrating the importance of "controlling the humor messages" (Haller and Ralph, 12). An important way these texts control the humor message is to promote pluralistic d/Deaf subject positions, not simply through performance and narrative construction, but through the value of lived experience. Deafness is not only part of the narrative landscape but integral to the artistic creation of each text. The fact that d/Deaf creators have composed each text means that the richness and dynamism of Deaf culture pervades every aspect of the storytelling. The peritext of *El Deafo* includes an acknowledgments page that states, "More important than how the hearing loss happened . . . is what a deaf person might choose to do with his or her hearing loss . . . there are lots of different ways to be deaf." This note from the author stresses that not everyone wants to "fix their hearing loss," while others "might think of their deafness as a difference, and they might, either secretly or openly, think of it as a disability." The inclusion of this note cements the central message of the story: d/Deaf experience is not universal or singular, nor is it synonymous with disability for everyone.

Kotsur's film generates a strong thematic message regarding the importance of "complete creative control" as art imitates life. There are moments in the film where the crossover between fiction and reality is highlighted. John Maucere is a Deaf comedian/actor who is renowned for creating the character SuperDeafy, who he plays in a series of webisodes. The opening scenes show SuperDeafy with adoring fans against the backdrop of a DeafNation event with Deaf performer, actor, and activist Marlee Matlin. Matlin, DeafNation, and Super-Deafy are popular icons of Deaf culture and provide a sense of credibility and authenticity to the film. The fact that the film is the first Screen Actors Guild commercial feature film in history to be executive produced, directed, and starred in by individuals who are d/Deaf (Propes, "The Independent Critic") is reflected in the strong social messages pertaining to inclusivity, access, and diversity symbolized by the film's closed captions, inclusion of characters who use ASL, and the speech bubbles during the television show.

Farber emphasizes this social function of humor in his discussion of "empathic humor," where "our failings are not merely shared but also to some extent redeemed" (78). The "payoff" of such humor stems from "*sharing* our foolishness, our failings, our ineptitude with a character who to some degree is able to draw our empathy" (76); this reassures us that we are not alone (78).

In the case of these texts, foolishness and failings are not associated with deafness but the challenging situations each character is placed in due to the society they live in. Suzanne Keen argues that the process of narrative empathy involves both affect and cognition because, when narratives invite readers to feel, they also stimulate them to think ("Theory," 213). Keen outlines a small number of narrative techniques that can generate narrative empathy, such as character identification ("Theory," 214) and narrative situation including point-of-view and perspective ("Theory," 219). The variety of ways each of the central characters negotiates being positioned as "other" has the potential to evoke a strong emotive response in readers and viewers. Just as narrative strategies evoke an affective response from readers, illustrations are capable of generating an empathic response by using a variety of visual techniques, such as body language, facial expressions, and color symbolism. The use of anthropomorphism, in particular, and the comic inversion of traditional schemata that relate human types to corresponding animal types (Keen, "Fast Tracks," 137) have not only a humorous impact but also an affective one.

Cece Bell employs anthropomorphism in her graphic novel by using rabbit characters and a cartoonish style to depict the experience of growing up with a hearing disability. In a recent interview for the *Guardian Children's Books* website, Bell recounts that she

> needed a good visual metaphor, and rabbits, with their big ears and amazing hearing, were perfect for that. Essentially, I felt like the only rabbit whose big ears didn't work—I had the ears for show, but little else. Also, drawing the cords of the hearing aid so that they went above my head into rabbit ears (as opposed to having them go into my actual ears) perfectly captures how conspicuous I felt as a kid (www.theguardian.com).

The comic inversion of a rabbit who has poor hearing, despite such giant ears, not only acts as a visual cue but as a way for young readers to understand what it feels like to be different.

TILTING THE KALEIDOSCOPE

The texts that I examine in this chapter highlight the social model of disability: the idea that "it is society which disables," "a society that discriminates, disadvantages, and excludes people with impairments . . . it does not make appropriate accommodations and gives preference to those without impairment" (Rice et al., 445). The texts that constitute my primary corpus support a social-model approach as opposed to an individualized/medical model that views disability through a pathological lens: "As a 'problem' evolving from the functional restrictions of psychological losses that arise from the disability . . . a 'personal tragedy' approach" (Durell, 20). These texts also illustrate the reality of living with a disability. They do not downplay the daily challenges that a person viewed as having a disability navigates. The challenges that d/Deaf characters experience arise from the restrictions placed on them by the society they live in. Representations of deafness that reinforce the social model can enable readers to identify normative social attitudes as a major cause of conflict for subjects considered to have a disability (Saunders, 8–9).

Sosie Simmonds in *Beauty Queens* evokes the social model of disability by reiterating how she plays her "part," "being the smiling, plucky, don't-worry-about-me, lip-reading Pollyanna" (136). Her analogy blends patriarchal notions of subservient femininity with the "saintly invalid" (Dowker, 1) archetype to criticize the narrow, repressive fictional and social spaces governed by normative aesthetics and expectations. It also reiterates the performative nature of social constructs as Sosie views herself as roleplaying in order to conform. Bray challenges the power of normative ideologies through a flashback to sixth grade when Sosie meets Fwanda, who is in a wheelchair because of cerebral palsy but "had not gotten the memo about how disabled people were supposed to be happy and noble all the time in order to make people without disabilities feel okay about being lucky bastards" (136). The obtrusive, caustic narrative voice and irreverent language reflect her resentment of the clear "us" and "them" social divide. The use of capitals to capture the teacher's demeaning approach when communicating with Sosie: "SHE MIGHT NEED A FRIEND HERE AT BRIGHT PROMISES ELEMENTARY" (137) and the sentimental, somewhat ironic choice of the title of the school, serve to mock the condescending treatment of the girls. The analogy "Mrs. Brewer thought she could pair disabled kids like socks" (137) interrogates the ingrained nature of ableism, even within educational institutions that aim to socialize children. However, this tendency to devalue disability experience, categorize and view all people with disabilities through a single lens, is dismantled by Fwanda, who refuses to "play."

Fwanda's characterization defies stereotypes of disability promoted by society and actively seeks to resist and rebel. Her opening lines to Sosie are to demand, "Stop. With. The. Bullshit" (137). Sosie retaliates with a string of forced clichés highlighted by the staccato nature of the sentences. "I choose to have a positive attitude. I don't let my hearing loss get me down. I can do anything a hearing person can do" (137). The credibility of her comeback is undermined by the cumulative (seemingly rote-learned) listing. Fwanda's campaign of resistance is captured through the language of warfare as she "[sticks] to her guns" and submits creative works with highly amusing and aggressive titles: "Hope You Enjoy Those Legs, Cheerleader Beyotch" and "Dear Well-Meaning Church Groups: Please Ask Jesus to Stop Dicking around and Get Me out of This Chair" (137). Her titles target the social power hierarchy from high-school cliques to the adult gatekeepers and institutions that continue to limit and devalue her because she is in a wheelchair. Her final line is as subversive as her opening one, starting "with 'F' and [ending] in 'Off'" (137), suggesting Fwanda leaves the school as she arrived, fighting social constructs, the language that labels, and the binary oppositions that classify and constrain. For Sosie, Fwanda's legacy is the power of emotion, specifically anger. The relationship shows Sosie that she does not have to be "everyone's good sport" or "the sweet girl mascot" (138).

Brenda Jo Brueggemann discusses the d/Deaf space as a "visual space—an eye space—and also too, an I-space" and reiterates we still have much to learn from each "eye" (perspective) and "I" (the personal) (41). She argues the expansive potential of this space "of potent possibilities, contained and yet kaleidoscopic in its perspectives" (41). She concludes, "There are so many ways to bump and see the same pieces again, but now all arranged differently" (41). Bell, Bray, and Kotsur employ a range of narrative and comedic strategies to highlight and examine representations of deafness to encourage young people to continue to shift their perspective when peering through the kaleidoscope and note the ways the colors blend but are capable of a myriad of color combinations. The humor in these three texts reveals the importance of resisting rigid representations of subjectivity that determine human variation as a disability (Lane, 359) and do not recognize d/Deaf people "as the possessors and protectors of a great cultural heritage, a beautiful language, numerous art forms, and an eloquent history" (Lane, 375). The power of defiance is harnessed by Bray's Sosie who, when her friend Jennifer equates her signing with a "secret code," (138) retorts, "It's not some cute code. It's a language. My language" (138). The possessive pronoun and high modality reiterate Sosie's pride as well as reinforcing deafness as culturally rich. Jennifer's apologetic "what's the sign for *asshole*?" (138) demonstrates the importance of contesting casual discrimination and the power of diverse narrative voices for challenging reductive discourses and instigating social change.

A narrative strategy employed by the texts to share the complexities of d/Deaf experience with readers is the intertextuality of the superhero genre and the comic manipulation of its generic conventions. The superhero motif is a common icon in children's literature, particularly for the empowerment of marginalized or subordinated figures. The comedy plays with iconography and plot trajectories associated with superheroes and the quest genre. In doing so, it functions to present an alternative worldview for readers, represent the power children are capable of, and challenge the notion and appeal of norma-tivity. Julius E. Heuscher argues that "humor and folklore lift us beyond the ordinary, blindly accepted limits of the everyday world" and suggests that "the state of unreality" created by a humorous situation is then the vision of a dif-ferent "world design" (1546). The texts use the superhero motif to challenge the stigma and oppressive social practices that limit d/Deaf subjectivity. However, Bell and Kotsur also demonstrate the limitations of this narrative strategy and the dangers of depicting d/Deaf characters as "superhuman" (Blaska, 2) or "extra-ordinary" (Brittain, 4) rather than multidimensional, complete with strengths and weaknesses.

The use of Batman and the superhero motif in Bell's graphic novel *El Deafo* explores the power of vulnerability and provides a way for Cece to understand the benefits of living with a hearing disability. The superhero motif presents a range of questions regarding vulnerability that is explored in all of the texts, specifically regarding viewing vulnerability as weakness. Rice et al. argue against associating vulnerability with disability (520). They challenge the Western world's privilege of "self-contained, autonomous, independent, and strong selfhood" and instead promote the vulnerable self and our shared human experience as a starting point to begin building a more equitable society (520).

For Cece, her superpower is the "SUPER HEARING" (44) that she gains from wearing her phonic ear, rather than conventional superpowers like the ability to fly, leap tall buildings, or have x-ray vision. Her "crazy technology" (44)—the phonic ear—equates to Batman's batarang or Wonder Woman's Lasso of Truth. Her alter ego encourages her to capitalize on the unique traits her disability offers and reframes her deafness from a weakness into strength. Bell draws on comic superhero dialogue ("holy hearing-aid, Batman") and iconography (a cape, gadgets, secret identity, a sidekick, etc.) to convey how Cece comes to the realization: "[I] can use my own crazy technology—the phonic ear—to turn myself into a superhero, too! My power? Super hearing!" (44). When Cece imagines herself as El Deafo or thinks about what Batman would do in her situation, the scene takes place in a green-colored, cloud-shaped bubble. This image contrasts with the black geometric frames of the rest of the graphic novel, suggesting that her alter ego is able to create a space that is defined by its capacity for personal liberation. Her flowing red cape and her body language—confident, with hands firmly placed on hips and a satisfied smile—represent the transformation of her embarrassment at wearing the phonic ear, to a sense of pride and contentment at the hearing abilities it allows her. Her daydream is then shattered by a large, onomatopoeic "POP" as a student infringes on El Deafo's blue cloud-shaped dream of amazing everyone, in order to ask what "those things" are in her ears (45). In the following frame (Figure 3.1), Batman

Figure 3.1. The loneliness of difference. *El Deafo*, page 46. Copyright © 2014 by Cece Bell. Image reproduced with permission of the publisher, AMULET Books, an imprint of ABRAMS, New York, NY.

Figure 3.2. Superdeafy. *No Ordinary Hero: The SuperDeafy Movie*. Directed by Troy Kotsur. USA: Douglas Matejki and Hilari Scarl, 2013.

replaces Cece in the superhero cloud-shaped bubble. His back is to the readers, and his shoulders are slumped: "Superheroes might be awesome, but they are also different." Cece steps from the cloud-shaped bubble into a transparent smooth-shaped "Bubble of Loneliness" (46). The various bubbles separate Cece from others and come to represent her fragmented subjectivity. Cece's vulnerability does not stem from her inability to hear. It stems from the exclusionary nature of the views of society.

The superhero motif is also integral to Kotsur's film because it examines the underpinning ideologies behind the joke. A study of the opening and closing shots of the film convey the potential of comedy to move beyond "zany" and the heroism possible when Tony chooses to "loose the wig" and step beyond the caricature. The opening shot is a close-up of feet in a busy, public space. As the tracking shot follows a pair of conservative shoes, it freezes on a pair of bright yellow vinyl boots, immediately distinct from the crowd. The shot pans upwards slowly to reveal SuperDeafy, a parody of traditional superhero characters—complete with a yellow cape, Elvis Presley-like wig, and a pair of crossed hands signing "I love you" emblazoned across his chest (Figure 3.2). The mid-shot of him gazing off screen morphs into a pixilated, slightly washed-out comic book frame (reminiscent of pop art) as the title of the film flies across using font traditionally associated with a superhero television series like Super-man. This parody has a nostalgic feel and certainly, as the movie progresses and the viewer witnesses SuperDeafy and his TV sidekick's "schtick," some of the humor that the SuperDeafy show generates begins to feel outmoded and parochial. This is reinforced by the growing dissatisfaction on an online message board criticizing the changing depiction of SuperDeafy: "He used to be funny and now he's stupid" and "He shouldn't make deaf seem like such fools." These young voices remind Tony of the power of representation and humor to both discriminate and liberate depending on its use.

Kotsur's "dynamic duo"—SuperDeafy/Troy and Officer Norm/Derek—symbolize binary attitudes pertaining to deafness and disability. The casting of Norm in his conservative blue police uniform establishes him as a metonym for authority figures and regulating social institutions in the world of the film—that is, discrimination that SuperDeafy and, symbolically, the d/Deaf community navigate on a daily basis and are sometimes forced to play along with. The clash of costuming indicates the clash of ideologies, where Super-Deafy provides color and warmth and Officer Norm orders and regulates (as one fan complains, "Officer Norm is always telling SuperDeafy 'No!' This is like all hearing people"). In an episode where Troy interviews a Deaf, female motor cross champion, Norm grunts, "Deaf girl can't ride no motorcycle," followed by a cartoonish montage where SuperDeafy and the champion fly through space on a motorbike whilst Norm chases them on a child's scooter that he can barely ride. The hero/villain dichotomy makes it clear which side (and ideologies) the young audience is positioned to align with.

SuperDeafy's slogan, "power at hand," increasingly promotes the potential of superpowers to "reinvent the wheel" and "change the system." Tony removes

Figure 3.3. Close of *No Ordinary Hero: The SuperDeafy Movie*. Directed by Troy Kotsur. USA: Douglas Matejki and Hilari Scarl, 2013.

the lycra in favor of a suit and moves into local politics. Power becomes about taking control of the ideological messages inherent in the superhero image, to "keep making kids laugh. But not make fun of SuperDeafy." The close of the film depicts Tony reaching for a SuperDeafy doll as the closed caption reads "whoosh" and the doll flies into his hand. The final shot is Tony gazing directly at the viewer with a smirk as he grasps the doll (Figure 3.3). The Deaf gaze has literally shifted, the audience is directly engaged rather than a passive observer, and Tony learns he can be both political advocate and "lovable buffoon." It is only now that he truly has superpowers. "The End" flies across the frame, closely followed by "And the Beginning." The open ending suggests the quest for equity, access, and inclusion is ongoing but that with the right balance of humor and activism, he will succeed.

CONCLUSION

When contemporary children's fiction seeks to represent d/Deaf subjectivity in a manner that subverts established (and marginalizing) ideological social paradigms, humor often plays a dual role. On one level, it functions to close the space between text and readers to encourage empathy and familiarity. However, humor also possesses the capacity to create distance; readers are forced out of the fictional world and into their own world to consider the ways in which power, equality, and tolerance operate. Such fictions do not treat children as "other"; instead they are child-centric in terms of their subject matter. That is, they construct the child figure as an agent of change and similarly position their readers in ways that require active participation, creativity, and critical thought.

NOTE

1. It is conventional to distinguish between "deaf" and "Deaf." First established by James Woodward, deaf referred to those who were audiologically deaf, and Deaf referred to those who use sign language as their primary language and identify with Deaf Culture (Lindgren, DeLuca, and Napoli, xiii)—a "linguistic, cultural minority group" (Pajka-West, 1). Brueggemann argues that "no one really seems to completely understand the differences and distinctions between the two terms" (34) and that "in the commonplace book of 'deafness,' things are not always clearly or singularly defined, designated, or determined as 'just' or 'pure,' or 'only' deafness" (32). For these reasons, this chapter will adopt the practice of using d/Deaf to "represent deaf, hard of hearing, and culturally Deaf people" (Lindgren, DeLuca, and Napoli, xiii).

CHAPTER 4

"The Deaf Man Turned a Deaf Ear"[1]

Metaphors of Deafness and the Critical Gaze
in the Works of la Comtesse de Ségur, 1858–1865

—Hélène Charderon

The experience of deafness is at the heart of four stories for children written by Sophie de Ségur, a popular nineteenth-century French writer. In the trilogy composed of *Les malheurs de Sophie, Les petites filles modèles,* and *Les vacances,* and in her later novel *Un bon petit diable,* various characters are shown as either deaf or victims of deafness—that is, being denied a voice. In this light, I propose to examine the extent to which such representations of characters "turning a deaf ear" deconstruct the power relations between adults and children, in the context of the process of civilization at work in these four tales.

Les malheurs de Sophie relates the life of Sophie from age three to four. Each of the twenty-two chapters is built around an anecdote relating some or other example of the little girl's mischief in order to foreground a corresponding parable based on her experiences, which gradually lead to her moral edification, symbolically allowing her to enter society and leave the family house in order to travel to America. *Les petites filles modèles* takes place after Sophie's trip: she now lives with her stepmother, Madame Fichini. Having been violently mistreated by her mother, Sophie continues to suffer at the hands of her stepmother, who finally abandons her to the care of Madame de Fleurville. From then on, Sophie is brought up alongside Camille, Madeleine, and Marguerite. Published a year later, *Les vacances* retrospectively fills the diegetic gap between *Les malheurs de Sophie* and *Les petites filles modèles*: as Camille and Madeleine's cousins come to spend the summer holidays with them, three characters, including

Sophie's cousin Paul, return after spending four years on an island as the result of a shipwreck that killed Sophie's mother and Paul's parents on their way to America. Finally, *Un bon petit Diable*, published six years later, recounts the adventures of a young Scottish orphan, Charles Mac'Lance, who is robbed of his inheritance and mistreated by his tutor, sent to a harsh boarding school, and has to learn to mend his ways in order to get on in life.

These four stories were published between 1858 and 1865. This is a transitional period in France from a political and a cultural point of view. On the one hand, the circulation of knowledge was greatly increased, but on the other, the state retained a very firm grasp on what could and could not be said and published. The historical and social context in which these four stories are inscribed is therefore essential to any analysis of the narrative function of metaphorical deafness as a means of deconstructing the power relations at stake, in order to foreground a potentially subversive reading of these works.

THE TEXTS AND THEIR CONTEXT

In Ségur's *Un bon petit diable*, the bell-ringer in Mr Old Nick's boarding school is deaf, which justifies his other role in this institution: he is the official whipper,

> in charge of administering whippings to the children. Because he could not hear the children scream, he couldn't be softened nor be swayed by promises, nor scared by threats, he carried out his duty with harshness and cruelty, which made the pupils hate him and the masters appreciate him. (158)

This character seems to embody the gap between two specific visions of the world, those of the adult and the child, who evolve alongside each other in the same environment but, arguably, apprehend and appropriate it in different ways. While the executioner is characterized as being literally deaf, Ségur's stories for children seem to be populated by hearing characters who "turn a deaf ear," thereby becoming deaf at a metaphorical level. Indeed, they *choose* not to hear, bringing deafness to the fore as a metaphorical means to undermine others' authority, or to deny others a voice.

Choosing to "turn a deaf ear" is particularly significant in the context of power relations between adults and children in these novels: Cousine Mac'Miche and Old Nick (*Un bon petit diable*), Madame de Réan (*Les malheurs de Sophie*), and Madame Fichini (*Les petites filles modèles* and *Les vacances*) each promote an education imparted under the threat of the whip, corporal punishment being seen as the only way to inculcate sound morals and social codes of behavior.

Therefore, they abuse their strength and power, denying any voice or agency to the child for whom they are supposedly responsible. Norbert Elias highlights the great influence of adults over children in the education process: "Partly automatically, partly quite consciously through their own conduct and habits, adults induce corresponding behavior-patterns in children" (Elias, 413). By portraying such undesirable educators, Ségur emphasizes the importance of suitable guiding figures in order for children to develop an adequate understanding of societal expectations. As a counterpart to such abusive adults, she creates disobedient child characters: Charles and Sophie seem to respond to the abuse of power by "turning a deaf ear" themselves, silently resisting the norms the adults try to impose upon them. This process varies, too: while Charles seems to do it on purpose, to challenge his cousin's authority, Sophie seems to disobey on pure impulse.

In order to understand its impact, it is important to consider the concept of deafness within the social and cultural context of the texts dealt with here. The etymology of the word "deaf" is quite telling with regard to its ambivalence: it does indeed denote the incapacity to hear, but also to speak, and is associated with ideas such as emptiness, insensitivity, and confusion.[2] The French word "sourd" is also ambivalent: etymologically it describes those "who cannot hear," but also "who don't want to hear."[3] In nineteenth-century France, deaf people were considered as subsocial, nearly subhuman. Their inability to hear (and even more so to speak) was taken to denote a lack of intelligence and morals. Correspondingly, deafness was regarded as a disease to be cured through the learning of speech, because only speech could help the deaf to improve their social standing by proving that they had intellectual capacities. According to Michel Foucault,[4] medical thought has a strong influence on social norms, and indeed, the *doxa* of the time held that the capacity to speak was inextricably bound to intelligence. Moreover, the nineteenth century was profoundly marked by the Industrial Revolution and the ideology of progress that goes hand in hand with it. In this context, the deaf, and even more so the deaf-and-voiceless, were thought to be defective, inferior, and as such, to be marginalized. If they could not prove their intellectual capacities through articulate speech, they were considered to be dumb, which shares the same etymological root as the word "deaf"[5] and which first meant "unable to speak," and then accreted the meanings "foolish, stupid, ignorant" in modern English in the early nineteenth century.[6] Hence arose a universally negative bias regarding the deaf community, who were heavily discriminated against on the grounds of their assumed intellectual and moral inferiority. Florence Encrevé talks about "social sidelining"[7] (Encrevé, 145), especially in the latter half of the century. Deaf people had to fight for their civil rights and for equality before the law, all through the nineteenth century. According to Adolphe Bélanger, "Until the end of [the nineteenth century] the deaf-and-mute were discounted by all the legislators on account of their disability and the neglect in which they lived" (Bélanger, 5).[8] Disability was simply not compatible with the ideology of progress.

According to the nineteenth-century historian François Guizot, "The notion of progress, of development, seems . . . to be the fundamental idea contained within the word *civilization*" (Guizot, 15).[9] The term has been defined by Norbert Elias as being a process: "The process of civilization is a change of human conduct and sentiment in a quite specific direction" (Elias, 403). This helps us to understand the marginalization of anyone not fitting the behavioral orientation imposed by society. Because of its resistance to change of condition, deafness was considered as an obstacle to the domination of culture over nature so dear to nineteenth-century bourgeois ideology. The Industrial Revolution that literally transformed nineteenth-century society was intricately bound up with hope in the future, a heuristic faith in the fate of human beings who would be able to master their environment thanks to new techniques. Within this debate, two opposed ideologies emerged: "In the nineteenth century, the chorus of voices was split between those extolling a better past and those celebrating a better future" (Elias, 505). Indeed, the industrial classes, in line with bourgeois ideology, focused on the future, while conservative aristocrats opposed the transformation of society through industrialization and endorsed an idealized heritage of the past.

In this respect, Ségur has traditionally been categorized among the more conservative aristocrats of her time—even though researchers have now shown that behind the distinctly conservative morals displayed in her stories for children, a more subversive philosophy seems to be lurking between the lines. A multilayered reading of the narrative function of metaphorical deafness reveals her characters to be indeed more complex than they seem at first sight, and it is the notion of "turning a deaf ear" that seems to bring their ambivalence to the fore.

THE NARRATIVE FUNCTIONS OF METAPHORICAL DEAFNESS

Ségur offers her readers two categories of adult characters: the good and the bad, those entirely unsuited to their roles as educators and those who are the perfect guiding figures. In *Un bon petit diable*, Cousine Mac'Miche is represented as a greedy, violent woman who does not hesitate to "abuse her strength and authority" (*BPD*, 52) because she thinks that using the whip on a child is "the best means of education" (*BPD*, 58). This attitude is mirrored in the (aptly named) Old Nick's school, where the students call their masters the "oppressors"

(*BPD*, 164), a clear acknowledgment of their habit of abusing their strength and authority. This is hardly surprising though, considering Old Nick's appeal to "order, under the beneficial regime of the whip" (*BPD*, 205). And indeed, violence against children occurs frequently throughout the story. Like the deaf whipper, adults "turn a deaf ear" to the children's arguments, and indeed to their needs. Charles is described as wearing "threadbare, worn clothes, like those of a pauper" (*BPD*, 29), and he sleeps in "a miserable bunk" (*BPD*, 70). Moreover, he is denied the right to speak when his cousin Mac'Miche won't listen to him: "Quiet! I don't want you to speak! I don't want to hear your stupid voice" (*BPD*, 92). Cousine Mac'Miche and the masters at the school are counterbalanced by good, generous, and compassionate characters who listen and help: mainly Betty, Cousine Mac'Miche's servant, who supports Charles against her mistress, and the judge, who helps Charles to regain his inheritance, which had been stolen from him by his cousin.

The trilogy of Sophie's adventures also contains several examples of abusive adults who "turn a deaf ear" to the child's well-being in order to impose their authority. Sophie's mother and later her stepmother promote violence as a method of education exactly like Cousine Mac'Miche and the teachers in *Un bon petit diable*. In chapter 18 of *Les malheurs de Sophie*, the narrator explains that "without saying a word, [Madame de Réan] took Sophie with her, and whipped her as she never had before. *No matter how Sophie screamed, begged for mercy*, she was harshly whipped" (*MS*, 181, my emphasis). This shows Madame de Réan's uncompassionate attitude towards her daughter, as, like the deaf whipper in *Un bon petit diable*, she frequently "turns a deaf ear" to her screams. Madame Fichini, Sophie's stepmother, is no better: after accusing Sophie of something she didn't do, she interrupts the little girl when she tries to defend herself, and instead of listening to her arguments, she "*didn't let her go on*; she rushed at her, grabbed her by the ear, dragged her in the room next door, and, *despite Sophie's protests and tears*, she started whipping her, beating her until her arms were weary" (*PFM*, 125, my emphasis). She too sees corporal punishment as "the only way to raise children; the whip is the best master" (*PFM*, 68). Here again, the contrast with good educators such as Madame de Fleurville and Madame de Rosbourg, who are deeply "outraged" (*PFM*, 126) by this "unjust and barbarous punishment" (*PFM*, 68), highlights the moral coloring of metaphorical deafness, mirroring the immoral image attached to the deaf community in nineteenth-century France. Therefore, metaphorical deafness can be read as a symbolical representation of the immoral dimension of these characters. Indeed, bad parents produce bad children, as the end of *Un bon petit diable* shows: "Severity makes people unhappy and nasty" (*BPD*, 403). On the contrary, good educators have a positive influence on their *protégés*:

"Sophie had been at Fleurville for two weeks; she was so happy that all her flaws and bad habits seemed to have receded" (*PFM*, 140).

As Ségur displays good and bad guiding figures and listeners, so too she creates two opposed categories of children: disciplined and undisciplined. Thus, in *Un bon petit diable*, Charles is opposed to his blind cousin Juliette, "who managed to change a true devil into a charming and excellent young man, thanks to the Christian gentleness and kindness that touches us and brings us back onto the right track" (*BPD*, 1), but when under the bad influence of his cousin Mac'Miche, he was becoming very impulsive towards her. Marianne, Juliette's sister, is very good to her and has been taking care of her since the death of their parents, which explains why, despite her disability, Juliette "never complains, never gets angry! . . . Always kind, always smiling!" (*BPD*, 34), whereas Charles, after the death of his parents, has been left in the care of villains. Apart from being occasionally violent when fighting back, he seems to mirror his Cousine Mac'Miche's tendency to deny him a voice by consciously "turning a deaf ear" to her: "Isn't it appalling, my dear Betty, that my cousin prevents me from being nice? . . . But I can't! With her, it's impossible! Ah! If only I could live with Juliette! How different I would be! How nice, obedient . . ." (*BPD*, 95). The influence of the guiding figure is therefore fundamental. Similarly, he "turns a deaf ear" to adults' orders during his stay at Old Nick's school. By leading the rebellion of the children against their "oppressors," he pursues the path towards complete mutism, becoming deaf and mute to the brutality of the masters. As a result, Old Nick announces he will "punish silence" (*BPD*, 184), an ironical counterpart to the guard, Boxear—"who lives up to his name!" (*BPD*, 185)—who had beaten Charles precisely because he had answered his question: "This is how we overcome smooth talkers (he pulls his hair); reasoners (he slaps him); insubordinates (he beats him with a ruler); revolutionaries (he whips him)" (*BPD*, 152).

Les malheurs de Sophie also offers several examples of Sophie disobeying her mother's orders, sometimes bringing Paul down with her, while her friends Camille and Madeleine are true "model children." Throughout her moral instruction, she questions various adults' commands, as she is obviously inclined to what Sigmund Freud calls the pleasure principle rather than to the reality principle. In chapter 20, Sophie and Paul discuss the matter of obedience and illustrate the difference between these two notions:

Sophie: "I'll try to mend my ways; I promise I'll try. But it's so annoying to obey!"

Paul: "It's a lot more annoying to be punished. And I've noticed that the things we are forbidden to do are dangerous; when we do them, something bad always happens to us, and then we're afraid to meet my aunt and Maman." (224)

Disobedience too can be read as metaphorical deafness, when children "turn a deaf ear" to norms the adults seek to impose upon them. The mistreatment experienced by the child characters shapes their attitude. Indeed, Sophie suffers very violent punishments, which explains why she is violent herself (to Paul in *Les malheurs de Sophie*, and to Marguerite and Camille in *Les petites filles modèles*). They are both denied a voice, which in turn explains why they more readily "turn a deaf ear" to the adults' voices, even at the risk of physical violence. Just as Sophie is denied the right to explain herself when accused, Paul, in *Les vacances*, explains that he endured emotional isolation, even though he may not have experienced harsh corporal punishment:

> No, my father d'Aubert didn't like me, and neither did my mother; when I wasn't
> with Sophie, I was very bored; I spent all the time with the servants, who mis-
> treated me, knowing that *nobody cared*. *When I complained*, Maman would say
> that I was a difficult child, that I was never happy, and *Papa would slap* me and
> *chase me out* of the living room. (*V*, 192, my emphasis)

Because they were orphaned, they both had experience of better surrogate parents, who were able to guide them towards the right path: Sophie, thanks to Madame de Fleurville, "was angry, she became gentle; she was greedy, she became sober; she was a liar, she became sincere; she was a thief, she became honest; finally, she was nasty, she became kind" (*MS*, 7). It is a long process: this behavioral transformation is only really accomplished at the end of the trilogy. Paul becomes a courageous young man under the influence of Monsieur de Rosbourg, his surrogate father, the epitome of the guiding figure. In this context, arguably, "turning a deaf ear" appears both as the symptom and the consequence of the children's resistance to the adults' abuse of authority in the power relations that are at the core of children's literature and may provide a powerful way to deconstruct them.

Norbert Elias defines the process of growing up as "the individual civilizing process to which each young person . . . is automatically subjected from earliest childhood, to a greater or lesser degree and with greater or lesser success" (Elias, 4–5). He explains that the impact of grown-ups in this process is fundamental:

> Since in our society every human being is exposed from the first moment of
> life to the influence and the moulding intervention of civilized grown-ups, they
> must indeed pass through a process of civilization in order to reach the standard
> attained by their society in the course of its history. (Elias, 5)

Ségur's characters arguably represent both categories: those who have successfully undergone the process of civilization, as well as those who have done so less successfully and are therefore unsuitable guides, and die in the end (Madame de Réan and Madame Fichini, Paul's parents and Cousine Mac'Miche). However, disobedient children are given a chance to mend their ways and live an honest life. The resistance to the authority of abusive adults tends to deconstruct the power relations between adult and child by providing a critical challenge to the social norms, when these seem questionable. As Juliette puts it in *Un bon petit diable*, children must obey their tutors: "He owes his cousin respect and obedience. . . . She is his tutor after all, she is the one who is bringing him up" (*BPD*, 50). However, this social rule is denounced and rejected in the stories where the tutors do not adequately fulfill their roles as guiding figures. In this sense, the narrative function of metaphorical deafness proves to be ambivalent. On the one hand, the immorality and insensitivity associated with deaf people helps to disrupt and deconstruct the prevailing power relations by character-izing the bad tutors as immoral and insensitive, unworthy of their social role, and therefore powerless. Unsuitable educators are indeed depicted as "barba-rous" (*MS*, 68), that is, uncivilized; moreover, "the mistreatment of minors is forbidden by law" (*BPD*, 60), that is, socially unacceptable—both characteristics mirroring the representations of the deaf community in nineteenth-century France. On the other hand, if children "turning a deaf ear" are judged by their tutors to be immoral or insensitive, the narrator (and the reader) will clearly come to the defense of these children: metaphorical deafness then becomes a mimetic response to the bad behavioral example provided by bad educators, which it highlights as unsuitable and alienating.

The issue of the suitable adult educator provides the reader with a critical perspective on the process of civilization, and more specifically, on the norms imposed on children by adult society. Ségur powerfully demonstrates that the process of civilization is rarely smooth and straightforward, but rather full of pitfalls. This is reminiscent of Ségur's own childhood: she was indeed ill-treated by a cold-hearted mother when she was a child. This biographical context may in part explain the frequency of visually violent scenes, especially in *Les malheurs de Sophie*, *Les petites filles modèles*, and *Un bon petit diable*, even though these works were dedicated to and written for children. In these stories, it seems that metaphorical deafness serves the narrative function of what Vladimir Propp calls a "mark": deafness can be read as the consequent sign of the "fight" (the previous function in Propp's classification) of undergoing the process of civilization with the wrong educator, which is reminiscent of Norbert Elias's comment on the painful learning to adjust to the social mold: "The learning of self-controls, . . . and the consequent curbing of more animalic impulses and affects—in short the civilizing of the human young—is never a process entirely without pain; it always leaves scars" (Elias, 416).

Young readers are therefore placed in the position of witnesses to the protagonists' plight. Ségur seems to play with the norms of texts written for children to adjust them to her own design: even younger readers can be confronted with visually graphic scenes, because it is clearly flagged from the very beginning that in the end, all will be well—Sophie will become "gentle," "sober," "sincere," "honest," and "kind" (*MS, 7*); Paul will become "excellent" (*V, 1*); and Charles will become "an excellent and charming young man" (*BPD, 1*). In the prefatory dedications addressed to her grandchildren, Ségur reasserts the traditional framework of the morality tale, displaying from the outset the moral qualities of the characters, whether natural or learned by way of moral lessons. If the readers can be reassured as far as the end of the story is concerned, unexpected scenes will unfold before their eyes, providing a no-less-unexpected and potentially subversive deconstruction of the prevailing power relations between adults and children, under the guise of traditional morality.

THE SUBVERSIVE POWER OF METAPHORICAL DEAFNESS

Ségur portrays a great variety of characters in her stories for children, and I can only allude briefly to some of them in this chapter. While admittedly the unsuitable guiding figures are capable of tremendous evil, by contrast with the compassionate, good educators, everything is not as Manichean as it seems. Indeed, the bad educators also prove themselves capable, if not of kindness, at least of some restraint, if only in the end, in the cases of Cousine Mac'Miche and Madame Fichini. Madame de Réan's characterization is even more nuanced: at various points in the story, she is also depicted as a loving mother. Conversely, the virtuous Mesdames de Fleurville and de Rosbourg occasionally prove to be capable of pettiness. And the same is arguably true of the younger characters: the disobedient ones mend their ways in the end, but all along the narrator depicts them as intrinsically good, while "model children" show that they indeed "have flaws" and are not perfect.[10]

The underlying message of this complexity seems to be a warning to readers not to trust appearances, not to take anything for granted. And here, arguably, lies Ségur's subversion: she calls on her readers' experience to decipher the critical gaze she brings to bear on social norms, hidden behind an apparently black-and-white portrait of different human characters, under the guise of a conventional morality tale. As John Stephens explains it,

> the subject position of a reader undergoes considerable change in a rereading of the text, from one of little power over the decoding of story to one of

considerable power, but the change nevertheless does not alter reader subjection
to the book's implicit ideology. (Stephens 1992, 277)

It seems that the representation of metaphorical deafness highlights Ségur's
double intention, as she addresses both children and adults. It is, however, the
rereading of her stories that foregrounds this potential subversive representation of social norms through the conceit of metaphorical deafness. A child
reader will not necessarily be aware of the irony underlying the stories, but the
adult can certainly discover it by rereading them. Indeed, using metaphorical
deafness as a narrative strategy helps the reader to adopt the point of view of
the marginalized, which proposes a distanced vision of the behavioral norms
and codes that are under scrutiny in the text, for example regarding the place
of corporal punishment.

   Arguably, the representation of (metaphorical) deafness can be construed as
what Philippe Hamon calls an "ideological contact point of the text" (Hamon,
24),[11] that is to say, a moment in the text when the dominant ideological discourse
can be questioned, when the author's own ideology is confronted, consciously
or otherwise, with the broader ideology of a given society at a given point in
time. Indeed, it seems that the use of deafness as a narrative strategy can be
read as a subversive gesture, made under the guise of apparent respect for the
rules of children's literature *qua* genre. If the bad characters are indeed punished and the good ones are rewarded in the end, the narrator seems to leave
clues for readers to question these codes. The notion of deafness itself bears
the weight of society's judgment, questioning the voice of the community by
ventriloquizing the marginalized. In the example cited earlier from chapter 18
of *Les malheurs de Sophie*, when Sophie is harshly beaten and denied a voice
by her mother, the narrator's comments, strategically held over until the end
of the sentence, are surprising at first sight: "Without saying a word, [Madame
de Réan] took Sophie with her, and whipped her as she never had before. No
matter how Sophie screamed, begged for mercy, she was harshly whipped, *and
we have to admit that she deserved it*" (MS, 181, my emphasis). This narrative
comment seems to express the standard point of view, that is, the *doxa*, through
the focalization of the mother. This is reminiscent of the general reassertion of
a belief in moral regeneration through corporal punishment especially prevalent in the second half of the nineteenth-century.[12] But the readers can witness
the ideological gap between the commonly accepted statement and another
underlying ideology, that of the author: the insistence on the violence of the
scene can be read as a hint of Ségur's own ideas about education.[13] Therefore,
arguably, the narrator's comments here leave a vacant, evaluative space for
readers to form their own opinions, guided as they are by the author's point of

view, which underlies the narrator's comments. As John Stephens has pointed out, "Point of view is the aspect of narration in which implicit authorial control of audience reading strategies is probably most powerful" (Stephens 1992, 26). Here, by "turning a deaf ear" to Sophie's screams of terror, the characterization of Mme de Réan opens up a space in the narrative for a marginalized point of view, which allows a critical response to the norm, precisely because it allows "ideology and its filtering effect [to be] glimpsed in the *gap* that lies between an existing model acting as a norm, and a given element" (Hamon, 14, *sic*).[14] In the example above, the norm would be the idea that "we have to admit that she deserved it," which is put in perspective with, and challenged by, the narrator's view on the scene: "[Madame de Réan] whipped her *as she never had before. No matter how* Sophie screamed, begged for mercy, she was *harshly* whipped" (my emphasis). In this way, the codes are transgressed, the *doxa* disrupted, and it becomes possible to read another story between the lines, *hear* another voice: the author's.

Metaphorical deafness is inextricably linked with transgression, at both the diegetic and the discursive level: adult characters turning a deaf ear transgress the codes of their educating roles and society's morals in order to wield power; child characters who ignore the adult's authority transgress the social norms regulating the power relations between child and adult. Through her comments, the narrator transgresses the apparent moral discourse displayed in the stories. There is a parallel between this act of transgression and a heuristic quest: it is precisely by deconstructing the norms of society that one can better understand them, and critically evaluate them. The process of civilization itself is arguably part of such a heuristic quest. Interestingly, in the context of Ségur's stories, metaphorical deafness is reminiscent of the Promethean myth, the myth of transgression *par excellence*. Indeed, it conveys the idea of transgressing the rules in order to gain power and freedom. Here, the reminiscence of the Promethean myth undermined within the representations of metaphorical deafness arguably deconstructs power relations—the apparently powerful adults become powerless, while the apparently powerless children become powerful. The transgression of established codes provides an external perspective on these social norms by defamiliarizing them: the representation of metaphorical deafness as a violent transgression of order brings this—usually naturalized—order, the *doxa*, to light and allows an ideological evaluation of its relevance. Here again, however, all is not black and white, and Ségur seems to confirm that the apparently coherent and fair conclusions of her stories can be questioned: if the aim of the quest is the suppression of uncivilized instincts, what Norbert Elias called the "drive impulses and inclinations" (Elias, 413), the means that are used to this end by unsuitable educators seem to be challenged by the narrator—and arguably the author—through the scars inscribed in the fabric of the text and upon the flesh of the victims, scars that are foregrounded by the marginalized point of view offered by the narrative strategy of metaphorical deafness.

CONCLUSION

If *Les malheurs de Sophie, Les petites filles modèles, Les vacances,* and *Un bon petit diable,* as children's stories, illustrate the triumph of victimized children over abusive adults, this generic norm can also be read as a deconstruction of power relations through the representation of metaphorical deafness. Indeed, the ambivalent narrative function of deafness can offer a glimpse of the author's own ideological and subversive discourse. It can be argued that "turning a deaf ear" tends to defamiliarize deafness, so that deafness in turn can be read as a defamiliarizing tool for questioning a given system of thought and representation.

The narrative use of metaphorical deafness, that is, characters "turning a deaf ear" to norms and morals, seems to question social and behavioral patterns. The resort to the *ab-normal,* the *ex-centric,* allows a marginal and critical point of view to be conveyed to readers, so that they can experience a necessary distance from the norm and reach a clearer idea of commonly adopted stances, which allows retrospective ideological evaluation.

Dealing with deafness, however, also means dealing with the issue of communication: "turning a deaf ear" implies denying the Other's voice because it represents a danger—a threat to one's power or to one's well-being, for instance. When mutual incomprehension between adult and child is at stake, it seems that the only solution to prevent such a "dialogue of the deaf" involves a restoration of the ability to speak and to listen. The ending of each of the stories I have discussed here suggests such a reconciliation, especially, *Les Vacances.* Because Sophie disobeys the order she had been given never to speak of the shipwreck, her voice is literally restored, along with her memory and identity, as she tells her story. In chapter 6, readers are informed that "Sophie was trying to remember her lost memories to tell them to her friends. . . . All these events came back to her so sharply that she did not understand how she could have forgotten them and never wished to speak about them" (*V*, 124). Further on, she explains why she never mentioned the shipwreck before: "I forgot many things because Papa had forbidden me to ever talk to him about this shipwreck and about my poor Maman, or to ever question him about his marriage with my step-mother" (*V*, 132). Here, the act of storytelling, as transgression, is a powerful tool in the restoration of her memory and therefore her social identity: as she remembers her story, she is no longer Sophie Fichini, but becomes

Sophie de Réan once again. Arguably, children's literature itself participates in this (re)conciliation between children and adults, since both, in fact, are being taught a lesson: if the child readers need to learn how to become civilized, the adult must learn how to accompany them effectively through the process of civilization. This too, it seems, is reminiscent of the mythical, and ambivalent, dimension of writing metaphorical deafness.

NOTES

1. *Un bon petit diable*, 194. All the passages from Ségur's texts are my translations. For the quotations, *Les malheurs de Sophie* will be referred to henceforth as *MS*, *Les petites filles modèles* as *PFM*, *Les vacances* as *V*, and *Un bon petit diable* as *BPD*.

2. Online Etymology Dictionary https://www.etymonline.com/word/deaf. Accessed 13 February 2018.

3. Centre National des Ressources Textuelles et Lexicales http://www.cnrtl.fr/etymologie/sourd. Accessed 13 February 2018.

4. See Michel Foucault, *Surveiller et punir*, 1975.

5. Online Etymology Dictionary https://www.etymonline.com/word/deaf and https://www.etymonline.com/word/dumb. Accessed 13 February 2018.

6. Oxford English Dictionary, *dumb*, 7 (b) http://www.oed.com.libraryproxy.mic.ul.ie,/view/Entry/58378?rskey=xSGJD0&result=1&isAdvanced=false#eid. Accessed 10 October 2018.

7. "La mise à l'écart sociale des sourds," my translation.

8. "Par suite de son infirmité et de son abandon, le sourd-muet, jusqu'à la fin du siècle dernier, se trouvait mis hors la loi par tous les législateurs," my translation.

9. "L'idée du progrès, du développement, me paraît être l'idée fondamentale contenue sous le mot de *civilisation*," my translation.

10. See *PFM*, Préface, 1.

11. "Les points d'affleurement privilégiés de l'effet-idéologie," my translation.

12. See Christian Molaro, "Education morale et éducation corporelle des jeunes des classes pauvres au XIXᵉ siècle. Entre conceptions théoriques et organisation sociale," 23–25.

13. The conclusion of *Un bon petit diable* is quite revealing of Ségur's philosophy: "Severity makes people unhappy and nasty. Kindness attracts, softens, and corrects" (*BPD*, 403, my translation). The passage from two qualifications ("unhappy" and "nasty") to three ("attracts," "softens," and "corrects") tends to endorse the superiority of kindness over severity.

14. "L'idéologie et son travail de filtrage se laissent donc appréhender dans l'écart qui existe entre un modèle construit, faisant office de norme, et un donné," my translation.

CHAPTER 5

Subjectivity, Theory of Mind, and the Creation of Deaf Characters in Fiction

—John Stephens

There is a group of cognitive processes that we use in our everyday lives but that people also use to build up their understanding of character and story when they are writing or reading fiction. The interactive components of these processes comprehend the narrative construction of a storyworld and its pro-tagonists. I have set out a core group of these concepts as a wheel in Figure 5.1. The process applies to any protagonist in any work of fiction, but for this study I have placed the thematizing of deafness and communication at the hub of the wheel, as these are the focus of this chapter. The characterization in fiction of a complex deaf protagonist, like any other protagonist, is an effect brought about by the interaction of the cognitive processes shown in Figure 5.1. These processes have been conceptualized variously in psychology, cognitive linguistics, and narratology and have some areas of overlap, but their most common point is that they enable readers to infer a larger significance than is literally present in the given data. It is a commonplace that readers find more in a text than appears to be there, and different readers find different things. This process of interpretation is parallel to and closely aligned with Theory of Mind (ToM), the cognitive ability most humans acquire to attribute propositional attitudes (beliefs, feelings, desires, hopes, fears, acts of imagination, and so on) to other people and then to use those attributions to predict and explain their behavior (Garfield, Peterson, and Perry, 495).

This chapter explores how d/Deaf characters are represented in two books of very different kinds. As its title indicates, Roz Rosen's *Deaf Culture Fairy*

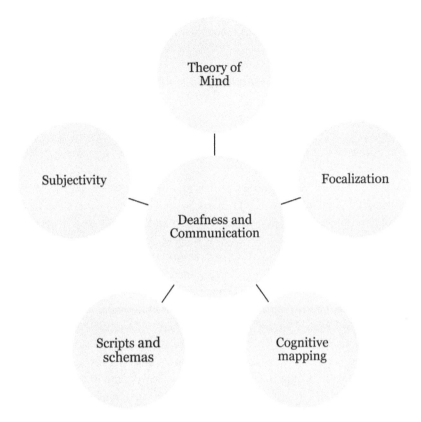

Figure 5.1. Cognitive processes for constructing character.

Tales (2017) is narratively, epistemologically, and ideologically positioned within Deaf Culture. Its retold stories are drawn from the fairy tale and fable canons, which have been transformed by replacing familiar protagonists with Deaf protagonists and nuancing events as Deaf experiences. Antony John's young adult novel *Five Flavors of Dumb* is a double-strand narrative that parallels the story of the infighting of a high-school rock band on its shaky path to acceptance and the coming-of-age of seventeen-year-old Piper Vaughan, who accidentally becomes manager of the band even though she has been moderately severely deaf since the age of six.[1] The contexts are family tension, peer relationships, and the rock-music tradition of Seattle from which emerged Kurt Cobain and Jimi Hendrix. Because her maternal grandparents were deaf, Piper is fluent in American Sign Language and often uses it to communicate with her mother and her brother, Finn, but with no one else. At school, where she is a top student, she "gets by" with the help of obsolete hearing aids she has had for seven years and an ability to "lip-read with Olympic precision" (13). Thus, like most postlingually deaf people, she has no contact with Deaf Culture.

THEORY OF MIND

Theory of mind emerged as a topic of interest to literary and cultural criticism around the beginning of the twenty-first century, and was apt to draw on research into the relative or profound mind reading deficits associated with autism, because, as Lisa Zunshine suggests, fiction "in many ways calls for the same kind of mind-reading—that is, the inference of the mental state from the behavior—that is necessary in regular human communication" (2006, 9), and autistic subjects characteristically seem unable to make such inferences. Writing in 1995, Francesca G. E. Happé documented twenty-six studies that demonstrate that a majority of autistic subjects fail a range of ToM tasks (844–45). Amongst scholars of children's literature, the best-known work of fiction that explores parallels between autism, Theory of Mind, and narrative strategies (in particular unreliable narration and the (non-)attribution of thought and feelings to characters) is Mark Haddon's metafictive, cross-over novel *The Curious Incident of the Dog in the Night-Time* (see Freißmann; Ciocia; Gilbert; Muller; Resene; Zunshine). There has not been a comparable work of fiction stemming from the extensive research into Theory of Mind in deaf children, and it is difficult to judge whether such research impacts on fictional representation or whether the typical maturation narrative trajectory from deficit to accomplishment replicates ToM deficit.

The key comparison in the research is the comparative performance in standard ToM tests of deaf native-signing children and deaf late-signing children. Deaf "native-signing children" are born to and raised by deaf signing parents and hence have a rich potential for communication from birth. Deaf "late-signing children" are born to and raised by hearing parents, and characteristically learn to sign after the age of six and do so at school rather than at home. ToM is generally perceptible in a child at around the age of four, and native-signing children perform in standard tests at a level equivalent to hearing children inhabiting a hearing environment. In contrast, late-signing children exhibit ToM at a much later age (Garfield, Peterson, and Perry, 507–8). It is argued that children develop a ToM of other persons' mental states because they are exposed to talk about thoughts and other invisible mental processes. Communication through signing supplies this exposure as effectively as speech in a hearing family. However, a deaf child in a hearing family may often have no easy means of communication with hearing family members and other children, especially about topics such as mental states, thoughts, and feelings, which may have no concrete referent. Communication is likely to be more functional, and hence these children, like children living in isolated families (Hollos and Cowan, 640), have specific difficulty in adopting the perspectives of others. These conclusions must be considered as tentative, since native-signers are rare among the deaf population as a whole (Woolf, Want, and Siegal, 769).

Although ToM is embedded in the fabric of narrative and has been of interest to researchers into the cognitive development of deaf children, it has not received any attention from scholars concerned with deafness in children's or YA literature. This is perhaps because it is implicit and not overtly thematized. An excellent example of active ToM in children's literature is the picture book *The Elephant in the Room* (2015), written by audiologist Jim Bombicino to promote awareness in both hearing and hard of hearing readers of the nature of communication when an interlocutor is using hearing aids. The book explores why the protagonist, Skyler, a hard of hearing boy, has decided it is too hard to converse with his hearing parents and siblings. Despite their best intentions, they are depicted as speaking too quickly, from too far away, with their backs to him rather than face-to-face, or not observing turn-taking amongst themselves, unaware that a hearing aid cannot separate out a specific speech signal from concurrent utterances. So, on this day, Skyler has given up. Conversation is the primary means for conveying ToM, but when Skyler mishears and tries a follow-up question, he is dismissed with "don't you worry about it" or "never mind." The visible elephant in the room, his little sister Maizy's stuffy, which runs a silent commentary on what is represented, comments, "But we do worry about it." The elephant's sensitivity to Skyler's thoughts and feelings is a projection of Maizy's unfolding ToM, which enables her first to perceive Skyler's frustration and then to adopt appropriate conversational strategies, which their mother recognizes as a model for the family. Maizy (and her elephant) thus bring into visibility the figurative *elephant in the room* of the book's title—the family's unacknowledged disregard of Skyler's everyday needs as a hard of hearing child. As an excellent example of how characters and readers employ ToM to reach similar conclusions, the book is a model of the functions of ToM in fiction.

The situation of a deaf child in an oral family is also depicted by Roz Rosen in her adaptation of Andersen's "The Ugly Duckling" (*Deaf Culture Fairy Tales*, 2017, 6–18). A pervasive theme of Rosen's collection, in which the politics of d/Deafness are brought into children's literature, is the long-running and often acrimonious debate over oral versus manual habilitation of deaf children: the stories unequivocally celebrate Deaf world culture, especially American Sign Language (ASL) as its flagbearer, and vehemently oppose any form of oralist education. Thus the core themes of Andersen's tale—"an uneasy outsider experiences the pain of a social world that will not or cannot accommodate him or her" (Wood, 199) and "one's true nature may not, at first, be easily recognized by self or other, but . . . one's value will become apparent if one endures" (Oroson-Weine, 19)—are adapted to express how a deaf character (Ugly Duckling) is encouraged by a signing cat to discover his own identity. Although the story is mostly focalized by the duckling, he proves to be ToM deficient, whereas the cat displays developed ToM and can guide the duckling's thinking. The duckling has been compelled by Dr. Quack (pun intended) to wear a rubber belt that prevents any use of his wings, which is one of the collection's many symbols for oralist bans on sign language, but the belt breaks as he matures into a mute swan (Cygnus Olor) and he learns to fly and uses his wings to convey meaning (as mute swans do). When he attempts to return to his duck family at the end of the story, it is his mother who tells him, "You're not one us . . . you belong with that flock over there" (18), and he is united with his biological mother. The story motif of the returned lost child, however, masks a more problematic outcome wherein a hearing family yields a deaf child to Deaf Culture. This outcome accords with the ethically problematic argument that because most deaf children are born to hearing parents, "most Deaf children do not belong to the same culture as their biologic parents" and belong intrinsically to Deaf Culture (Lane and Bahan, 304).

Theory of Mind has been attributed to fictional characters throughout the history of the novel but may take specific forms in the case of deaf protagonists. Piper Vaughan, protagonist of *Five Flavors of Dumb*, exhibits some crucial examples of mind-blindness, although readers might attribute these more to her social reticence because of her deafness than to the onset of deafness postlingually at the age of six, by when she would have normally developed ToM. Further, readers will be more likely to read the story as an example of a recognizable plot structure, a coming-of-age story that focuses on Piper's struggle to understand herself and the social ecology she inhabits. ToM functions in conjunction with such familiar scripts (that is, dynamic narrative elements that express how a sequence of events or actions is expected to unfold). Readers work interactively with scripts because not every action in the causal chain that constitutes a script needs to be included for the script to be realized. Rather, readers infer the complete script from a core element and identify unexpressed causal links between events (Schank and Abelson, 38; Stephens, "Schemas and Scripts," 14).

A COGNITIVE MAP OF DEAF CULTURE

An interplay of familiarity and novelty can be especially evident in adaptations of well-known stories such as fairy tales and fables, as in Rosen's *Deaf Culture*

Fairy Tales. Because Deaf characters and Deaf experiences (often as outcomes) have been interpolated into the familiar scripts and schemas of these stories, reader expectations about the components of a fairy tale or folktale world have been displaced by a cognitive map of Deaf Culture. This map begins to unfold with the first adapted tale, "Little Red Riding Hood." All of the stories begin with an initial capital rubric in the form of a hand using ASL fingerspelling, so the first word of this story, "Little," begins with the sign for L. Readers unfamiliar with the sign are thus encouraged to deduce that this is the L sign, which is easy to do from context, and perhaps to begin to familiarize themselves with an ASL fingerspelling chart. By the last item in the book they will have learned A, D, I, K, L, O, and W. The opening story then proceeds to depict an idyllic scene in which Red Riding Hood and her deaf mother share an affectionate signed conversation before the familiar script unfolds to the point where the wolf is about to eat the little girl.

> But Little Red Riding Hood held out her palm and stopped him. She signed, "Are you Deaf? You sound different from the other wolves."
> "Me, Deaf?" thought Big Bad Wolf, "aha, that's it." (4)

At the tale's close, the woodsman is repelled by Little Red Riding Hood and her deaf Grandma as an interloper from the hearing world, and the two then elide the Wolf's twofold difference—he is a nonhuman animal and is deaf—and induct him into Deaf Culture by sharing food and teaching him a mantra that expresses Deaf agency: "Nothing about us without us!" The story thus establishes two key elements of a cognitive map of Deaf Culture, the centrality of signing and Deaf agency, whereby public policies impacting upon the lives of d/Deaf people "could be shaped with the active involvement of deaf people rather than for deaf people" (Holcomb, 472).

The conclusion to the first tale also signals that *Deaf Culture Fairy Tales* is grounded upon a Deaf-centric epistemology. Thomas A. Holcomb argues that a deaf epistemology is analogous to various minority epistemologies that consist of "theories of knowledge created by members, about members' modes of knowing, for the purpose of liberating members" (Holcomb, 471). Paddy Ladd suggests that Deaf epistemology also reaches out to hearing people to enable them to understand "Deaf ways of being in the world, of conceiving that world and their own place within it, both in actuality and in potentiality" (19). An essential element of Deaf epistemology that appears in *Deaf Culture Fairy Tales* is that the felt experience of individuals outweighs scientific research.

The formulation "Deaf ways of being in the world" implies the existence, as a work in process, of a cognitive map. The concept of cognitive mapping originates as a spatial application and refers to the cognitive or mental abilities that enable us to collect, organize, store, recall, and manipulate information about the spatial environment. In a wider meaning, it describes how individual subjects experience everyday life in relation to larger conditions of existence that are grounded in proximal phenomena—the mundane and local properties of *here, now, this*—and range through sociality to distal phenomena (*there, then, that*), which are global and even transcendent (see Stephens, "Cognitive Maps"). Both senses point to the way settings are interpreted when they are focalized by characters within the text and thus represent embodied experience of physical and/or social landscapes. This mapping of space, and particularly in relationship to the narrative representation of *place* and people located within that place, overlaps with social ecology, which enquires into the interdependencies of place and the social and cultural networks that shape the cognitive development of a person. Piper Vaughan's deepening understanding of rock music and life in Seattle (*Five Flavors of Dumb*) is a good example of this interaction between cognitive development and social ecology.

The core of social ecology is the concept of well-being or flourishing in the interactions of people with the surrounding world: that is, interactions with habitation (environment) and social, institutional, and cultural contexts and the bearings such interactions have on notions of wholeness, humanness, natural-ness, and place in the larger order of things (Stephens, "Cognitive Maps," 243). The fictive representation of such interactions may be positive or negative, or, as in *Deaf Culture Fairy Tales, Five Flavors of Dumb*, a picture book such as Jim Bombicino and Gildas Chatal's *The Elephant in the Room* (2015), and probably most fiction for young adults, may represent a struggle to maintain well-being in the face of hostile or chaotic forces. Rozen's "Little Red Riding Hood" depicts such hostile forces in two stages as, first, the Wolf is marginalized by his deaf-ness and, second, by the unreflective attempt by the woodsman to intervene in and disrupt an emerging Deaf community. In contrast, the map incorporates the physical landscape by linking the houses of Red Riding Hood's mother and her Grandma by the bread and jam made in one house and consumed in the other and by the use of ASL to affirm a strong sense of belonging.

Each entry in Rozen's collection adds another component to the cognitive map, retrospectively framed by the concluding piece, which, as the author describes, "Weaves and links actual milestones in Deaf history into a story-like series of positive accomplishments" (vi) and acts as a foundation for Deaf-centric epistemology. It rounds off a sequence of stories that offer readers an account of how Deaf characters in various situations constitute a map of how to live well. A recurrent theme is the century-long impact of the resolution to ban sign language in the education of children passed by the 1880 Milan International

Congress of the Educators of the Deaf, or, as Rosen puts it, when "the world plunged into darkness" (124). The implacable opposition to communication other than sign takes many forms through the collection and pervades its cognitive map. One of the most acerbic examples, "The Emperor's Clothes," draws on popular understandings of Andersen's familiar tale to transform it into an allegory that asserts that oralist practices are fraudulent. Andersen's tale is usually understood to show how people can believe a lie even while they know it is a lie, or, as Hollis Robbins expresses it, "The weavers are not really producing anything. They are rogues and frauds profiting from the insecurity and gullibility of others" (62). To the Emperor's vanity Rozen adds a speech impediment that "the proprietor of the Bell Tailor Shop" (68) undertakes to cure. Given the context and the repetition of "Bell" seven times in nine lines, it seems obvious that satire is directed at the Alexander Graham Bell Association for the Deaf and Hard of Hearing (AG Bell), whose stated mission is "to ensure that people who are deaf and hard of hearing can hear and talk."[2] The tale concludes with the humbled emperor's decision "to put his money into bilingual education for everyone instead of squandering it all on fancy clothes" (73).

The cognitive map of *Deaf Culture Fairy Tales* embeds its characters within a Deaf world or in an enclave that remains separable. The deaf pigs in "The Three Little Pigs" thus surround their brick house with commercial enterprises—a bakery; a hardware store; and a combined coffeehouse, bookstore, and tutoring business, all of which interact with the local hearing community. Within the cognitive map their situation is grounded in proximal phenomena—family, peers, and friends ("Big Bad Wolf learned how to sign and became good friends with the three pigs"), home, and physical environment: "the house had a fine doorbell that flashed a lamp to alert residents if somebody was at the door" (57). More distally, the map includes the wider local community, whose members visit the pigs and "buy some rolls, coffee, books and gadgets." Some of Rosen's tales focus on societal expectations, beliefs, and values. Deaf Snow White, for example, is forbidden by her stepmother to sign—"My dear child, you must hear and speak to survive in this hearing world" (36)—and formal bans on sign language are a pressure point in "Hansel and Gretel" and "The Town Mouse and the Country Mouse." Deaf subjects are often mistreated by the hearing and excluded from social interaction ("Snow White," 36).

In contrast, other tales depict utopian communities or societies, usually described in a version of the formula, "There is equality, full access, social justice and love for all creatures. Everyone signs there" ("Beauty and the Beast," 118). The epitome of this strand is "The Princess and the 20 Mattresses": in this tale, a "Deaf-friendly and people-friendly country" (60), whose official languages are sign, fingerspelling, and English, is ruled by a family that has been deaf for

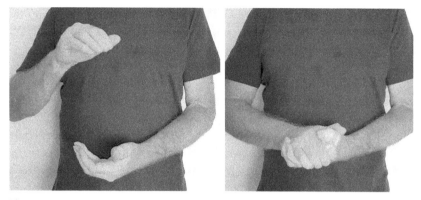

Figure 5.2. American Sign Language: *marriage / marry* (image supplied by author).

generations. The royal family "had to make sure that their children, who would become kings, queens, and heirs, inherited pure Deaf blood and were Deaf. This meant that they heard absolutely nothing. The less one could hear, the more pure one's Deaf royal blood was" (60). This curious situation appears to be a parody of some tenets of the early twentieth century American eugenics movement, which proposed a ban on marriage between deaf people (see Greenwald and Van Cleve, 37–42). For the unknown young woman to be deemed a suitable bride for the royal prince, she has to pass four tests rather than one as in the pretext, "The Princess and the Pea." These tests involve: competency in sign language and English; Deaf-centric wisdom; kindness and humility; and the Deaf royal blood test (that is, the twenty mattresses test).

The "Deaf-centric wisdom" test is also a test for readers and reflects the blurb on the back cover of the collection that describes it as "designed for the reader who uses American Sign Language or wants to learn about sign language and Deaf culture." The test pivots on supplying a punchline for an amusing story told by the King. The underlying script is derived from the movie *King Kong* and tells how a gorilla the size of a tree, and who is also an ASL user, captures a "lovely scientist" and asks her to marry him. Ordered to complete the story, the princess replies, "When the gorilla asked the scientist to marry him, he accidentally squashed her when he signed MARRY." The answer demonstrates that the princess is clever and witty, but readers who don't know ASL won't grasp the full humor of the joke unless they research the sign used (see Figure 5.2), which is made by lowering one hand to gently grasp the other hand. The "mattress test" entails that the princess is kept awake by a small object at the bottom of twenty mattresses, as in the tale's pretexts, except that a wooden tongue depressor has replaced the traditional pea. Used by speech trainers to explain where and how similar sounds such as "k" and "g" are made in the mouth, the depressor is anathema to Deaf Culture, and a "true blood Deaf-centered Princess" would be sensitive to its presence.

As the tales, and other components of the collection, roll into the summary Deaf history that brings closure, the historical sweep over two thousand years asserts a persistence of nascent Deaf culture. Regardless of context, throughout the collection "Deaf" is always capitalized, claiming all deaf people for Deaf culture. Further, Deaf-centric epistemology is grounded in the belief that members of Deaf Culture establish a truth based on their cultural beliefs and experiences. This particular cognitive map encompasses the description of deaf epistemology laid out by Holcomb:

> Deaf epistemology provides knowledge on how deaf people can best compen-
> sate for their limited hearing access. Deaf epistemology provides knowledge on
> the solutions for successful integration into society. Deaf epistemology provides
> knowledge on how family dynamics within families with a deaf child can be
> enhanced. The vast knowledge generated by the collective experience of deaf
> people, all of whom have varying degrees of hearing and speaking capabilities,
> has the potential to provide the truth needed to achieve improved educational
> success for all deaf children. (476)

FOCALIZATION, THEORY OF MIND AND SUBJECTIVITY IN *FIVE FLAVORS OF DUMB*

Five Flavors of Dumb is not situated within Deaf Culture, although Piper Vaughan, the seventeen-year-old protagonist, defines her deafness as "moderately severe." As first-person narrator of the story, Piper nevertheless exemplifies what Donna M. McDonald defines as "an immersed participant in the deaf experience (i.e., the insider's view)" (464), and by the close of the novel is moving toward bimodality-centered communication. Written by a hearing author with the support of deaf informants, the novel depicts Piper's experience of life in a predominantly oral/aural world and represents her everyday mode of communication as a form of *total communication*, which advocates the use of a combination of methods to communicate. Having lost her hearing postlingually, and having already become fluent in sign language to communicate with her deaf grandparents, Piper at age six was equipped with a range of communication options, although these do not render her life in a hearing community unproblematic. Sign language is only used by her mother and reluctant younger brother (but not her father), her hearing aids are borderline obsolete, and her unusually high skill in speechread-ing depends on the understanding and cooperation of any interlocutor as well as her ToM ability. Piper considers herself the class nerd, sitting at the front of the class and gaining the highest marks while she nurtures an ambition to attend Gallaudet University. However, her life is thrown into confusion when she discovers that, in order to pay for a cochlear implant for Grace, her profoundly deaf baby sister, her financially straitened parents have raided the college fund bequeathed by her deaf grandparents. Thus, while the novel's plot revolves around Piper's efforts to meet a challenge to manage "Dumb," a school rock band, a wide range of deafness issues are introduced and become prominent if the novel is read as deaf-themed.

Rosen's cognitive map can be interpreted as a collage of Deaf subjectivities, although separately they lack subtlety or complexity. Thus when Snow White rejects the Prince, closes the lid of her glass casket, and goes back to sleep, the dwarfs explain, "Snow White loved being Deaf and using sign language. Upon being liberated and finding her Deaf identity, Snow White did not want to go back to her old way of life" (43). In contrast, *Five Flavors of Dumb* refuses to position Piper's different hearingness as the defining element of her subjectivity, her sense of who she is and of the choices she can make and act upon. Her subjectivity is mutable, changing from time to time and in response to different social contexts such as her clashes with her family, her role as band manager, the "girl time" she comes to spend with female band members Tash and Kallie, and the times she spends demolishing her friend Ed at chess, for a long time (in her most acute failure of ToM) not knowing that he hates the game but plays so he can be with her. Deafness functions differently in different contexts and its significance changes. For example, after the band has imploded during its first television appearance the three girls go together to a café.

> We huddled at a table next to a bay of windows. A month before, Tash and Kallie would have piled onto seats without a thought for me, but now they sat beside each other on one side, with me on the other, so that I could follow the conversation more easily. Such a small gesture, but it meant everything. (219)

Such small gestures acknowledge Piper's deafness without making it the point of the scene. The point here is rather that three seventeen-year-old girls who didn't think they liked one another are dismissing their differences and beginning to bond. Such gestures become larger when Piper learns that her father and Ed are attending a class to learn how to sign, and baby Grace is the star pupil. Future membership of a small signing community adds another nuance to Piper's subjectivity.

In the café scene, Piper as narrator describes an action and supplies her ToM interpretation of Tash and Kallie's behavior from the perspective of her deafness. When we refer to processes of mental mapping such as "getting inside a character's head," we are talking about theory of mind, and this is a key part of the cognitive processes employed in constructing the illusion of complex characterization. As I said above, subjectivity is a product of the constantly changing relationships a person has with the multiplicity of social discourses he or she engages with—that is, the "subject positions" that a person occupies from moment to moment and from which subjectivity is negotiated through interrelationships. In this simple but subtle example, Piper's deafness is mediated through an intersubjective moment in which deafness is acknowledged as an everyday facet of her being. Attribution of subjectivity to fictive characters pivots on the representation of thoughts, feelings, emotions, and intentions, and this again comes down to theory of mind.

FOCALIZATION AND FIRST-PERSON NARRATION

The precursor and still the basis of theory of mind in fiction is the concept of focalization—that is, the technique whereby events, actions, and so on are presented from the point of view of a narrator or of a character within a story as if in the process of physically perceiving these phenomena. In principle, subjectivity is mainly attributed to a character in fiction if that character is depicted as a significant focalizer, because that is the principal means whereby interiority can be indicated. Focalization is signaled primarily by perceptual nodes—seeing, hearing, smelling, feeling, thinking—and is a very fluid process.

First-person narration, as in *Five Flavors of* Dumb, is narrator-focalized—while the thoughts of other characters may be accessed through their speech and reader application of ToM to their behavior, the viewpoint of the narrator dominates the narrative. In the following scene, close to the end of the novel, the band has secured a gig as warm-up to a highly successful group, but Josh, their narcissistic lead singer, has decided to leave the band and destroy it by ruining their performance. Piper has decided at the last minute to replace him with Kallie, even though Kallie's musical skills are poor, and play air guitar herself to make up the five performers required by the contract she has signed. The extract begins at a moment when Josh, having invaded the stage, snatched the microphone, and shouted abuse about the band, is about to be removed by bouncers.

> The bouncers [launched] themselves onto the stage at the very moment an earsplitting shriek filled the air.

> At first I assumed it was more feedback from the microphone, or maybe an
> alarm. It was high-pitched and piercing, and even though I didn't know where it
> was coming from, my immediate response was to press my hands against my ears
> to make it stop. Everyone else on stage was doing the same thing too—all except
> Kallie, whose body resembled a coiled spring, face twisted in anger. In her hand
> she clutched the microphone, shoved so far into her mouth it looked like she was
> making up for skipping dinner.
> That sound was *Kallie*? (*Five Flavors of Dumb*, 331)

The mixing of physical sensation and thought processes is characteristic
of the representation of complex mental states. Readers don't need to think
about what the text is doing or how it aligns the reader with the focalizer
because the processes are simple and don't demand attention. On the other
hand, this extract includes a good example of how focalization, by aligning
reader and focalizer, contributes to the gap-filling activity performed by readers. Piper hears the intensity of the sound, despite her imperfect hearing aids,
an intensity expressed in the impulse shared by all on stage to cover their ears.
Then she *sees* Kallie, the exception, and readers employ ToM to make sense
of Kallie's posture and expression. The awkward variation of the simile cliché
"like a coiled spring" draws attention to the fact that the image is conceptual
rather than visual, but thereby emphasizes the idea of potential energy waiting to explode. Piper's other analogy—"like she was making up for skipping
dinner"—is discordantly comical and helps emphasize the chaos of what is
happening, until Kallie's wild scream reorients the scene. In a brief discussion
in his essay "The Thinking Mind," Uri Margolin suggests that focalization is "a
purely literary technique," but the process itself is an integral part of human
cognition and "definitely possesses psychological reality" (283).

The cognitive map that emerges from the novel is quite dissimilar to that
of Deaf Culture. Piper's limited hearing pervades the text, but apart from
Josh, who nowhere attracts reader empathy, other characters rarely use it to
diminish her. She herself uses it strategically, as a weapon against her parents
or when she asks brother Finn to sign interpret for her in situations she could
manage with speechreading and her residual hearing, but in which she wants
to slow proceedings, as when negotiating the contract for the band's major
concert appearance. The novel rejects any assumption that a deaf person
will necessarily be isolated in hearing society, and Piper's own expectation is
likewise dismantled. The paradoxical situation wherein she had undertaken
to manage a rock band when she could not hear the music and knew almost
nothing about rock culture becomes part of the structural arc expected in a
young adult novel. The novel's close does not deliver the triumphalism often

expected of disability scripts (McDonald, 463). Rather, the transcendent level of the cognitive map, that is, the band's fervent acceptance by an audience of a thousand and Piper's epiphany as she mimes on stage—"what emerged was a me a thousand times more powerful than Piper Vaughan. I was Piper Vaughan, guitar hero–spiritual descendant of Jimi Hendrix and proponent of pure anarchy" (322)—is balanced by Piper's renewal of her intersubjective roles as a daughter, a big sister, a member of a signing community, a girlfriend, and an admirer of the complexity she has found in her female friends.

CONCLUSION

Like most young adult novels, *Five Flavors of Dumb* is double-stranded. The story of "Dumb," the rock band, follows a familiar underdog script wherein an unpromising group—a sport team, some dancers, or some musicians—are inspired to improve their personal skills and learn to work together, and if the outcome is not always a triumph, it is at least satisfactory. The second strand, here a familiar coming-of-age script, is thematically imbricated with the first because Piper is central to both and her personal life follows a parallel trajectory from a state of (self-perceived) lack attributed to her deafness to a state of mature well-being. Further, the band's triumphant public performance displaces any reader expectation that Piper will also achieve a public triumph as well as her enriched subjectivity.

The grounding of *Deaf Culture Fairy Tales* in Deaf-centric epistemology means that the two books are largely ideologically incompatible, since *Five Flavors of Dumb* is firmly positioned within majority hearing culture. The novel in effect dismisses some major concerns of Deaf Culture by representing them in their most successful manifestations. Piper's speechreading ability is far above the median but, most significantly, baby Grace's cochlear implant during her first year of life is without problems, and it is implied that she will hear and develop speech at the same rate as a typically hearing baby.[3] That she is also learning Sign, and at one year old is developing Sign faster than speech, is presented as a practical decision to ensure that the whole family can sign, not as an alternative to speaking, and it is affirmed by the consequent strengthening of the bond Piper feels with her little sister. In contrast, *Deaf Culture Fairy Tales* makes several jibes against alternatives to sign: a final example is the oralist Witch in "Hansel and Gretel," who claims credit for convening "a congress . . . against signs," and after her death the children find her treasure chest "full of gold coins and notes of praise from ear horn companies around the world." The obsolete ear horn (last manufactured in the early 1960s) here symbolizes hearing technologies in general.

To put *Deaf Culture Fairy Tales* and *Five Flavors of Dumb* side by side, along with their strategies for representing deaf characters, has proved to be an instructive exercise because the cognitive maps that constitute their representations of Deafness and deafness, respectively, are so different. *Deaf Culture Fairy Tales* shows a propensity to assume an essentialized Deaf identity and thus to perceive hearingness as a threat; written from outside Deaf Culture, *Five Flavors of Dumb* simply assumes that deaf people and their social relationship are very diverse—diverse, as Sutton-Spence and West put it, "in their audiological profiles, their social affiliations, their education, and their language choices, as well as in terms of class, ethnicity, sexual orientation and so on" (422–23). The two works are thus positioned at opposite ends of the spectrum of creative representations of deafness and Deaf culture.

How readers engage with the characters in these works is mediated by Theory of Mind, which enables inferences to be made from the presented data. A key aspect of our ability to explain people's behavior in terms of their thoughts, feelings, and beliefs is that within culture we employ scripts and cognitive maps in common, and as part of ToM we expect other people, and this includes fictional characters, to make much the same inferences as we do. Rosen uses this cognitive practice to position readers to align with her Deaf Culture ideology, whereas John invites readers to apply ToM to Piper's hopes, fears, and frustrations to map her own development of an enhanced ToM, which is her coming-of-age into a state of mature well-being.

NOTES

1. Moderately severe deafness indicates a hearing loss range of 56–70 dB. Persons in this range are apt to use powerful hearing aids in combination with speechreading. Some people also sign.

2. In a "Position Statement" released in 2008, AG Bell inclines toward *total communication* and expresses acceptance of multiple approaches: "AG Bell recognizes that there are various options regarding language choice, including spoken and signed languages throughout the world. AG Bell also recognizes that there are numerous communication approaches and educational methods that incorporate audition, signs, and various combinations of both speech and sign. . . . With respect to American Sign Language (ASL), AG Bell acknowledges ASL as a language in and of itself. AG Bell also recognizes ASL's importance in Deaf culture as a unique feature, and a language that many take pride in learning. AG Bell does not believe that ASL should be prohibited or restricted as a choice, nor does AG Bell advocate against learning ASL as part of a child's overall development if that is what the child's parents desire." https://www.agbell.org/Advocacy/American-Sign-Language

For an astute analysis of ideas explored by Bell himself and ideas erroneously attributed to him, see the article by Gallaudet University historians Brian H. Greenwald and John

Vickrey Van Cleve (2015). In defense of Bell, they write, "Bell's acceptance of the common view of deafness as a tragedy, and as a "defect" that a progressive society ought to remedy, has influenced historical memory and overshadowed his actual words and deeds. It explains at least in part his continued vilification in deaf community literature" (43).

3. This level of success does occur, but not invariably. The strong opposition to cochlear implants maintained within much of the Deaf community for almost thirty years (Lane and Bahan; Ladd, xx) has now largely dissipated, reduced to the ethnocide argument: if increasingly sophisticated implants can "cure" deafness, then Deaf Culture may disappear. Although the argument has persisted into the twenty-first century (Baynton 2008; Sparrow 2010), Christianson and Leigh concluded from a large survey that "opposition to pediatric cochlear implantation within the deaf community is giving way to the perception that it is one of a continuum of possibilities for parents to consider" (2004, 673).

CHAPTER 6

"The Only Thing You Can't Do Is Hear"[1]

Hurt Go Happy by Ginny Rorby

—Helene Ehriander

Hurt Go Happy (2006), Ginny Rorby's novel for young readers, tells two interrelated and analogous stories and in doing so sensitively connects two important areas. First, through the struggle of deaf protagonist Joey Willis to be allowed to learn sign language, it engages with a long-standing controversy in deaf education between the aims and claims of oral education and those of sign-language-based education. The former, whose proponents are known as "oralists," generally aims to integrate deaf children with majority culture by teaching them to lip read, whereas proponents of sign-language-based education initially aim to introduce deaf children into Deaf Culture (Lane, "Constructions," 173–75). The second narrative strand concerns a young female chimpanzee with a highly developed grasp of American Sign Language. This strand not only interacts with the oralist/manualist debate but also introduces questions about personhood, that is, an individuality of combined body-mind being. The historical context of *Hurt Go Happy* is thus important. Published in 2006, it was written after the twentieth-century projects involving chimpanzees and sign language had run their course, but when Roger Fouts's *Next of Kin: My Conversations with Chimpanzees* (1998) was still current. Second, the controversy over the language and communication to be used to educate deaf children, whether signing should be included, and to what extent, or whether a totally oral approach should be used (Gregory et al. 1998, x), was still very alive, although shifting toward a total communication approach.

The account of the life and death of Sukari, the chimpanzee, is embedded within Joey's story, and so, like many other multistranded narratives, the two characters are represented through different narrative modes. The framing strand is pervasively focalized by Joey, a mode established by the opening paragraph of the novel, whereas in contrast Sukari is not a focalizing character and her thought processes are available only by what other characters and readers can infer. Joey fights to gain agency over her life and succeeds, but Sukari, as a nonhuman primate in a human environment, has no control over what happens to her. By the close of the novel Sukari has died as a consequence of vivisection, and Joey is about to embark on a successful professional life. Joey is thus a character with whom readers may empathize, but Sukari can only be an object of sympathy and compassion, which is in line with the novel's advocacy of greater awareness of nonhuman-animal well-being.

The two strands are from the outset connected through Sukari's grasp of sign language and Joey's desire to learn it. However, Joey's mother, Ruth, has adopted a hardline oralist perception of sign language as primitive and repugnant, and dismisses it as "a language a monkey can learn" (94). Girl and chimpanzee are also linked by discrimination because of their otherness, which only Joey overcomes. Ruth's attitude is a continuation of oralist attempts to extirpate sign language, a campaign that developed in the late nineteenth century and carried weight well into the second half of the twentieth century. As Douglas C. Baynton explains, the argument against sign language emerged from an historically situated construction of deafness that embraced fundamental issues such as what distinguished humans from animals, and civilized people from "savages," and what "nature" and "normality" meant (1). Ruth holds to a view that sign language marks its users as less than fully human. She also makes an assumption common amongst oralists that Joey's younger brother will be impeded in learning to speak if he starts signing.

The novel's opening chapter informs readers that thirteen-year-old Joey has been almost completely deaf for six and a half years and that she sometimes feels so insecure that she has heart palpitations and sucks her thumb at night. One day in February 1991, when she is out picking mushrooms close to her home in Fort Bragg in California, she strays onto the property of Charlie Mansell. He upbraids her for trespassing, but when he realizes that Joey is deaf, it is the start of a friendship between them, and he brings her home to meet Sukari. Charlie grew up with deaf parents and has worked as a doctor in Africa, where he rescued Sukari in Cameroon when her mother had been killed by poachers.

Social norms are grounded in binary constructions such as ability/disability, in which disability is the contested and stigmatized opposite of ability (Garland-Thompson, 523; Lane, 174; Ehn and Löfgren, 38). Joey is at the intersection of two discourses, in one of which she is perceived as disabled and thus "the Other" since she lacks an ability that it is "normal" to have, while in the other discourse, that of Deaf culture, she gains access to a language that is competent, energetic, and participatory. Charlie, who possesses knowledge and personal experience of deafness, fights so that Joey will acquire a language and be able to take part in social activities. He speaks on her behalf, and he makes her understand that although she is deaf, she is not helpless. In this chapter I investigate how the discourses that define Joey's deafness are constructed and how she is marginalized in many contexts and defined in terms of her deafness, encountering what is called ableism—social prejudice based on her hearing impairment (Campbell 2009). I mainly focus on power orders and communication perspectives, viewed in relation to the vulnerability that Joey shares with Sukari. I also discuss the ability to communicate with sign language that is attributed to Sukari and compare the fictitious chimpanzee with the real Washoe (1965–2007), the first chimpanzee to learn American Sign Language (ASL): their ability to express themselves by signing has a significant relationship to research on the cognitive abilities of chimpanzees.

LISTENING WITH YOUR EYES

Joey's deafness makes her mother overprotective and controlling, which restricts Joey's freedom of action: "It seemed to Joey that her mother treated her as if she'd stopped aging when she stopped hearing" (15). Moving alone outdoors near the house where they live is a measure of how narrow her world is, and even this little excursion from home makes her mother anxious. Charlie represents a broader outlook, both geographically and mentally, and he is kindly disposed to humans and animals alike. When the book begins, Sukari is about three and a half years old. She lives with Charlie like a member of the family, has a highly developed signing ability, and displays an impressive capacity to make herself understood. She can articulate in a nuanced way both what she is thinking and her relationship to things in her physical environment. Through communication with Sukari Joey is introduced to sign language and its potential for her. Communication with Charlie, which he mostly does in writing, is important so that Joey can see a world outside her own and believe in her own abilities.

As Jean Webb argues, "The question of who or what it is to be 'normal' frequently arises for adolescents and young adults. For the medically defined disabled child, all of these matters are exacerbated" (Webb, 282). Joey is an ordinary young girl on her way toward adulthood, but she is grappling with the difficulty that her functional variation involves and with the trauma that caused her deafness. In depicting Joey's everyday life as a deaf child, Rorby reflects feelings of hopelessness and solitude that stem from the experience of living in the cultural world without full access to systematic communication. Ruth is determined that Joey should be mainstream educated and advances the argument that, as Donna Mertens frames it, "opportunities for social interaction with normally hearing peers benefit hearing-impaired students by providing them with an experiential context in which to develop social skills necessary for functioning in the world" (15). However, as Mertens and others conclude, students do not find mainstreaming a positive experience unless support services are available, the student is able to voice and lip read, signing is an option, parents are involved, and teachers and peers demonstrate appropriate deaf awareness. Joey's experience is not like this: although she is intelligent and ambitious, she cannot cope in school because teachers and classmates constantly forget and talk with their backs turned to her. The FM system she wears in school sets her apart and adds to the social isolation. At home, because they cannot afford a hearing aid (which Ruth also opposes because it would make Joey's deafness visible to other people), Joey can lip read neither her kind, supportive, and well-meaning stepfather, who has a droopy moustache that hides his mouth, nor her little brother who cannot talk clearly enough yet. Joey is alone because of her deafness, left like a helpless outsider and totally dependent on her mother. When Joey has met Charlie and Sukari and started learning a few signs, her mother is angry and forbids her to use sign language in the home.

> But her mother turned. "We'll get you more therapy." . . . "But, Mom, they can't talk to me. I can't read their lips or very many other people's. I don't hold conversations with anyone but you, and Charlie because he writes his half."
>   "Well, practice more. If you get better at reading lips you can talk to everybody in the world and nobody has to learn that stunted language." . . . "I don't want to argue this with you again. Sign language is not the answer. Use it to talk to that chimp if you want to, but don't use it in public. People will feel sorry for you." (106)

At first readers can easily get the impression that Joey's mother is stigmaphobic, that is, desperately wanting Joey "to be included under the umbrella of the 'normal'" (Bérubé, viii), but it is later disclosed that she has a different primary reason for wishing to conceal Joey's deafness, that is, guilt over failing to protect her from her violent father.

In Joey's thirteen-year-old body, both personal negative experiences and socially constructed patterns are inscribed. Both of these are reproduced at the beginning of the novel, but when with Charlie's help she starts to take power

for herself and breaks free from the restrictive discourse of disability, her deafness is transformed into something that transgresses boundaries. The narrative
of her body is charged with meanings that the spoken word suppresses, and
this narrative only makes itself heard in dreams or when the body reacts out
of fear. Joey and the people around her are part of a culture of silence and
they have an ambivalent relationship to the damaged body. The real truth
is that Joey's deafness is a result of domestic violence, and her mother has a
guilty conscience because she was unable to leave the brutal alcoholic father
who abused his daughter. Deafness is thus not something she was born with
or acquired through sickness, but something imposed on her through an act
of power, as her father dominated both Joey and her mother by threats and
violence. Moreover, her guilt-ridden mother has told Joey to explain her deafness as a result of meningitis to protect the mother from accusations by other
people. Joey is part of an order of power in which she belongs to a social class
with no education or financial resources, where her mother and she herself
have been abused by the violent father, as a result of which she has become
disabled, a constant reminder of the guilt she bears. Joey is also in a power
structure where she is defined by being a girl and a child, who needs care and
protection, and who cannot make decisions about her own life. The patterns and
memories carried by her body become clear in an episode when she is chased
by a tramp, who is actually harmless but finds amusement in frightening her.
She feels afraid and vulnerable, and the traumatic memories are reawakened,
but when she has calmed herself, she chooses, as always, not to be a victim.
She tells the man that he is like her father and that her father made her deaf:
"I'm not afraid of you. You can't hurt me" (196).

An aspect of the parallel stories of Joey and Sukari is that they share the
experience of violence and abuse, which is depicted as memories that provoke
bodily reactions and have left their mark on the body. Sukari has had a panicked fear of dogs since she was just a few months old, and she experienced the
trauma of seeing her mother killed by the poacher, so Charlie assumes that the
hunter used a dog. This brings up the controversial question of what kind of
memory animals have, but there is little doubt that an animal's ideas concerning what will or will not happen, and how to accept or avoid this happening,
are acquired, and the animal involved draws on memory to process a mental
event that denotes the conceived situation and its possible outcomes (Kiley-
Worthington, 10). The memory is stored and Sukari experiences a "recognition
memory" (Shettleworth, 23) when she sees a dog, even if it is only in a picture.
Sukari's ability to remember can be compared with Joey's traumatic memory
of the event that caused her deafness. Rorby's construction of Sukari's memory
does not represent it as episodic memory ("a replaying of events from [the]

past in order to re-experience them," Andrews 75) in the same way as Joey remembers when her father caught her and beat her with the leg of the stool. Joey evidences autonoetic consciousness, whereby images enter conscious awareness and there is a strong sense of the self in the past. In contrast, it could be the trauma and her unconscious that makes Sukari afraid when she sees a dog and thinks that it will bite her, which may not indicate that she remembers and understands the connection between the poacher's dog and her own fear.

Joey eventually manages to convince her mother to let her learn sign language, and she gets close to both Sukari and Charlie, who sees her as the grandchild he never had. Charlie gives Joey support and explains to her mother what it means to be deaf; he tells her that sign language is a real language, which means that Joey can participate in society: "Deafness *is* different, dammit. And for Joey it is normal not to hear. But she's missing so much more because you're trying to pound her deaf ears into hearing holes. She is what she is. Let her be deaf" (117). Learning sign language also helps to end Joey's isolation; once she has "come out" as deaf and starts using sign language, it turns out that many people she meets in different situations can communicate with her because they know other people who are deaf and have learned sign language for their sake.

When Charlie dies, no one can look after Sukari properly and the chimpanzee ends up in a research laboratory where she is subjected to experiments that subsequently lead to her death from liver cancer at the age of ten. Before that, however, Joey, who is about to start veterinary school, finally discovers that Charlie has left a foundation not just to finance her own studies but also to support Sukari. Joey can rescue Sukari from the laboratory and organize a better life for her in a park during her last four years. The story deals with the problem of what it means to be powerless and to need someone else to speak on your behalf and look after your rights; in the research laboratory the scientists have not even understood that Sukari is trying to communicate with them. The novel also problematizes what it means to have a chimpanzee as a pet, which is permitted in the USA, and how it is impossible to keep them when they become sexually mature and strong. For Sukari, being rescued from life as a young orphan in Africa to end up as a pet in California, wearing a t-shirt and diaper, means that as an adult she becomes a subject of animal experiments, a far too common "solution" for the many "surplus chimpanzees" that grow from small and cute juveniles to unruly and unmanageable adults. The novel also describes how Joey and the attorney who helps her contact various places in the hope of finding somewhere she can stay, only to find that there are already more than enough unwanted chimpanzees who have grown too big for the movie industry, for advertising photography, or for skating at children's parties. The photograph on the cover of the Swedish translation, which shows a girl sitting with a chimpanzee in her lap in a domestic setting, is therefore highly problematic, sending signals that run counter to the explicit intentions of the story. Furthermore, it is worth noting that the girl's hair has a reddish tone and she has freckles on her nose, which makes the reader intuitively think of the only girl in Sweden hitherto who has been allowed to have a monkey, namely, the fictitious Pippi Longstocking.

"A LANGUAGE A MONKEY CAN LEARN"

The novel is grounded on Sukari's ability to communicate through sign language, and to do so in a sophisticated way, although not all researchers in the field agree that this is possible (Rendall and Owren, 157f). In *Fundamentals of Comparative Cognition*, Sara J. Shettleworth poses important questions about the cognitive processes involved in animal communication: "Which are shared with human language, and what can the answer to this question reveal about how human language evolved?" (Shettleworth, 101). She also emphasizes that the capacity for language has traditionally been regarded as the great difference between humans and apes/primates, and that experiments conducted during the twentieth century have only reinforced this view: "the concepts expressed in language would be meaningless to a creature that does not already have them or something like them" (Shettleworth, 116f.). This also raises questions about how things can be measured and how one can assess the results obtained (Martin and Bateson 2007). The problem affecting all studies of animals' linguistic abilities is that humans are the yardstick with which they are compared—and thus always deemed inferior. It is the chimpanzees who are expected to learn our language, and it is by the results of these experiments that their skills are judged; this is also a question of power and our perception of ourselves as being on a higher level and of greater value.

Perceptions differ as to whether chimpanzees, and other primates who have learned communication through sign language actually understand what they say or if it is all a result of operant learning, where the animal is rewarded for doing something right and can then make associations and imitate the right sign in the right situation. Naturally, it is often the people who train the animals that understand them best, which might indicate that there is a high degree of relation and interpretation in the communication, and that the animal trainer sees and understands what he or she wants and consequently sees abilities that do not exist. Another criticism is that it is only the animal trainer who can communicate with the animal, and that the situation is reminiscent of the horse Clever Hans, who in fact was just responding to his owner's signals

(Andrews 2015). Yet I think that the situation is much the same regardless of who is communicating and how the communication takes place; parents understand their child because they have developed shared signals and references, although an outsider only hears that the child is trying to say something, and Joey communicates most easily with her mother because they have always been close to each other and have no difficulty interpreting each other. Another important factor in this connection is that it is easy to judge a person by his or her linguistic ability. A deaf person risks being perceived as uninterested, inattentive, or downright stupid for not being able to follow a conversation. Joey says on one occasion when a train attendant treats her condescendingly, failing to realize that she can lip-read: "*The only thing you can't do is hear,* Charlie had written. 'I'm deaf, not retarded,' she snapped. 'Don't talk to me like that'" (213). It is not my intention to rank the different functional variations but rather to show how power and language go together. Moreover, in this context it is complicated if an animal is given the tools to express thoughts and feelings, since this can upset a power hierarchy that is fundamental for our society, according to which humans are above nonhuman animals and feel entitled to rule over them and to use them for his own purposes.

SUKARI'S LINGUISTIC ABILITIES

Sign language is not an international language, although the existence of sign language families or clusters enables varying degrees of mutual intelligibility between users in different countries: for example, the Danish family—Denmark, Norway, Iceland, Greenland and the Faroe Islands—shares a high mutual intelligibility; and the BANZSL family—British Sign Language, Auslan, and New Zealand Sign Language—is about 70 percent mutually intelligible (McKee and Kennedy, 43–73). However, sign languages from different families are not mutually intelligible. In the novel, Sukari uses ASL, American Sign Language, which is used by deaf people in North America. Sign language, just like spoken language, is supplemented with facial expressions and body language to make it easier for the receiver to understand. Sukari's first sign to Joey is I-SEE-YOU (22) and subsequently she appears to understand when Joey tries to pronounce her name, because she pulls down her diaper and shows the fine white hairs on her bottom; in Swahili Sukari means "sugar" and her name is a nickname for "sugar-butt" (21). This might suggest self-awareness, as Sukari knows what she looks like from behind (Andrews 2015). The signs that Sukari use include: FRIEND, TICKLE, HUG, DOG, CAT, GIVE DRINK, GOOD GIRL, TOILET, and HELP (which are written in capitals in the novel). When Joey first mees her she knows a total of 25–30 words and concepts (27). These are relatively simple and can be used directly to link words with actions and to ask for things: GIVE DRINK (236). It is more problematic with the words/concepts FRIEND, HURRY, and TELL SORRY, which have a higher degree of abstraction. Sukari also understands some spoken language, and Charlie explains in writing to Joey how this is possible, comparing this with Joey's little brother who is two and a half years old:

> *Even though babies can't understand what we say, they figure out what we mean from our facial expressions and the words we repeat over and over. It's how children learn language. It's the same with our pets. They don't have to understand every word to get what we mean. We say, "Are you ready to eat dinner? Do you want to go for a walk?" and they probably hear blah, blah, blah, eat, blah, blah, blah, walk."*
>
> Joey laughed. "That's just what I do. Catch a word or two and figure the rest out." (23, italics in the original)

The reader can assume that Sukari has learned sign language in the same way and that she has learned it parallel to spoken language and in order to reinforce and clarify the spoken words, and—not least of all—so that she herself can answer and communicate.

Sukari's language has the correct syntax for sign language, and it is important to point this out because sign language does not always have the same syntax as spoken language, and because signing chimpanzees have no knowledge or sense of grammar and syntax. An example is when Sukari signs to Joey: GOOD GIRL YOU. COME HUG (234) and says about herself: GOOD GIRL ME (236). By way of comparison, Kathy Lawson, a sign language interpreter who helps rescue Sukari from the research laboratory, signs to Joey: "MOTHER OKAY NOW. KNOW-WHAT? IN HEART, PROUD YOU, THINK ME" (233). What is a challenge to discuss is that Sukari is also able to communicate rather advanced abstractions. She has two animal friends: a kitten that she calls Hidey because it once hid so that she couldn't find it, and a turtle. Sukari also understands quite a lot of human language and can respond to spoken language with sign language, as in the following passage where Sukari shows her turtle to Joey:

> "That's not a turtle, silly," Joey said. "That's a seashell."
> Sukari drew her lips back and shook her arms. TURTLE HIDE, she signed.
> Joey grinned. "If that's a turtle, where are its head and legs?"
> Sukari jumped up and down.
> "Okay, okay." Joey lifted the abalone shell. Beneath it was Sukari's tortoise in a hibernating torpor. I-SEE TURTLE, Joey signed. (63)

Charlie explains to Joey that Sukari has given him a name: "*She calls me turtle because I'm slow*" (27). This means that a chimpanzee is able to follow a chain of thought: a turtle is slow, Charlie is slow, therefore Charlie is (like) a turtle. This chain of thought could also be perceived as an association: they are both equally slow. One may wonder whether this also entails an awareness in Sukari that she can move faster. One of the words she likes to use is HURRY; from the perspective of cognition this might indicate an awareness of herself as being fast while others are slow, which could be interpreted as a consciousness of her own body and her own abilities.

Sukari can also comprehend her own reflection in a mirror and thus has self-awareness (Andrews, 70–72). At the end of the story, when Joey has rescued her from the research laboratory, Sukari is given raisins as a present and then she rubs the identification tattoo on her leg and signs first DIRTY TEETH and then DIRTY. HURT THAT (230f.). They go to a motel to have a bath and Sukari does all she can to wash away DIRTY HURT: "Joey couldn't stand watching Sukari try to scrub the number off her leg" (231). After a lot of washing she is dried, groomed, and dressed, after which Joey "lifted her so she could see herself fully clothed and wearing her cap in the mirror over the sink. For a moment Sukari stared at her image, then lightly touched the reflected face. Joey felt tears threaten until Sukari pointed to herself in the mirror and signed, DEVIL THERE WANT RAISIN" (232). Sukari calls herself a "devil" when she has been mischievous or "bad," or when she is dissatisfied with herself, which can be interpreted as a negative experience of herself, likewise presupposing self-awareness.

Sukari's way of naming the kitten is in line with the way Koko the gorilla (1971–2018) names her first kitten All Ball (since it was small and round) and a later kitten Lipstick (an orange cat with a pink nose and lips). Yet another example, which is like Koko the gorilla's perception of the kitten Lipstick's lips, is seen when Sukari names an orangutan that she meets in the sanctuary park RED BOY (243). She ought to be able to work out with no difficulty that he is male, but what is her perception of the color red? She does not need to see the same red color that a human does, but she must be able to understand that red is an umbrella term for colors within a certain color range. If she has learned, for example, that a certain ball is red, it is still quite far removed from the reddish-brown color of Chris the orangutan boy.

What no one can explain to Sukari by signs or spoken language is that Charlie has died. She sat beside him when he passed away one stormy night and has thus seen him die and seen him dead, but despite this she keeps on asking where he is and whether they will go to see him. Joey tries to explain that he is now inside their hearts and that he is HIDING (253). Sukari can remember other things that have happened and she recognizes people she has met before, but she obviously does not understand what it means to be dead.

CHIMPANZEES AND SIGN LANGUAGE

Quite a lot of research has been done in the field of chimpanzees and sign language. There is a study by Shoji Itakura of a chimpanzee's ability to learn personal pronouns, and there are studies of chimpanzees' ability to learn a limited amount of sign language (ten signs) based solely on human speech (Fouts, Chown, and Goodin). The chimpanzee studies, which can often be perceived as unethical and disrespectful, have nevertheless generated extensive knowledge of our closest nonhuman animal relative. We consist in large measure of the same DNA, chimpanzees know much more than what is required for survival, and they are surprisingly like us humans (Fouts 2000).

The pioneering and best-known study of chimpanzees and sign language began in the mid 1960s and was called "Project Washoe." The chimpanzee Washoe (ca. 1965–2007) was the first nonhuman animal to learn ASL, and then she taught this sign language to her adopted son and two other chimpanzees. This study "indicated mental powers of generalization, abstraction and concept-formation as well as an ability to understand and use abstract symbols. And these intellectual skills were surely prerogatives of *Homo sapiens*" (Goodall, 24). Washoe was taught only whole signs and no experiments were performed with finger spelling.

This project, led by Allen Gardner and Beatrice Gardner, clearly showed that ASL is a suitable form of communication for a chimpanzee, and that when the chimpanzee gains access to a mode of communication, a considerable level of two-way communication can be attained (Gardner and Gardner 1975). The three methods used by the scientists to teach Washoe ASL were: imitation, operant conditioning whereby the right sign led to reward and reinforcement, and "babbling." "Babbling" means that the researchers tried to notice and capture all kinds of hand movements and perceive them as a sort of babbling that could subsequently be developed into signs. The latter method worked least well, and it was obvious from an early stage that the other two were much more effective, useful, and appreciated by Washoe. All three methods were based on the methods that we know human children use when learning language. They babble to explore different sounds, they imitate other people's speech, and they receive different forms of reward when they succeed. In Washoe's case the reward was that she was scratched when she did right. Her interest in being tickled and scratched was an asset here, and it was used as a form of reward in the operant learning (Gardner and Gardner 1969). The research findings show that Washoe was capable of learning a large number of signs, and when she died at age forty she knew over two hundred signs and had also taught sign language to other chimpanzees.

The most remarkable and surprising thing about these studies, in my opinion, is not that Washoe and other chimpanzees are able to learn a number of signs but that they can use them in metaphorical senses and in meaningful combinations (Gardner and Gardner 1969). The words that Sukari learns in the novel correspond well with the words used by Washoe in reality. Washoe managed to name many objects, to ask for them, to talk about them, and she developed something that can only be called "communication," although there are critics who view chimpanzees' ability to use sign language as "empty words" and pure imitation, something that is learned but without any thought behind it (Andrews 2015). Sukari also likes to be tickled, and the way she learns new signs also conforms to the methods of the Washoe project, *imitation* and *instrumental conditioning*. It is thus plausible that the fictitious Sukari can name the cat Hidey because it has hidden from her, or that she tries to associate the slow turtle with its slow owner. Washoe the chimpanzee has evidently served as a model for the Sukari of the novel, but with the important difference that Washoe had a much more dignified life, even though one may question the ethics of research that involves keeping chimpanzees in captivity in unnatural environments. On Washoe's gravestone at the Chimpanzee and Human Communication Institute there is an inscription: "May all beings be free," which shows that the scientists in the project were aware of the ethical dilemma.

GIVING VOICE TO THOSE WHO CAN'T SPEAK FOR THEMSELVES

There is an obvious problem in bringing together in the text a chimpanzee and a deaf girl, since it can easily be assumed that the parallels between them indicate that they are equivalent to one another, but a reading of *Hurt Go Happy* that implies that *deaf* people and chimpanzees have the same linguistic and cognitive abilities would be a grave misinterpretation. Although Rorby affirms on the one hand that human beings and animals have the same value and that it is not acceptable that humans use animals for their own purpose, and on the other hand that animals can think and feel much more than most people assume is possible, she does not contend that a chimpanzee's linguistic ability enables employment of sign language at a high level. What Joey and Sukari have in common at the start of the novel is their vulnerability, as each is always at the mercy of other people's decisions. Charlie meant well when he looked after Sukari, and Joey's mother tried in her misguided way to protect her daughter and bond with her as compensation for not having saved her from her father in time.

As the novel unfolds an important distinction emerges: as Joey becomes more articulate, she develops increasing agency. She is strong and intelligent and rebels against her mother instead of passively accepting the role assigned to her; her mother waited far too long to end the destructive relationship, and Joey shows with her actions that she does not intend to wait until everything is too late. Joey's mother sees her as damaged and disabled and wants her to try to make her disability invisible, whereas Joey increasingly views herself as deaf but not helpless. Her aim is not to become "normal" but to live a life that realizes her full potential. She refuses to be regarded as a victim, and she chooses not to be bitter. She acquires a language, puts her fears behind her, makes her way in the world, finds new friends, and gets a prestigious education. Here Joey is to be regarded as a role model and a "supercrip" who does not let her damaged body be an obstacle or define what is possible. At the same time, the author underlines that chimpanzees are our nearest relatives, with whom we share much of our DNA, and that they have considerable cognitive abilities as regards language, awareness, and emotions, which humans can understand and interpret if the chimpanzees are given expressive linguistic tools, but confined in the human world they are deprived of agency. Nevertheless, the fact that they do not possess the same linguistic skills as humans does not mean that we have the right to treat them without respect or use them for our purposes. Ginny Rorby is giving voice to those who cannot always speak for themselves since the power structures tend to place them in subordinate positions: the disabled, children, and animals. A great deal has happened since 1991, when the novel takes place, but many of the questions raised in the story have their counterparts today, which makes the story relevant as regards functional variations and ableism, and vulnerable children and animals alike.

NOTE

1. The title of the chapter is a quotation from a main character, Charlie, who bought a book about sign language for Joey in which he wrote: "*To Joey Willis, remember all you are unable to do is hear. Love from your friends—Charlie and Sukari*" (85). The book's title, "Hurt Go Happy," is American Sign Language for "the pain has ended." *Hurt Go Happy* has won several awards, including the American Library Association's 2009 Schneider Family Book Award.

PART 2

Deaf Cultures in Visual Texts

CHAPTER 7

"We Are Just as Confused and Lost as She Is"

The Primacy of the Graphic Novel Form in
Exploring Conversations around Deafness

—Sara Kersten-Parrish

In her Newbery Honor winning graphic novel *El Deafo* (2014), Cece Bell uses both images and text to portray how losing her hearing at the age of four changed the trajectory of her "normal" childhood experiences. For a book aimed at young readers, ages eight to twelve, the story is narratively complex. Bell crafts her story through the inclusion of multiple layers of narration that effectively move beyond showing and telling readers about a disability experience and instead—through vivid color, use of speech bubbles and illustrations, manipulation of graphic novel elements, and the numerous story arcs—invite readers to consider circumstances with which they might not be personally familiar and think about what it was like for Bell growing up deaf in a hearing world. In stark contrast to other middle childhood books on disability experiences, *El Deafo* moves away from a medical view of disability, wherein disability is broadly depicted as a defect within the person that needs to be "cured or eliminated if the person is to achieve full capacity as a human being" (Lane, "Deaf People"; Lane et al.; Siebers, 3). Instead of attempting to represent the entire deaf community, Bell focuses only on her singular lived experiences and invites readers to understand the point of view of one deaf person.

El Deafo tells the story of Cece, the author, who lost her hearing due to spinal meningitis at the age of four. Her story is told through anthropomorphized rabbits and takes readers on a journey with Cece as she is outfitted with hearing aids, enrolled in a new school, and begins to deal with the difficulties of being deaf in a hearing world. At school she wears an FM system called a Phonic Ear that enables her to better hear her teacher. Her teacher wears a microphone that amplifies and directly sends her voice to Cece's ears via a battery box connected to wires. Because she is depicted as a rabbit, the wires lead all the way to the tops of her ears. It is not discreet but instead is obvious—a constant visual reminder that she cannot hear on her own. When she realizes the Phonic Ear device gives her the superpowers to hear her teacher in any situation and from any location in the school—including the hallway, when a teacher is talking to another student, or even in the bathroom—she adopts a superhero persona to separate and elevate her situation from her hearing peers. She names this persona El Deafo, and it soon provides a space of confidence that helps her confront and deal with the difficulties that come with being deaf in a hearing world. This alter ego allows her to voice her real thoughts and feelings when confronted with ignorance and misunderstandings due to her disability, as well as deal with situations typical to growing up such as making friends and first crushes.

I argue that the graphic novel form is well suited to initiating and exploring conversations about the deaf experience. I first describe and analyze the structural elements in *El Deafo* that invite a closer and more communal reading process for those unfamiliar with this particular disability experience. Then, I describe the conversations a group of undergraduate students, all of whom are hearing, had while reading the book. It is precisely because *El Deafo* is a graphic novel, instead of traditional text-only book, that it invited the students to explore and have conversations about marginalized and inaccessible subjects (Blaska 2004; Davis, *Enforcing Normalcy*). As a female who is profoundly deaf like Bell, this experience placed me in the "traditionally marginalized" category that my students were learning about, creating a shared connection that allowed my students to reconsider their own assumptions about deafness/disability and the graphic novel.

GRAPHIC NOVELS AS AUTOBIOGRAPHY

There is a rich history of the graphic novel as autobiography, especially a rich history of women using the medium of comics to tell their stories. The unique combination of text and visual images "denies any collapse between autobiography and autobiographical subject" and connects the various explorations of the textual content with the emotional connections of the visual images (Gardner,

Projections, 131). Thus, in the graphic novel memoir, the subject is not silenced or marginalized. Hillary Chute ("Comics Form") argues that graphic novel autobiography, which she calls graphic narrative, is distinctly feminine. When reading an author's story, readers see the handprint of the author throughout the story, and the author's past, present, and future is represented through the combination of the verbal and visual. The female author has control over the story she is telling, and in graphic novel form, she is able to self-articulate her own story. Susie Bright states, "There is literally no other place besides comix where you can find women speaking the truth and using their pictures to show you, in vivid detail, what it means to live your life outside of the stereotypes and delusions that we see on television, in shopping malls and at newsstands" (7). The verbal and visual nature of the form allows authors to "literally recapture" their individual experiences, reconceptualize their pasts, and give voice to traumatic experiences (Chute, *Graphic Women*, 2).

Bell's recent graphic novel memoir, *El Deafo* (2014), joins the ranks of *Persepolis* (Satrapi 2003), *Fun Home* (Bechdel 2006), and *Smile* (Telgemeier 2010) as memoirs written by women that effectively and powerfully use the graphic novel format to share the author's story. These graphic narratives often explore traumatic events in the authors' lives. Yet the value of the form, the dual nature between verbal and visual, lies in its ability to continually convey the presence of the author and her story. Therefore, the trauma is not the entire story, and the author simultaneously erases conceptions that she is her trauma and points to the female subject as the object of the story, thereby redefining what it means to tell an autobiographical narrative. The complex layering of illustration and text helps readers rethink the representation of trauma, moving away from common ideologies where the subject is secondary and invisible. Instead, the medium bears witness to the woman "registering its difficulty through inventive textual practice" (Chute, "Literature," 459). Specifically, in *El Deafo*, the invitation to read Cece's experiences of losing her hearing and navigating life moves the reading beyond a vicarious and disengaged experience to an experience that demands interaction and engagement.

In the comics form, words and images are integrated "so completely that the story cannot be told another way" (Brenner, 257), yet in a graphic novel memoir this integration is taken further because, instead of a separation between narrator and subject, it creates what Jared Gardner (*Projections*) refers to as a "communal enterprise" as the text and the image work together to challenge the very idea of representation. Instead of an outside narrator talking about a subject, which creates a distance from and disengagement with the topic represented, the relationship between the text and image are jointly connected, as readers must use both media to further work through the experiences of the autobiographical subject. This "communal enterprise" of graphic novel and autobiography has been called an autography.

There is a tactility to autography, as authors are physically drawing themselves on paper, creating embodiment through their self-representation and the creation of their story (Chute, "Comics Form," 112). The authors, then, are recreating themselves and their stories for their readers, "resurrect[ing] and materializ[ing]" their history (Chute, "Comics Form," 112). The visual elements of graphic novels, specifically the concept of line that separates graphic novels from films and novels, makes readers cognizant of the author/artist, making his/her gaze the gaze by which readers experience the story (Gardner 2011). This relationship between author and comic, author and reader, and reader and comic demands what Hillary Chute calls a "physical intimacy with the reader in the acts of cognition and visual scrutiny" ("Comics Form," 112).

In the contexts of autography and stories of disability, this representation takes on another character. Describing what she calls the visual gazes of disability, Rosemarie Garland-Thomson states that the "history of disabled people . . . is in part the history of being on display, being visually conspicuous while politically and socially erased" ("Staring," 56) in a system of representation wherein visual representations of disability rarely ever consider the whole body of the disabled person. Thierry Groensteen argues that the comics form makes erasure of the narrator impossible because each image "does not take its place, but is added to it in the mode of accumulation, collection, with the totality of images remaining easily accessible at any time" (*Narration*, 82). This union between stories of people who have been historically erased within a comics form that does not allow for such canceling of the body, privileges autography as a well-suited form, which is used very effectively in *El Deafo*.

This literary/artistic form discourages disengagement, sentimentality, and sensationalism, as the story becomes both a verbal and a visual story, as the telling of the story becomes part of the story itself, reminding readers that this is a story told by someone. The story is not shown through a "lens of unspeakability or invisibility," but instead constrains readers to consider how individuals are situated within specific narratives (Chute, "Literature," 459). Bell's use of the images, panels, speech bubbles, and other numerous graphic novel elements, including gutters, the use of space and font styles, gives her comic the ability to "spatialize memory" (Chute, "Comics Form," 108). The emotional landscape of the form and the story is a form of visual and embodied witnessing, making visible the author first, and trauma second. It is Bell's manipulation of the layers of narrative in conjunction with the graphic novel elements in this autography that causes readers to make connections among the verbal and visual, physical and emotional. Additionally, as Chute argues about Lynda Berry's *One Hundred*

Demons (2002), *El Deafo* also "demands to be understood in its entirety as a physical, aesthetic object, where the text begins and ends is not discernable" ("Comics Form," 112).

El Deafo provides multiple spaces to read and live the literature. According to Rudine Sims-Bishop, children's literature has the possibility to be a window into unfamiliar experiences; a mirror reflecting back recognizable experiences; and even a sliding glass door where readers can walk through to become part of the world the author has created or described. Thus, in the context of the class reading *El Deafo*, the book becomes a vehicle that creates a collective bond of understanding multiple experiences.

ELEMENTS OF NARRATION

As an autography *El Deafo*, operates on many layers and develops themes through multiple lenses, creating what Scott McCloud calls "thematic triangulation" (*Reinventing Comics*, 34). Readers see the illustrations, the narrative, and the spaces between the images and words. The text becomes a map to differing points of view, and a map to the author's own experiences. Much like Satrapi in *Persepolis* (2003), Bell triangulates between different versions of herself in order to effectively reveal a well-rounded testimony of her childhood. Robyn Warhol states that in reading autography, the narrative occupies three levels: the world inside the story, the world inhabited by the narrator, and the visual elements (5). In *El Deafo*, the world inside the story is depicted through the speech bubbles of dialogue explaining the events as they are happening. The narrator is shown in various ways: through the explanatory rectangular boxes positioned at the top of the panels, and in the moments when the narrator enters the story to educate or further explain a moment in time. Lastly, the visual elements like the dream sequences, Cece's asides, and the depiction of all the characters as anthropomorphized rabbits produce, contradict, and reproduce varying perspectives; they, as Chute describes the pictures in the comic form, "move rather than merely illustrate the narrative" ("Comics Form," 108). These elements are connected to the writing and convey different characters' outlooks, provide information that contrasts with the visual images, and emphasize new understandings. Additionally, because Bell was in charge of creating all of these elements, they become more representative of the emotions and associations in each scene. Furthermore, the visual modes Bell uses are more effective in conveying the emotion and reality of a scene than the use of realistic images would be. For example, when Cece sees a friend, Martha, across the street, the thought bubbles reveal that Cece is lonely and really wants to meet her; additionally, when Martha calls across the street, the speech bubble seems to be filled with gibberish, showing that Cece cannot understand her from so far away. The interactions among these various elements connect the world inside the story to the world inhabited by the narrator to the experience created for readers.

TEXTUAL AND VISUAL COMPLEMENTATION

World Inside the Story

The world inside the story, sometimes called the intradiegetic level, is the one in which the narrator exists within the storyworld of a book. In *El Deafo*, the interior story is that of Cece, the author's representation of her younger self, as a child from the moment she loses her hearing to her later elementary years. This level is depicted by the speech and thought bubbles, the words spoken and thoughts realized by the characters within the chronological timing of the story. Readers see Cece losing her hearing, getting hearing aids and a Phonic Ear system, and trying and failing to make new friends in real-time through this level. They experience her successes and frustrations as she does, yet it is the combination of the world inside the story and world inhabited by the narrator levels, overlapping with the third, visual level of autographical narration, which deepens the conversations surrounding Cece's hearing loss. Bell further manipulates this intradiegetic level with her illustrations. The speech bubbles do not always clearly articulate what is being said as they are sometimes empty or filled with nonsense words, providing hints into how Cece is hearing or not hearing and understanding the world around her. The added visuals allow readers to experience Cece's frustrations with hearing and communicating with her hearing peers, while also making the connection that the experiences of the child Cece, as she stumbles through communicating, are also those of the adult Cece, the author, Bell (Fig. 7.1).

Outside Narration of the Story

As the second level in graphic novel narration, the outside voice narrating her own story, the author, Bell, as extradiegetic narrator, focalizes the events transpiring through the images on the page (Horstkotte and Pedri, 335). There are two versions of outside narration within *El Deafo*. The first is depicted in the yellow rectangular boxes positioned at the top of panels where Bell tells her story in first person. The second version is when Bell as author enters into the storyline to further explain an event within the story. This is depicted both

Figure 7.1. Uses of speech bubbles to convey different ways Cece hears and understands others. *El Deafo*, page 16. Copyright © 2014 by Cece Bell. Image reproduced with permission of the publisher, Amulet Books, an imprint of Abrams, New York, NY.

through visuals and text as Bell uses the younger version of herself to interject
and provide needed asides. This dual narrator role serves multiple purposes
and does not rely solely on a description of her deafness.

In her first version of outside narration, Bell provides context and background
for the story, setting the scenes and helping readers get their bearings on the
visuals depicted in the panels. For instance, the book begins with Bell narrating, "I was a regular little kid." She goes on to explain and show how exactly
readers might connect with her "regularity," depicting scenes where she plays
with her mother's belongings and watches television with her siblings. Then,
as this outside narrator, she shifts the story by stating, "But then everything
changed." Within this version of outside narrator, the following pages switch
into two layers of narration: Visually, we see the child Cece dealing with the
overwhelming experience of being thrust into a world without hearing, but the
narrator reminds us that those remembrances extend to her life as an adult as
well. Yet, this "everything changes" does not come across as normalizing, making
light of disability or saying life is "normal" when you do not have a disability.
Instead, these scenes stress that the emotions, thoughts, feelings, and changes
in relationships that result from dramatic life events are both universal and,
specifically in the case of Cece, filtered through a layer of disability.

In the second version of the world inhabited by the narrator, Bell inter-
jects herself within the framework of the storyline to help explain situations
and events surrounding her deafness, which may not be intuitively obvious
for hearing readers. For example, it is not intuitively obvious that speaking
loudly, overly slowly, or even over-enunciating does not help people with
hearing loss. Thus, Cece halts the current storyline of learning to lip read as a
means of communicating with hearing people by coming in with "placards"
that clarify why certain ways of conversing actually create barriers instead
of opening up lines of communication. Again, the author combines this
narrator-inhabited world with visual elements showing characters talking
in those inhibiting ways. Thus, an illustration of a character (Cece's father)
with a large mustache is accompanied by Cece holding a placard saying,
"Mustaches and beards are bad news! Sorry, Dad" (32). On this one page, you
have narrator Bell stating that she "made many discoveries about lip reading" while child Cece is depicted holding signs explaining what difficulties
present themselves with lip reading.

Visual Elements

The third narrative level inhabited by autography, according to Warhol, is the
visual elements. Readers do not solely read the text of a graphic novel, but need

Figure. 7.2. Readers actively participate in reading this panel, trying to decipher what is being said. *El Deafo*, page 20. Copyright © 2014 by Cece Bell. Image reproduced with permission of the publisher, Amulet Books, an imprint of Abrams, New York, NY.

to take in the visuals in order to complete their understanding of the narrative (Postema, 494). McCloud (*Understanding Comics*) argues the interaction between words, images, line, speech bubbles, and icons contributes to the understanding of comics. Each panel and layer of narration works to convey Cece's frustrations as she puzzles her way through this new, exasperating world post hearing loss; they show how Cece responds to a particular situation while simultaneously enlightening readers to how she *really* felt during that incident. In *El Deafo*, the visuals do more than depict the characters or events. They help readers move beyond any preconceived notions they may hold about hearing loss and deafness. Additionally, the form necessitates reader involvement by requiring readers to actively contribute to the language of comics in order to engage (Groensteen, *System*).

To represent the different ways of hearing inherent in being deaf, Bell uses word balloons in various creative ways; for example, when someone's voice is fading out, the text starts fading away in the book. Moreover, early on in the story, readers see Cece outfitted with a hearing aid. Bell does not solely rely on a singular mention and depiction of the hearing aid, and instead draws Cece with the large aid strapped to her chest and a thought bubble thinking, "I can Hear! But what are they saying?" (20). And, in the background of the panel, behind Cece and her new hearing aid, are nonsense words scrolling across the page (Fig. 7.2). Readers then may pause, and "imaginatively compensate" for this lack of recognizable words, but cannot, because, like Cece, they may be able to "hear" the sound—see the words on the page—but also, like Cece, cannot decipher what is being said—realizing the words on the page are nonsense (Groensteen, *Narration*, 70). In this way, readers are actively involved, using the information in the word balloons to construct a complex understanding of her experience. In other words, Bell is making her readers work a little (McCloud, *Understanding Comics*, 89).

El Deafo is drawn in a rather simple, cartoon style. The characters, as anthropomorphized rabbits, are not realistic portrayals of rabbits or even humans, but are drawn with sparse lines and little detail. This simple style contributes to what McCloud (*Understanding Comics*) calls an amplification through simplification, as comics artists can magnify the meaning of a text in a way realistic images cannot. Since Bell's story is not one most are familiar with, her decision to eliminate the realism in the images, deemphasizing the appearance of the physical world, places the story in the "world of concepts" (McCloud, *Understanding Comics*, 43); in this case, the concept of hearing loss and how that changes one person's daily interactions. Yet, even though the story is a singular story, it also, through the choice of line, allows readers to see themselves in similar situations. McCloud argues if a subject is realistically drawn readers are "far too aware of the messenger to fully receive the message" (*Understanding Comics*, 36), thus the iconic cartoon style of *El Deafo* allows readers to put themselves inside the story. Bell continues to use visual elements to guide readers in understanding that hearing aids only increase the volume of sound but do not provide clarity when she depicts Cece having a conversation with a friend, Emma. In each panel, Emma is shown offering a different beverage, like orange juice, where the speech bubble is in direct contrast to the offered object showing that, while Cece can hear Emma, she cannot understand her. Why would Emma hold a carton of orange juice and offer "shoes . . ." or hold a can of cherry pop and offer "Jerry's mop"? Readers are also privy to Cece's thoughts as she visualizes a pair of shoes and a mop with a nametag for Jerry while conversing with Emma. It is confusing, yet readers, while having the benefit Cece does not have of seeing Emma's offered drink and Cece's misheard offer, are aware Cece cannot understand what Emma is saying (25). Attentive readers will begin to grasp that lip-reading is largely contextual, since the lip position is identical for "juice" and "shoes" and for "cherry pop" and "Jerry's mop," as is subsequently explained (29). Such lack of clarity "can also foster greater participation by the reader and a sense of involvement" as this necessitated involvement of readers can create an emotional charge between subject and topic (McCloud, *Understanding Comics*, 133). The difference between hearing and understanding is made apparent through Bell's use of the visual elements and eliminates a need for a reader to have specialized knowledge of deafness. Or, as Chute states, "Comics accommodates the interaction between the seeable and the sayable without attempting to smooth over the gap of reality that each puts into motion" ("Comics Form," 116).

Additionally, to mitigate the social difficulties and insecurity of being different and not knowing who she is, Cece adopts a superhero persona, El Deafo, who looks like Cece wearing a red cape. There is a common motif in superhero comics, which often feature protagonists who suffer trauma that imbues them with special powers (Duggan, "Traumatic Origins"). Because trauma dismantles the idea that we are ourselves, and "[makes] us question who we are, what we are worth, and how we fit into society" (Duggan, 53), it makes sense that Cece created this totem to help her make sense of this new world around her. El Deafo takes on the form of a transitional object, negotiating the space between Cece's reality and her fantasy (Curtis, 30–31). Also, whenever El Deafo enters her psyche, Bell frames the panels with a cloudlike outline foregrounding the moments Cece adopts this persona (Figure 7.3). This manipulation of the frame around the panel provides what Groensteen (*System*) calls an expressive function of the frame. The cloud-like outline signals that Cece is stepping out of her current situation and is providing an interpretation of the scene via her alter ego, El Deafo. It serves, in a way, as a punctuation mark—focusing on a specific emotion, shaping a mood, and crafting a point. Whenever it arises, it alerts readers that Cece is making sense of her environment. Within these frames, El Deafo allows Cece to give voice to the frustrations she faces as she educates her friends and deals with her insecurities. This additional testimony allows readers to step outside the storyline by putting the story on pause and creating a space for them to step in, see, and consider Cece's struggles. For example, when Cece leaves a sleepover early because her deafness makes her feel isolated, El Deafo comes in and states what Cece wishes she could: "don't ever call me your deaf friend again!" (101). While the sentiments may seem sharp, they are the universal frustrations of people who have been hurt by the callous words of others and allow readers an additional means of connection

Figure. 7.3. Cloud-like outline that frames the panel whenever El Deafo appears. *El Deafo*, page 69. Copyright © 2014 by Cece Bell. Image reproduced with permission of the publisher, Amulet Books, an imprint of Abrams, New York, NY.

to Cece's emotions. Making friends, having a crush, and feeling lonely are common experiences to everyone, and these universal emotions push against the idea that Cece is defined by her disability. McCloud states, "There's only one power that can break through the wall which separates all artists from their audience—the power of understanding . . . Today, comics is one of the very few forms of mass communication in which individual voices still have a chance to be heard" (*Understanding Comics*, 196–97). In this manner, *El Deafo* not only educates readers but also invites them to feel the loneliness and isolation that can come with being deaf. The images simultaneously convey power and information alongside the text, and the book realizes Sims Bishop's sliding glass door analogy, inviting readers to understand one person's experiences while also making connections to their own experiences.

These levels of narrative within autography call attention to the act of storytelling, thereby making the story the focus of readers' attention instead of the subject. Warhol argues that this complexity of narratology within autography "adds unanticipated dimensions" to the current body of memoir literature because in this medium, the writing, drawing, and "autograph of the self" all indicate an authorial imprint on the text (1). Additionally, the book, already being an interactive object, becomes even more so when considering it through the lens of physical disability. Conversations surrounding disability can be difficult and fraught with misrepresentation, and more is needed in the current body of literature on disability experiences in order to have those discussions. However, *El Deafo* does not simply tell a disabled experience. Because the author is imprinting her story on the pages in multiple ways—text, illustration, and narration—it invites conversations about disability, specifically deafness, which is the focus of the remainder of this article.

DEPICTIONS OF DEAFNESS IN CHILDREN'S LITERATURE

Characters with disabilities have largely been absent or misrepresented in children's literature. As Cynthia Neese Bailes observes, readers are positioned to see the world through the eyes of the writer (16, this collection), so when characters with disabilities are depicted as supporting characters, when the story is not told from their point of view, or the emphasis is on the medical condition of the disability, readers get an incomplete and inaccurate understanding of what it means to live that particular disability experience. Particularly, in what is called the medical model of disability, books portraying the deaf experience tend to focus on one's limitations and depict the individual's deafness as a problem that needs to be fixed. In fact, in books depicting deaf and/or Deaf characters, those characters seem to be isolated from society, placed in positions to be pitied, and shown to be able to use communication strategies used by hearing people. The emphasis on "society's prioritization of normality," creates a divide between the "disabled person" and nondisabled members of society, cultivating condescension and pity, and neutralizing the complete aspects of the individual (Eyler, 320; Kunze, 305). Interestingly, the vast majority of these books were written and illustrated by hearing people (Golos and Moses, 281).

The other model of disability, the social model, emphasizes disability as a social construct. Disabilities are not one's impairments, but instead occur "when society restricts or impedes" the individual, limiting and excluding them from society (Eyler, 320). For example, in *El Deafo*, Cece's impairment is her hearing loss but her hearing only becomes a disability when she, for example, tries to watch television with her siblings and cannot due to the lack of closed captions. In the medical model, disability is depicted as something to be treated and fixed by doctors, but in the social model, disability becomes a problem to be solved by society (Wheeler, 339). Both models, though, can be effectively combined to guide readers to understanding the realities of people with disabilities. For instance, early in the story, Bell shares Cece's family's decision to purchase and have Cece wear hearing aids and use a Phonic Ear system at school. A medical model reading of this scene may claim her family was trying to "fix" her. Yet, as Tobin Siebers (*Disability Theory*) argues, exclusive use of the social model can deny the realities of the body. In *El Deafo*, Bell reveals the complicated emotions and situations Cece experiences when confronting the difficulties in her hearing loss as well as challenging society's preconceived notions of deafness.

El Deafo firmly places the main character's deafness in the center of the story and thus challenges earlier disability literature that precludes the character's agency. The visual nature of the graphic novel form does not allow readers to forget who this memoir is about: a young girl exploring what it means to be deaf in a hearing world. Rosemarie Garland-Thomson states, the "way we imagine disability through images and narratives determines the shape of the material world, the distribution of resources, our relationships with one another, and our sense of ourselves" (Disability, 523). Bell reshapes and embodies notions of disability through her use of the comics medium. Her use of the language of comics helps focalize Cece's story, calling attention to multiple perspectives and focusing on the myriad ways Cece encounters, interprets, grapples with, and understands how society hinders, ignores, and sentimentalizes her experience. The book works to destabilize ideas of normalcy. This effectively provides a window into a new experiences while also holding up a mirror to readers' own perceptions and misconceptions.

METHODOLOGY

Because I saw this book as an example of my own story as a deaf woman, and because of the ways in which the book uniquely invites deeper explorations into conversations and understandings around disability due to its three levels of narration via its graphic novel format, I shared this book with a class of undergraduate students. My qualitative research was conducted during the 2015 school year in a university-level Children's Literature course at a large, public Midwestern university in the United States. There were thirty students from a variety of socioeconomic statuses, ethnicities, and university majors and interests taking the elective, general education course. The course required students to read ten middle childhood chapter books, including *El Deafo*. The initial goals of the study were to critically engage not only a text about a disability perspective, but also the graphic novel form as a means of telling an autobiographical story. Terms commonly used to describe approaches to understanding disability (medical model and social model) were also introduced. To describe the medical model, I used Simi Linton's explanation: "The medicalization of disability casts human variation as a deviance from the norm, as pathological condition, as deficit, and significantly, as an individual burden and personal tragedy" (11). The social model states that disability is instead "created by a society that is predominantly able-bodied" (Neithardt, 4) rather than a person's difference or impairment. I acknowledged the complications in defining and the tensions between the two terms but sought to provide introductory definitions within the parameters of the class and semester. Prior to reading *El Deafo*, students were introduced to *Wonder* (Palacio 2012) and several picturebooks on various disability experiences, which prompted discussion about how disability is portrayed in children's literature. These conversations provided a framework for students to think critically about disability representation in children's literature.

Other class periods were spent on studying the graphic novel form. Students explored graphic novel features such as the gutter, speech bubbles, font, and how text placement can impact, change, and drive the storyline forward. The students applied this knowledge when reading *The Arrival* (1996), Shaun Tan's wordless graphic novel, analyzing how those visual and textual features impacted their reading of the story. The time spent studying graphic novels helped students understand the impact that those features had on emotions, pacing, the passing of time, and the arc of the story line.

With this beginning theoretical knowledge of graphic novels and disability education, the students were able to use a critical lens when reading *El Deafo*. Before attending class, students were asked to read the book and create a blog post describing their reading. During the ninety-minute class period, time was provided for dialogue about the novel, and the students further responded to the book through a personal response and a creative visual representation of themselves while reading the story. I observed and participated in the students' discussions, classroom writings, and reflections on *El Deafo*. However, I was careful to not interject my own experiences into the classroom discussions, only offering up my experiences as a person with a hearing loss when asked. Otherwise, the student reactions to the book were entirely self-driven.

READER ENGAGEMENT

I was in a unique position to explore not only how I perceived the book in relation to my own deafness, but also to see how my students began to notice, consider, and challenge their own beliefs about deafness through their reading of this graphic novel. We were problematizing the idea of identity, specifically identity in relation to disability. When discussing the intersection of identity and literacy, Sarah McCarthey and Elizabeth B. Moje assert, "Identity matters because people can be understood by others in particular ways, and people act toward each other depending on understandings and positionings" (228–29). My students' identities as abled-bodied readers of predominately text-based literature were being challenged through this discussion. Their responses to the book showed how they wrestled with their own misconceptions surrounding both graphic novels and deaf experience. Some students wrote they had never picked up a graphic novel because it looked silly, or they felt the pictures did not add to the story. Yet, they soon came to recognize how the narratological elements in graphic novels were an integral part of this story. This book challenged previously held notions about hearing loss and reshaped their own abled-bodied identities. For example, students thought hearing aids allowed deaf people to hear exactly like they can and did not realize the difficulties inherent in social situations. During our large group discussion, one student bluntly said, "I had no idea this is how it was for deaf people." They acknowledged this autography opened dialogue into deeper understandings of what it means to live with a hearing loss. Through its graphic format and multiple layers of story, *El Deafo* compelled these readers to participate actively in Cece's struggles, loneliness, and quests for friendships. Students made connections between the visual elements and their means in showing Cece's perspective. The book became a tool for change, altering perceptions and opening dialogue, ultimately making way for new understandings. Many students shared this was the first graphic novel they had ever read, even acknowledging that "*El Deafo* was a different reading experience compared to 'traditional' books" they were familiar with. Instead of relying only on text to read a story, the students now had to consider the features of the graphic novel and its illustrations in conjunction with the text in telling the story. While my students were not able to name Warhol's three levels of narrative within the book, they recognized the book was told through different layers of narration: the visual, the text, and the combination of the two. Students admitted the visual elements not only created a positive and more enjoyable reading experience, but also provided the space to encounter and learn about life involving disability. Moreover, through the study and discussions, the students grasped how the combination of the visual with the other two levels of narrative made it the best way for the author to tell a story on disability. For example, in discussing the thought bubbles, one student noted they "were crucial to the story because they provided information that might not have been assumed otherwise by the reader."

In a conversation about Bell's use of the speech bubbles in the story, the students astutely recognized Bell was manipulating the speech bubbles to not only visually present the story, but also to narrate elements of the story particular to one's experiences with a hearing loss. When other characters' speech bubbles were blank, indicating Cece could not hear what was being said, my students could not read what was being said either, clearly expressing Cece's perspective and making it my students' perspective as well. Unique to graphic novels, these visual elements and the layer of the narrator inside the story acted as a guide to Cece's experiences. The narrator welcomed students in. One student made the connection between the book's graphic format and its ability to help her experience the story:

Whereas a chapter book would have just said, "I couldn't hear anything," we see people talking but no sound coming from their mouth. We also see the text start to fade as her hearing does. This puts the reading in Cece's perspective better than a chapter book could have. We are just as confused and lost as she is in that moment because we have no idea what the people are saying either.

This embodiment happened again when Bell drew speech bubbles filled with nonsense words, as students had to work to decipher what was being said, just as Cece does. When bubbles were drawn with all capital letters to indicate someone shouting or the author visually depicted over-enunciation through long, drawn-out words, students commented that *El Deafo* moved beyond "telling the story as most books do, but makes you part of the story." In talking about the role of silence in narrative, Davis defines silence as the "absence of sound" and the "absence of voice" ("Deafness and Insight," 891) and notes that in printed text silence is often, ironically, indicated by language. In *El Deafo*, silence is represented through the visual manipulation of the speech bubbles and, because readers see what she cannot hear, understand, or communicate, they too are forced to consider an experience of deafness.

In these examples, the specifics of Cece's difficulty with communication as an individual with a severely profound hearing loss were made known to readers through the book's use of image and text. Chute posits that, in the process of reading the "nonsynchronous" pairing of the verbal and visual, a reader "not only fills in the gaps between panels but also works with the often disjunctive back-and-forth of *reading* and *looking* for meaning" ("Literature," 452). Students negotiated the fusion of text and image, reading and looking for meaning amongst the contradictory and "confusing" pairing between the verbal and visual. Because of this continual interaction between reader and story, Cece's story was never silenced, and the text instead created a close, communal relationship between the hearing students and the deaf autographical subject.

READER INTERPRETATIONS OF GRAPHIC NOVEL FEATURES

Bell chose to depict the characters in *El Deafo* as anthropomorphized rabbits with tall ears, and in the case of her story-self, tall ears that do not work. When she wears hearing aids and her Phonic Ear system, the aids are fitted at the very tops of her tall ears, making them impossible to ignore and, consequently for readers, difficult to forget who and what the book is about. Students said the visual depiction of the ears and hearing aids "was most significant . . . [because the ears] were very prominent and identifiable." They also saw a connection between the prominence of the hearing aids and how Cece felt wearing those hearing aids, remarking that the depiction was a representation of how her classmates saw her, and also enabled readers "to see how Cece felt when others saw her." Indeed, Bell stated she wanted the cords of her Phonic Ear to be extremely visible in the book because that is how she felt they looked in real life: "noticeable and very embarrassing" (Interview with Bell, 2014). In this way, Cece is never "sanitized" for readers, rendered more palatable for hearing individuals, or depicted as other than human, as disabled characters often have been historically portrayed in literature (Davis, *Enforcing Normalcy*; Neithardt; Garland-Thomson, "Politics of Staring"). Additionally, in contrast to other books on disability, Cece is not depicted in a manner to garner amusement, wonder, or pity. Instead, she is transformed from a character with absolute difference to one whose disability is just another variation in the human form, One student commented on the benefit of the graphic novel form in serving as a continual, visual reminder of Cece's hearing loss in conjunction with her feelings about being deaf when she said, "In a normal [text based] novel, this image may be forgotten over time," whereas, in "a graphic novel, you see it in every panel and therefore, you develop an empathetic understanding of the character."

Another connection the students made was that, while the prominence of the ears and hearing aids helped them not forget Cece, the fact she and the other characters were rabbits did not distract them from the story. In *Understanding Comics*, McCloud contends that the simplification of cartoon renderings eliminates a barrier between the character and readers, allowing readers to see themselves within the story. Because Bell did not depict Cece as "other" and instead depicted her as an individual with the same feelings, issues, and relationships as others around her, the students felt they were never reminded that all the characters were rabbits. They were instead invited to embrace a realistic visual rhetoric of disability. The differences between able-bodied readers and disabled character were minimized, avoiding differentiation, and instead continuity was created between reader and character, McCloud stresses that the simplicity of cartoons focuses readers' intentions on the ideas of the character because "cartooning isn't a way of drawing, it's a way of seeing" (*Understanding Comics*). Additionally, Groensteen argues, "a claim to truthfulness is not necessarily to be equated with the most realist possible graphic modalization" (*Narration*, 112). Students said they saw themselves in Cece and remarked that, while they were not deaf like Cece and would never be able to fully understand all of her experiences, they also had experienced many of the thoughts and emotional and relational experiences Cece had.

IMPLICATIONS

In her study exploring how 5th grade students engaged with graphic novels, Ashley K. Dallacqua ("Exploring Literary Devices") discussed the process readers take when reading both the verbal and visual components of such texts. Readers are engaged in a complex reading process when they "oscillate" between print text and image, and, as a result, "a reader must contribute to the story, participate, in order for the story to take place" (370). My university students also had to "participate" in their readings of *El Deafo*, as the structure, narrative layers, and combination of the verbal and the visual forced them to slow down and consider not only her story but their own conceptions about an outside experience, like deafness. This encounter was a powerful one for my students; one that I could easily see used with elementary school children. McCloud, in talking about minority representation in graphic novels, remarked that it is "possible for members of the majority to go for months or even years" without engaging with people in minority groups, including those with a disability (*Reinventing Comics*, 105). He contends that writers of graphic novels have long argued that comics could be written by and appeal to people outside of the majority (105). Engaging students with texts like *El Deafo*, from a young age, could provide another avenue to consider, discuss, and grapple with life experiences outside their own.

Research shows students are successfully engaged with graphic novels in elementary classrooms (Dallacqua, "Literary Devices"; Dallacqua et al., "Using Shaun Tan's Work"; Carter), and spending time with such texts has many additional benefits beyond content and disciplinary instruction. In my study with Dallacqua et al., 2015, I found 3rd grade students engaged deeply with Shaun Tan's wordless graphic novel, *The Arrival* (1996), and its themes of immigration. The students considered their "own likely thoughts and feelings within such a context as a way to extend their understanding of such experiences [immigration]" (212). This kind of experience could easily be replicated with *El Deafo*, as the text lends itself to the type of close reading that results in empathy.

With the recent proliferation of graphic novels for children, elementary students may be more familiar with the comics form than my university students, but providing the needed understanding and vocabulary on graphic novels—space, gutter, speech bubbles, font, and the use of the visual images—will provide students with the framework they need for exploring texts like *El Deafo*. Additionally, a useful starting point for discussion about understanding differences would be Rudine Sims Bishop's influential metaphors of mirrors, windows, and sliding glass doors. Teachers could begin this discussion by using picturebooks that touch on different cultures, races, abilities, and experiences before using *El Deafo*.

With this type of foundation, teachers can allow students time to explore and talk about *El Deafo* since the universal experiences Bell encounters in her elementary years, such as bullying, making friends, and being lonely, are emotions with which many children are also familiar. This commonality could provide a way in for students to begin to think about the perspective presented in the story, especially since some children may not be exposed to or even know anyone with a hearing loss. Asking students to create their own superhero persona, to point out the many ways communication is explained, or to discuss and write about new realizations could be a means for helping them consider their own thoughts and feelings as they interpret, extend, and create meaning about the book. Most importantly, *El Deafo* can provide a space for them to develop empathy and expand their thinking around hearing loss and deafness.

CONCLUSION

As someone who is deaf, it is easy to tell people facts about my deafness: I wear hearing aids. However, it is not easy to help people understand the complicated nature of deafness: wearing hearing aids does not mean I automatically understand people. Moreover, it is complicated to convey the feelings that come along with my disability: I frequently feel isolated while wearing hearing aids precisely because, while they help me hear, I often do not understand what is being said. Thus, when I read *El Deafo* and saw Cece in her "bubble of loneliness" I instantly connected to that emotion in the book, having experienced my own bubble due to similar circumstances as Cece. Numerous situations that were deftly and humorously explained through the visual features, such as the difficulties in lip reading and clarifying what is being said, not only reflected my experiences but also gave voice to a marginalized experience accessible to readers unfamiliar to these experiences. Children's literature has long been recognized as a means of helping readers get a glimpse into those complicated experiences and feelings that are not always articulated or voiced in society. *El Deafo* begins to do that for a long neglected and misrepresented population, those with disabilities. Beyond being a piece of literature that is a window into a new, potentially different, experience, its complex text and graphic elements engage readers. As a result, *El Deafo*—a piece of literature, a memoir, and a graphic novel—begins to allow for conversations beyond the facts of a disability. The layers of narrative, illustrations, and other features of graphic novels guide readers through complex questions regarding the hidden nature and emotions someone with a disability may experience. Showing, instead of telling, creates a personal reading experience, allowing readers a glimpse into the life of Cece. Readers are invited to take on the author's gaze as they, collectively, walk through Bell's experiences growing up deaf. Furthermore, Bell depicts a variation of all readers' experiences, those with hearing and those without—growing up, going to a new school, making friends, feeling lonely—but all filtered through the added layer of disability, allowing for students to make a lived experience of deafness more comprehensible. This medium allowed me to see myself inside of a story for the first time and prompted discussions among and with my students that otherwise might never have occurred.

CHAPTER 8

Childhood Spaces and Deaf Culture in *Wonderstruck* and *A Quiet Place*

—Vivian Yenika-Agbaw

In the introduction of her edited book, *Secret Spaces of Childhood* (2003), Elizabeth Goodenough posits that during childhood children move in between "secret spaces," which "may be found inside, outdoors, or in the middle of nowhere—in a tree fort, snow igloo, or beneath the stairs" (2). These spaces afford them opportunities for adventure away from the prying eyes of adults, affording them alternative worlds and/or spaces within which they can reclaim their autonomy as children. These spaces, which might also be fraught with danger, enable them occasions to be vulnerable and problem solve, as they imagine they are in control of their world even if momentarily. For deaf children this sense of adventure that conveys their independence takes a different dimension as, unlike their hearing counterparts, they also have to understand the risks inhering in the reality of their silent world. But they remain children first, and deaf second, and as such are often curious about their surroundings within urban, suburban, or rural settings. Exploration of these worlds often transforms their childhood significantly, satisfies their curiosities, and stimulates their "sense of wonder" (Tribunella, 67). For deaf children the wondrous spaces might be shrouded by a larger Deaf Culture of silence, enabling them to further convert the spaces into more personalized private spaces that allows them to shut out the rest of the world. In this chapter, I argue that Ben and Rose, co-protagonists in Brian Selznick's *Wonderstruck* (2011), and Regan Abbott, a major character in John Krasinski's 2018 movie *A Quiet Place*, are portrayed as children with agency whose deafness does not interfere with their imagination of childhood spaces, the affordances of such spaces, or their sense of wonder. Thus, as child flâneur and flâneuse (Tribunella, 66–67) they wander through urban and/or rural spaces navigating and/or creating secret spaces that empower them to imagine alternative ways of being in spite of the blatant risks. These ways of being may include the ability to code switch from childhood to Deaf childhood. In this chapter, I extend the concept of flâneur, historically conceived to be associated specifically with cities, to include rural settings that are central to Krasinski's *A Quiet Place*. I reference this concept primarily because the children tend to roam around modern cities and/or rural pathways. In so doing, they learn more about their society.

THE TEXTS

Visual narratives that feature deaf child characters such as Selznick's young adult graphic novel and Krasinski's horror movie are rare. It therefore does not surprise scholars with interest in children's literature and disability studies that both texts are generating lots of conversations within pockets of communities in North America. In the UK, there is also excitement about Rachel Shenton's *The Silent Child* (2018), which won an Oscar in the Best Short Film category. Unlike the other two primary texts under discussion in this chapter, Shenton's overtly probes the "assimilation perspective" whereby a deaf child's hearing parents push more for speech therapy than for the child to learn British Sign Language (BSL). For Rachel Fenton, director of the short film, it was an opportunity to educate the community about deafness and Deaf Culture especially in regard to deaf children's access to education (https://www.youtube.com/watch?v=XogZnFPRPfI). Neither Selznick's novel nor Krasinski's movie adopts this direct advocacy approach to deaf children and Deaf Culture. Rather, each centers the deaf character as a child with a rebellious spirit—children who are not willing to accept the perceived "limitations" of deafness within their fictional society. Their characterization thus affords them ample opportunities to self-actualize.

Published in 2011, Selznick's *Wonderstruck* won the 2012 Schneider Family Award for its depiction of d/Deaf culture. It explores two parallel stories that eventually converge at the end to make a statement about the evolution of societal treatment of deaf children in the 1920s in comparison with the 1970s, when eleven-year-old Ben Wilson's story begins in Gunflint Lake, Minnesota, with a series of misfortunes including the death of his mother and the loss of his hearing. Ben has no clue who is father is. Now living with relatives, he misses his mom and so visits his old home frequently; and on one such visit he finds an envelope amongst his mother's belongings containing a "small blue book,"

Wonderstruck, with an inscription that reads, *"for Danny/Love, M"* (96). His quest to reach Danny on the phone costs him his hearing in the one good ear.

The novel tells parallel stories of Ben and Rose in three parts: part one sets the scene—alluding to the cultural scene of raising deaf children during the 1920s; part two presents the co-protagonists as defying societal expectations for deaf children; part three merges the storylines with the co-protagonists both appearing in the verbal and visual texts. And this is where readers learn the female co-protagonist's back story (see pages 508–9).

The story of Rose, whose name is only hinted at (316) until part three when she and Ben meet, opens in Hoboken, New Jersey, in 1927. Narrated in black-and-white pencil drawings, it parallels Ben's story that appears in print. However, the visual narration withholds the information that the woman she searches for in the city is her mother, and instead builds suspense by deliberately misleading readers to deduce she is a fan searching for the actress and movie star, Lillian Mayhew. Through textual messages that are embedded within the visuals, we learn that Rose is not allowed to leave the house. She gets tutored at home; but every so often she sneaks out to watch a movie starring Lillian Mayhew. On hearing that Lillian now stars in a show in New York City, she goes to find her, when it is disclosed that Lillian is her mother and does not want her there (274–91). So rather than returning to Hoboken, New Jersey, Rose runs off to the American Museum of Natural History, where her brother Walter works.

Krasinski's *A Quiet Place* (rated PG-13), in contrast, is a science fiction movie set in the future. It recounts the story of a family of four living in an upstate New York town, where they are hunted by alien creatures that are highly sensitive to sound. To survive, they must live in silence. The Abbott family uses American Sign Language (ASL) to communicate as their daughter is deaf. When the movie opens viewers witness the death of the family's youngest son whose toy space shuttle triggers an attack from one of the monsters. This scene establishes an underlying tension between the father and his deaf daughter, Regan, who had returned the toy to her brother after their father had advised against him playing with it. The story thus wrestles with the tensions of maintaining silence in a hostile environment and of functioning as a family unit that must contend with a restricted idea of childhood and the social needs of their growing children.

SPACES FOR/OF CHILDHOOD

Both texts depict spaces for childhood in terms of "imaginative and physical freedom" (Kennon, 28). In such spaces children are capable and roam freely, although sometimes they find themselves in trouble. Amongst the many spaces of childhood readers encounter in *Wonderstruck*, the most memorable is the America Museum of Natural History. This is where a significant part of the story occurs. The secret spaces of interest within this museum include the diorama exhibit of the wolves that remind Ben of those foreshadowed in his dreams; and the Cabinets of Wonders Rose rushes through as she escapes from a museum official. For Regan in *A Quiet Place*, the rail trail bridge, the sandy path between the corn fields, and the corn silo are significant spaces for transformative childhood experiences. These are spaces that come to be associated with Regan's doubt of her father's love, her assertion of her independence, and her recognition of her father's unconditional love for her.

SECRET SPACES

I open this section with an excerpt from the manifesto "A Credo for Deaf Americans (1995), by Frank James Lala, Jr.:

> It is our right to be the uncommon and noble silent minority
>   If we can, we seek opportunity, not security
>   We don't wish to be "kept" citizens, humbled and dulled by having the state
> look after us
>   We want to take the calculated risk to dream and to build, to fail and to succeed

The protagonists in these texts manifest similar sentiments to those of Lala's "Credo" as they strive to create secret spaces in which their childhood can flourish. In Selznick's *Wonderstruck*, the American Museum of Natural History is a space of wonder and inquiry for both Ben and Rose. Perceived in Ben's mind as a "castle from a fairy tale" (311), its affordances are endless for the co-protagonists. It is also an ultimate destination for the flâneur and flâneuse protagonists, as each finds his/her way through New York City in search of a parent to affirm their sense of being. When the bus from Minnesota arrives in NYC,

> Holding his suitcase, he [Ben] stepped off the bus into the rank, hot station . . . He followed the crowd through the vast red and gray spaces of the station . . . It was so quiet. And then Ben remembered that he still couldn't hear . . . He followed the rush of people around corners and down the escalators until they all came to a set of big glass doors leading outside into the bright light of morning. (242–43)

Once out on the street, he noticed everything including the surrounding filth and smells. It was his first time in the city.

Ben looked around in astonishment. Taking in all the colors and smells and movements, he felt like he'd fallen over the edge of a waterfall. He was sure he had never seen this many people in his entire life on Gunflint Lake. Everyone everywhere seemed to be a different color, as if the cover of his social studies textbook had come to life around him. (264)

The text emphasizes the sensory aspects of his experience, as is typical of Deaf Culture. He cannot hear the sounds but notices every tiny detail of his immediate environment and makes comparisons with his hometown. New York City itself momentarily becomes a big secret space for this child. But what intrigues him the most is the "magnificent" (320) museum he notices across the street. The visual sights he observes on his wanderings around the city in search of the Kincaid bookstore also reflects his flâneur status. But once inside the museum his imagination illuminates the magical quality and possibilities within that space, which enables him to reflect more on his childhood and where he actually belongs.

At Hoboken, NJ, Rose's secret place is the cinema where she often watches silent movies to feel her mother's presence. The transition eventually from silent movies to "Talkies" later demanded that the theatre be upgraded to accommodate the new technology. This shift in technology also ends Rose's desire to go to the cinema and fuels her need to connect with her mother in person.

When Rose disembarks the ferry, holding her suitcase, she runs across streets to the theatre where her mother, Lillian, was slated to perform "My Mother's Advice" (246). Unlike Ben, she gets the physical location right and actually meets the parent whose company she seeks. But when her mother fails to welcome her as envisioned, Rose sneaks out of her mother's dressing room and meanders off to the American Museum of Natural History in search of her brother, Walter. As she wanders through the museum, she is mesmerized by the different exhibits, which pique her curiosity. The experience spurs her to write a note pondering where she actually belongs: "I wish I belonged somewhere" (351).

The challenges both children experience on their way (separately) to the museum as well as encounters with unique artifacts in the museum impact them significantly. For Ben, first, it is frustrating that he has not been able to locate Danny in Kincaid bookstore as he had anticipated. When the contents of his suitcase spill over, "Ben bit down his lip to keep from crying again" (321); but the frustration does not deter him from his original mission of tracking down Danny, his father. However, finding himself in the museum, a major "secret place" in the novel, enabled opportunities to carve out a new space for childhood through his encounter with the wolf diorama, which deepens

Figure 8.1. *Wonderstruck* Left: Wolf image at opening (detail); Right: Wolf image at close (detail). Copyright © 2011 by Brian Selznick. Reprinted by permission of Scholastic Inc.

his understanding not only of wolves, which had petrified him in his dreams, but also of himself. He is frightened of these wolves but is full of awe at their beauty and natural prowess.

> Looking at the diorama, Ben felt the hair on the back of his neck stand up. His suitcase dropped from his hand.
>
> He was staring into the shimmering lights of the aurora borealis cascading across a painted night sky. Beneath the blue light of an unseen moon, two wolves were running across a snowy landscape, heading right for Ben. A terrible shiver rippled through him.
>
> It was as if someone had cut out the dream from his brain and put it behind glass. (359)

The novel opens and ends with almost isomorphic black and white illustrations of the wolves that appear in Ben's dreams (see Figure 8.1), but the first version is low in modality and fuzzy, in keeping with Ben's inability to make sense of his dream. By the end of the novel, when he has discovered that the dream is a memory of the diorama that connects him to the father he never knew, the modality of the image is closer to photo-realism: the head of the wolf is finely detailed, the Aurora Borealis in the background is clearly visible, and the trees in the middle ground are now identifiable as birches. These framing images have a metafictive effect, in that they encapsulate Ben's cognitive and emotional growth during his journey of discovery.

For Rose, the museum is a place and space in which she is certain she will find someone who loves her: Walter. This quest and conviction take her to the physical place and emotional/psychological spaces, which combined become a secret space for her childhood to flourish. Thus, it is a space that promises love while displaying artifacts that amaze her and further empower her to ponder her place in the larger universe. The exhibits tower over making her look and feel small next to the exquisite objects. She is a child flâneuse within the museum roaming its spacious hallways and appreciating the extraordinary exhibits. Pages 314–15 of the novel depict a postcard photo of the American Museum, while on pages 318–19 Rose looks at the postcard while standing in front of the "real" museum (but which is overtly a drawing). The photograph of the museum, is dated "February 1927," and addressed to Miss Rose Kincaid. It also bears the message "Happy Birthday Rose, love Walter." The effect of this *mise en abyme* (here, the placing of a small copy of an image inside a larger one) foregrounds how the Museum represents the greater or primary narrative level of the novel, not just as a site in which crucial events from each of the narrative strands occur; but also as the sweep of historical time over fifty years that embraces the lives of Rose and Ben and perhaps a hint at a formal emergence of Deaf Culture, as affirmed by eight openings devoted to ASL finger spelling near the close of the book (592–607). At a lower narrative level, Rose enters the museum to seek help from Walter, while fifty years later Ben stumbles across the museum in search of Kincaid's Bookshop. In terms of narrative causality, Rose's action sets in train a process of self-actualization that leads to her becoming Ben's grandmother, while Ben's time in the museum enables him to learn about his parents and to find Rose.

The affirmation of the past as meaningful for the present is made in the exhibit the "CABINETS OF WONDERS: HOW MUSEUMS BEGAN" (400–401), which becomes a secret place where Rose hides from the museum guard (part of her leg is visible as she slips behind the central display). In this room, dwelling within history, she is drawn to the myriad images that surround her and ponders the significance of each piece until Walter retrieves her.

There is no museum in the movie, *A Quiet Place*, but the setting of the abandoned town can be perceived as a museum of sorts. With the town's declining physical and economic state on display, the Abbotts appear to be strolling through a live museum. Various parts of the town hold significance to the family. For Regan in particular, specific places and spaces are of great importance. By the end of the movie they have contributed in transforming her childhood or rather adolescent experience. Of particular note is the rail trail bridge that opens with the death of her brother, Beau. This spot becomes a secret space where she pays homage to sort out her mixed feelings toward her father, as she suffers from the guilt of having given Beau the battery-operated space shuttle, a toy that also epitomizes childhood.

The movie introduces this tension early by foregrounding that Regan is a doting big sister who is deaf. In her attempt to do right by Beau, in order to preserve his childhood in the midst of the horror that was their reality, she is oblivious to the consequences of the child's desire to have a functioning space shuttle and so instead endangers him. In Beau's fantasy, the space shuttle toy transcends its practical purpose as a play object. It is a tool with the potential to liberate them from their current plight. But in reality it is an object—a toy—that causes his death—hence the contradictory nature of secret spaces reminiscent of childhood. These spaces hold dreams and possibilities of endangerment for all children. This is noticeable in the early part of the movie. Because he is a child the family does not take Beau seriously and so even though his father confiscates the toy with the batteries removed and placed separately elsewhere, they underestimate his attachment to the plaything.

The pathway between the corn fields also functions as a secret place for Regan. It is a place of wonder where she appreciates the natural beauty of the surrounding corn fields even though she knows full well that it is unsafe to be out there by herself. There is a parallel here with Ben becoming lost in the museum, as these fields are also a place to retreat. For instance, after a brawl with her father, who prefers to take his unwilling son fishing instead of his daughter who loves the outdoors, Regan seeks solace in the fields. When she lies on the sandy pathway between two corn fields with eyes closed that space becomes personal and private. Holcomb (2013) notes, "privacy is only possible among Deaf people when visual access is blocked" (215). Thus, by shutting her eyes, she removes herself from the surrounding environment and retreats into a private world where she could imagine her world differently. This brief tranquility allows her for a moment to enjoy being a child away from the insufferable gazing eyes of her father who constantly fusses—reminding her to wear her cochlear implants constantly and to be quiet, as well as telling her what not to do, where to go and where is off limits. However, it is disrupted when her cochlear implant picks up a shrill sound from a monster close by.

SPACES FOR FRIENDSHIP: NEW AND OLD

The texts also depict secret places as spaces where new friendships are culti-
vated and old friendships reaffirmed. The American Museum of Natural History transforms Ben's childhood by allowing for a new friendship to blossom
between him and Jamie, the son of a museum employee; it becomes a place of
wonder where anything can happen based on Ben's imagination as the boys
embark on a treasure hunt. Jamie's intimate knowledge of the museum enables
him to help reconstruct an experience that is personal and meaningful to Ben.
Their meeting is random, but their friendship is based on childhood interests
and trust. Ben asks, "'Why did you pick this diorama to meet me at?'" (366)
Although he could not understand what the boy was saying because of his loss
of hearing, he eventually figures this out. "Of course, the wolves on the box had
given the boy the idea to meet him here!" (367). Guessing that Ben might be
deaf, "The boy reached into a pocket and pulled out a spiral-bound notebook
and a green pen" and wrote: '*Are you deaf?*'" (68).

Ben's friendship with Jamie develops exponentially throughout the novel.
Over the course of this friendship they learn more about one another, and
Jamie, surprised that Ben can speak and yet cannot sign, teaches him how:

> Jamie started making strange shapes with the fingers of his right hand. When
> Ben didn't respond, Jamie wrote, *"Don't you know sign language? I learned the
> alphabet in school."*
> Ben shook his head.
> *"Why not?"*
> Ben touched his ear. "It's only been a month," he said
> "What happened?" Jamie asked. (568)

And he explains.

Finally, it is a space that introduces Ben to a new family member. Eastland
summarizes this succinctly:

> In that same museum, where years ago a friend took Selznick on a backstage
> tour, he places Ben and Rose. They are amazed and sometimes scared by what
> they find. Ben comes across a diorama in the Hall of North American Mammals,
> showing wolves that look just like the ones that plague his dreams, and Rose
> enters an exhibition about that Renaissance precursor to modern museums:
> cabinets of wonders, or *wunderkammer*, rooms filled with sundry curiosities
> arranged to tell a story . . . The museum also figures as a place where they find
> another kind of wonder: friendship and even new family.

Ben went to New York City in search of his father but ends up with a deep understanding of his family's genealogy in addition to gaining new relatives and cultivating new friendships.

The friendship motif plays out differently in *A Quiet Place*, for the isolation of the family doesn't allow Regan to make new friends. Rather, she and her younger brother, Marcus, reaffirm their sibling friendship and she comes to appreciate her father's love for her through this emotional reconnection. This happens when they are trapped in a corn silo, a dangerous space that also furnishes them an opportunity to reflect about their family situation and her relationship with their father. In working together to survive in the belly of the corn silo where they are cornered fleeing from the sound sensitive creature, Marcus reassures her that their father does not blame her for Beau's death. Lee Abbott's ensuing self-sacrifice so the children could live conveys this love to Regan and empowers her to join forces with her mother to reclaim their home from the invaders.

Both *Wonderstruck* and *A Quiet Place* succeed in constructing spaces for childhood that encourage wonder and nurture friendships. They also offer readers some insights into Deaf culture depicting characters who are not preoccupied with their deafness, for it is a way of life that is central to their very existence.

DEAFNESS AND DEAF CULTURE

In the introduction of his anthology on disability, Lennard Davis contends that "To understand the disabled body one must turn to the concept of the norm, the normal body," noting further that "the problem is the way normalcy is constructed to create the problem of the disabled person" (1). "An important consequence of the idea of the norm [is that it divides] the total population into standard and nonstandard subpopulations" (3). As mentioned earlier, Selznick and Krasinski diverge from this way of thinking by positioning the humanity of deaf children at the center of their narratives, especially in regard to their desired childhood experiences and the need for varying degrees of autonomy.

Selznick's narration of Ben and Rose's stories identifies two ways deaf children make decisions about their lives in spite of hearing people's expectations. Both long for parental figures and so do what I consider the logical thing—go on a quest to New York City, with hopes of being reunited with these parental figures. Normalcy is captured in their actions as children desiring the company of a parent. However, Selznick draws attention to each character's deafness as it pertains to the historical period. For instance, from Rose's activities in the visual narrative it is difficult to tell that she is deaf. But later in the novel when

Figure 8.2. Lillian and Rose in Lillian's Dressing Room. Copyright © 2011 by Brian Selznick. Reprinted by permission of Scholastic Inc.

she tells Ben her life story she goes into details about her treatment as a deaf child, including the common experience of learning sign language from other children at a school that banned signing.

Readers notice her sneaking out of her bedroom window to go to the cinema unbeknownst to her parents or guardians. That image of her engaging in that act implies that it could be any child, just as her abrasive encounter with Lillian (see Figure 8.2) also demonstrates how deaf children were treated in the 1920s, as Rose subsequently explains to Ben.

Looking closely at the facial expressions in Figure 8.2, readers notice there is some tension between the two females: Lillian, the older woman has her left hand on Rose's shoulder in a dominating gesture, an indication that the older woman might feel angry because the girl is there. In contrast, Rose's eyes widen indicating disbelief at what she might be hearing. In that space, they share an intimate moment, and though the reader has no idea about the nature of their relationship, he/she can figure that they know each other. This is confirmed by the textual correspondence between the two females. The dialogue between this unnamed girl (who we've now come to understand is Rose, Ben's grandmother) and Lillian when they finally meet in New York City in her dressing room runs thus:

What are you doing here? (274/5) [Lillian]

   I miss you, momma! (278/9)

   I am working! I said I would visit you next month. You know you aren't
allowed out. (282/3)

   Please don't make me go back (284/5)

   We've discussed this enough. It is too dangerous for a deaf girl to be outside
alone. You could be hit by a car or kidnapped! (286/87)

   So could anyone! (288/9)

Throughout the "conversation" Rose positions herself as a child who happens to be deaf and for whom deafness is not a limitation. Their correspondence through the written word implies that sign language might not be a mode of communication available to them (Rose later recalls that at this time she had never met another deaf person).

In regard to Ben, readers are told early in the novel that he lost all of his hearing postlingually, as opposed to Rose, who was either born deaf or lost her hearing prelingually. He wrestles with this new reality as he recalls what had happened: "They ran so many tests in the hospital and discovered the lightning had damaged his ear drum. Ben looked down at all the silent shoes in the station and up at all the silent mouths. What would life be like if his hearing never came back?" (243). Despite this brief moment of reflection, he does not see his deafness as a limitation. Instead he is learning fast to expand his modes of communication beyond speech, and eventually beginning to communicate through American Sign Language (ASL)

Selznick acknowledges the role that the documentary *Through Deaf Eyes* (2007) plays in his depiction of deaf characters and Deaf culture in the novel. Through this research, he also came to understand that the Deaf are a "'people of the eye'" (Minzeshelmer 2011), a concept he integrates consistently in the illustrations focusing on the eyes of the characters, starting from the eyes of the wolves early in the novel to the illustrations of Ben's bonding with Rose toward the end of the novel. The documentary, spanning two hundred years of Deaf Culture in America, presents the history from the Deaf perspective. According to the WETA press release in 2007, "The documentary takes a straight forward look at life of people who are part of the cultural-linguistic group who use American Sign Language and often define themselves as Deaf with a capital, and cultural 'D'—and deaf people, who for a variety of reasons, do not identify with the Deaf cultural community" (*Through Deaf Eyes* website). Professor Samuel Supalla whose interview segment appears early in the documentary elucidates the sense of normalcy that permeates his Deaf Culture community, and in a way frames the documentary. He notes,

There was a little girl; a neighbor girl who always came and played with me and we used gestures with each other. One time I went over to visit her and I saw her using her lips to communicate with her mother. They weren't using their hands at all. And so I ran home and asked my mother what was happening:

- *Why aren't they using their hands?*
My mother said: They are hearing.
  - *And I said, oh, well, what are we?*
She said: Daddy and I are deaf; you are deaf; your brothers are deaf.
  - *And I said: is everyone deaf? Is that little girl the only hearing girl in the world?*
She said: No, Everyone else is like them
  - *And I said, Oh now, I get it"*

Selznick (2011) channels Deaf Culture in *Wonderstruck* through historical accounts, using Rose's character as a vehicle for how things were in the 1920s compared to how they had changed in the 1970s. In *Wonderstruck*, therefore, he is able to weave in sentiments conveyed in the documentary about the passage of time, changes in technology such as moving from the use of Sign Language to educate youth to oral language that forces deaf children to learn how to speak, and back to sign language; changes from silent to sound movies that widened the gap between deaf and hearing worlds as conveyed in the illustrations, and finally, changes in governmental policies. It therefore isn't surprising to learn that Ben is not familiar with American Sign Language (ASL). For one, he only became profoundly deaf a month previous to the time of the narrated events, and since he had some hearing in one ear he would be considered an oralist; but his communication repertoire continues to expand as he finds his way in the city. The last sets of illustrations indicate Ben finally learning to Sign: "Ben could feel the letters vibrating on his fingers. *My Friend* (608). Thus, he is embracing a new language that presents him other ways to communicate.

This graphic novel about deafness and Deaf Culture, written by a hearing person, could be problematic, since many might be skeptical, and rightfully so, regarding Selznick's knowledge about the subject. Anticipating this, the author/illustrator did his research. Euan Kerr, Arts Reporter of MPR news in St. Paul, MN remarks, "Selznick knew [the subject] had to be handled sensitively. He wrote the story after extensive research and interviews. He also had his work checked and double-checked by members of the deaf community" (Euan Kerr 2011). Perhaps this is why his work has been well-received with minimal controversy from the deaf community. Ann Claire LeZotte (2016), a white Deaf author, observes:

What makes it [*Wonderstruck*] different from other books about the d/Deaf experience written by hearing authors? Simply this: Selznick approached the project not as a writer who wanted to write about characters with disabilities, but as a writer delving into an historical novel about Deaf Culture and language. This is what makes the book so enjoyable and authentic.

Unlike *Wonderstruck*, in which characters grapple with the expectations of the hearing world, *A Quiet Place* overlays a silent world upon the world of sounds that is depicted as violent to human existence. In this setting, American Sign Language (ASL) is pivotal to the communication process and serves as the preferred mode of communication for the Abbotts whose daughter is deaf. It is a story of how her hearing family and she in particular survive in a soundless world. It is also a story of her tumultuous relationship with her father, stemming from her view that he bears a grudge against her for Beau's death. Additionally, she is female and deaf and that is how her father sees her. From his perspective as the patriarch, Regan should stay indoors and work closely with her mother learning how to be female; as a hearing person, he is anxious about how her lack of hearing may predispose her more to the dangers of being killed by the alien creature that hunts them; as a father, he worries about her wandering away from their parental supervision. All these anxieties Regan believes stifle her growth as a person and so she rebels.

The family in the movie primarily utilizes American Sign Language (ASL), thus placing Regan, their deaf daughter at the center of the story. Holcomb (2013) contends that, "Whether as a teaching philosophy, a linguistic right, or simply a communication mode, ASL is considered to be the primary cultural marker of the Deaf community" (131).

In the movie, it is hard to know how early the family learns to communicate [native-deaf signing versus late deaf signing] with Regan through sign language. However, for the father, it is still important that Regan wears cochlear implants so she is more aware of her surroundings. This technology that is developed to improve her hearing of sounds also poses a problem, as it can be perceived as an attempt to normalize Regan. But her intimate knowledge of how friction from the technology can be irritating to the ears enables her to convert her cochlear implants into a weapon that together with her mother's excellent gun skills are able to kill one of the creatures (and thus gain valuable knowledge about how to fight back).

Using a real-life deaf girl adds more authenticity to the movie. Nevertheless, Pamela J. Kincheloe (2018), a member of the Deaf community and a professor at NTID, does not believe that the movie depicts a "truly deaf-centric world." Rather, she argues that

In the end, it is not the ability to speak silently through ASL that saves the Abbotts . . . It is that other symbolic piece, the cochlear implant, that saves the day. It is one of the very first things we see in the movie; we see it even before we clearly see Regan, or any of the other characters. It is the *implant*, not the signing deaf person, that is heroic.

Although Kincheloe has a point, I would add that the presence of mind that enables Regan to understand that the "screech of technological feedback" might be the key in getting rid of the creature is commendable. This insight derives first from her experience of trying to minimize the pain that comes from the technological feedback when wearing the cochlear implants, and then from her consciousness of her surroundings, as she is able to notice the question posed by her father on his lab wall, "What is the weakness?" Placing herself in the creature's shoes, she comes up with the obvious answer: it does not like sound. In their list of "13 Things They Learned about *A Quiet Place* from John Krasinski," Travis and Hewitt (2018) mention,

> Sound was always intended as the creatures' weakness, as well as their hunting super-power, but Krasinski tweaked the source of the offending sound in his script re-write to tie thematically back in to the father-daughter relationship . . . "I needed the girl who thought she was the black sheep and the reason for all the horror to be the reason they survived. I needed her biggest weakness to be her superpower."

Ultimately, Regan and her mother destroy the creature as the movie comes to a close. Nevertheless, alignment of the experience of being deaf with that of a creature who destroys humans at the slightest sound can also be problematic as it can suggest that deaf people may be construed as less than human.

CONCLUSION

On the whole, the deaf child characters are portrayed as audacious and resilient children with a healthy sense of wonder. In the case of Ben and Rose, they must contend with the demands of the hearing world as they forge secret spaces for childhood that nurture imagination and create possibilities for them as children who happen to be deaf. In Regan's case, silence is the norm, but the greatest threat stems from a creature that is sensitive to sound. She is granted agency to use her intimate knowledge of the potential of cochlear implants, their shortcomings, and her intuition regarding how the technology can better serve her family to outsmart the creature that terrorizes them. She imagines the possibilities and acts swiftly. In short, the young protagonists in these texts seek the opportunity to be children rather than security as Deaf children; they thus assert their "right to be an uncommon and noble silent minority" (Holcomb, 61). They are rebellious characters that strive to create identities that are not limited by deafness as perceived by the larger hearing community. For Davis, texts such as these "reverse the hegemony of the normal and institute alternative ways of thinking about the abnormal" (12). They turn the table on what it means to be "normal"!

CHAPTER 9

(Mis-)Communication Scripts and Cognition in Japanese Deaf Fictional Film *A Silent Voice* (Koe no Katachi)

—*Helen Kilpatrick*

Although Japan has a rich source of "disability" narratives that have developed intertextually over time through a blend of international and local cultural sources, the depiction of Deaf culture in modern Japanese film and television drama productions has regularly been (unconsciously) portrayed from a dominant hearing perspective. This view paints Deafness as a disablement to be overcome or cured. Such a view is rejected by the Japanese (and international) Deaf community, which, having its own customs and language, self identifies as bilingual and bicultural. Fictional films, in contrast with documentaries that are more expository in nature, can promote audience mental and affective activity, which can help counter such "disability" perspectives and foster understanding about less familiar social groups. Despite a fin-de-siecle boom in disability and Deaf-culture film and television that helped inform the dominant Japanese hearing community about Deaf culture, there have since been more documentaries than fictional dramas. Until recently, the latest feature film was *Yuzuriha: To Another You* (Yuzuriha: Kimi mo mata tsugi no kimi e), which commemorated the 60th anniversary of the Japanese Federation for the Deaf in 2009.[1] Of late, this hiatus in fictional drama has come to an end with the 2016 coming-of-age *anime* (animated film), *Koe no Katachi* (henceforth, *A Silent Voice*).[2] In linking the issues of (physical) deafness, marginalization and gender in a romance drama between a deaf girl, Nishimiya Shōko, and hearing boy, Ishida Shōya, this film confronts many intercultural communication issues. Because dominant hearing perspectives can become evident through (mis-)communication scripts, especially those between romantically involved hearing and hearing-impaired characters, and because such relationships have pervaded Japanese Deaf Bildungsroman film narratives, this chapter focuses on the communicative successes and failures in potential romance scenes between the two young protagonists. The analysis demonstrates how narrative processes can operate to counteract dominant perspectives and foster communicative skills between different communities, but especially those between the hearing-impaired and hearing people.

This examination employs a cognitive narratological exploration of the anime in order to expose how dominant hearing perspectives and misunderstandings about Deaf culture can be driven or challenged by audience mental activity and affect, rather than plot alone. Cognitive narratology deals with the "nexus of narrative and mind" and focuses attention on the role of stories in the development of social and self-perception (Herman 2009, 30–34). Such a literary approach applies equally to watching film because a cognitive perspective examines how fictional characters, readers and viewers perceive what other characters think. That is, watching or reading any such text requires theory of mind (ToM), the "cognitive ability to explain the behavior of other people by attributing to them mental and emotional processes (thought and feelings, and so on), as well as attributing states of mind to oneself" (Silva 2013, 161). As with all human culture, communication between hearing-impaired and hearing characters relies on the capacity to "read" minds, which, because of the hearing impediment, can heighten awareness of other communication strategies and "signs." By exposing the metaphorical aspects of the capacity to "hear" as the capacity to understand in a less binary, more embodied way, this chapter demonstrates how culturally specific communication situations in the anime interrogate the idea of Deafness as a physical disability. Through the imaginative and affective capacity to see, listen and experience, audiences can reflect upon, ascertain, and *feel* how cultural disability schemas and scripts are reinforced or challenged.

Every fictional representation is about communication and understanding, and while fictional film and media with Deaf characters have an important role to play in increasing the profile of the hearing-impaired and Deaf culture (Maher 2010, 142), they can also model and provide alternative cognitive strategies. Because films with Deaf protagonists depict how fictional minds communicate beyond the "verbal norm" (Palmer 2004, 53) to convey communicative interaction and thought processes, their filmic techniques emphasize theory of mind processes. In other words, narrative understanding of Deaf fictions not only relies on acknowledging and following different forms of nonverbal communication such as sign language, but also on accessing a higher mental capacity to make inferences about the subjective feelings and experiences in the minds of the fictional characters. Cognitive processes are heavily situated in Deaf communication exchanges because the characters must operate in a bilingual and bicultural capacity in the process of developing their subjectivities. Watching and understanding the interactions among characters in fictional dramas with Deaf protagonists can thus provide an embodied or affective experience of mental and bilingual communication processes for understanding others, which is higher than that of common monolinguistic or auditory communicative behavior. Cultural (mis-)understandings among characters who are attracted to (or often initially repulsed by) each other emphasize the complexities of theory of mind—or "minds" as per Keith Oatley's (2014) term. Whereas to understand the events in everyday fictional dramas viewers need to mentally attribute feelings, thoughts, emotions and motivations to the characters, Deaf communication exchanges emphasize different strategies that can lead, through cognitive processing, to a greater appreciation or intensified experience of how it feels to live as a Deaf person.

As David Herman (2013) suggests, narrative is a mode of representation tailor-made for gauging the felt quality of lived experiences, and of having and knowing a mind. Recent research has shown how the cognitive process of mirror neuron functioning can affect observers emotionally or bodily when they have understood someone else's action. This process applies to understanding the actions of fictional characters. Lisa Zunshine (2014) explains that such understanding will "resonate" in the observer's motor system because "the brain does not seem to distinguish between you doing something and a person [who] you observe doing it" (65). Even whilst comprehending that the characters are fictional, in order to understand and enjoy a narrative an audience must use mental processes to comprehend and experience the expressive modes the characters are trying to communicate (or veil). The strategies deployed in imaginative engagement with the mental states of participants in projected social situations connect, then, with viewers' own states of mind. Viewing alignment with or rejection of the represented characters' actions and thoughts facilitate audience experience of other people's emotions. Exploration of how protagonists are affected and how viewers access and interpret given information helps explain how mental activity can influence social and self-reflection, particularly on Deafness. Watching Deaf film narratives requires reflection and acceptance or rejection of, for example, the disability model.

Any such social or self-reflection requires access to a combination of previous cultural or stereotypical knowledge and concepts, including those about

Deafness or disability, which the mind then processes, often unconsciously, as it interacts with new and unfolding circumstances and situations. Attitudes to disability, which are reflected in, brought to or affected by films for example, often rely on unconscious associations with preexisting disability scripts. As David Herman (2013) explains, schemas and scripts represent stereotypical and expected information. Whereas a schema guides expectations about more static concepts such as a classroom or a prison cell, scripts guide expectations about more dynamic processes such as what may happen while ordering food in a restaurant or walking a dog. In the case of Deaf romance situations in film, any viewer, whether hearing or nonhearing, will have some kind of preexisting schema for a Deaf person and some kind of preexisting script for how a romance may evolve. Both would then subconsciously come together and be processed against unfolding scenes in the narrative. Further, as Monika Fludernik has indicated, narrative deviations need a "human (anthropocentric) experiencer" (1996 13) to fill in the gaps in expectations to deduce what others are thinking. Following on from this observation, David Herman explains that scripts are particularly useful for understanding how narratives "focus attention on the unusual and the remarkable" (2002 90). In the case of *A Silent Voice*, the "remarkable" interactions fit within a common Japanese disability script that has developed historically and intertextually through, for instance, fictional narratives, myths, and other social discourse.

Some cultural background about dominant Japanese narratives of disability and Deafness contextualizes how the anime promotes the deductive capacity to understand Deaf culture and prompt an affective viewing experience. As Arran Stibbe (2004 24) suggests, in cases where people have little personal experience with Deaf culture, especially if the hearing-impaired are segregated as has been the case in Japan, knowledge of the minority culture may be acquired through literature, film and other media. When people from Deaf and hearing cultures interact, they not only need to communicate through different forms of language but also different suites of cultural understanding, which derive from separate sets of knowledge and experience. Watching films can thus go beyond understanding any given narrative to build and develop a store of cultural experiences for future application to new life situations and experiences.

Japanese scripts for Deaf characters have evolved through a medical model that regarded any disability as a pathological disease and kept the afflicted segregated and invisible in society and media (Stibbe, 21). The Japanese disability script can be considered to have originated from early myths and legends that later filtered into mainstream television documentaries, dramas and film then blended with a new awareness of Deaf cultural issues that developed in the 1970s. As Karen Nakamura (2006, 31) indicates about the latter period,

legal rights and social recognition began to increase through the social disability activism in Japan. This activism resulted in a boom in Deaf drama in
the mid-1990s (see Maher 2010; Stibbe 2004; and Valentine 2001, 707), but as
Carolyn Stevens suggests in relation to Japanese cultural attitudes to disability,
any such progress had been made against a long background of disablement
in Shintō and Buddhist mythology (2013, 24–27). Stevens draws links to early
myths and legends that demonstrate both positive and negative associations
with disabilities. She notes tropes of abandonment, worship, propitiation, and
negative (Buddhist) karma attributed at birth and usually seen as a curse but
sometimes a blessing. In Japan's Shintō creation myth, for example, Izanagi and
Izanami, the husband/wife, brother/sister pair who created the Japanese islands
and deities of the universe, also produced then abandoned a limbless child.
When the same child resurfaces in later cultural texts it has evolved into Ebisu,
the god of the sea, who is Deaf as well as physically impaired, but "cheerful
and pleasant" (25). As Stevens indicates, these traits are similar to stereotypical,
"idealistic characterizations of people with intellectual disabilities, who are
often described as charmingly innocent and childlike" (25). This categorization
coheres with a standard schema for a Deaf character in modern Japanese film,
which involves "the stereotype-that-never-ends: that people with disabilities
are childlike and innocent" (Maher, 151). Schematic characterization can also
include the Deaf protagonist's isolation, silence (a particularly Japanese moral
virtue that is often seen as indicative of the "true" inner self), selflessness,
martyrdom, and perseverance (*gaman*) (Valentine, 714–17). Stevens further
refers to eighth-century legal documents that elucidate pragmatic appraisals
of disability that are similar to today's welfare criteria in their concerns with
the ability to live independently and earn income. As Masao Kato (2010 134)
observes, ancient Buddhist beliefs (of *karma*, for instance) are still part of
"daily vocabulary," embedded in "ordinary" people's understandings of health
and medical risks along with basic knowledge about genetics.

Early Japanese texts are not the only source of cultural scripts and attitudes
to disability. Films and dramas with Deaf characters, which brought Deafness
into the mainstream, also access European intertextual tropes. The 1995 television drama series *Heaven's Coins* (Hoshi no kinka), for instance, takes its name
from the Grimm tale, *Die Sterntaler* (The Star Coins), and directly references
the story and its themes of abandonment in the first episode (Valentine, 714).
The Deaf female protagonist's (hearing) male love interest narrates his version
of the tale to her in one scene, and in another, her foster father reveals to her
that she was abandoned by her mother at birth, explaining that she must not
get her hopes up about the man of her affections, a regional medical physician.
The doctor is considered to be out of her reach, not only because of his higher

status, but also because of the competition with other (hearing) women, any of whom would supposedly make a more suitable wife. Predictably, then, he leaves her to pursue work opportunities in the Tokyo metropolis. This "abandonment of the deaf" trope continues throughout the entire series, which had two sequels in 1996 and 2001 respectively (Valentine, 714), and in many other mainstream Deaf films.

Besides the abandonment script, dramas from this time stereotyped hearing-impaired characters or situations in other ways. Although there was an increasing number of deaf characters in television film and dramas from the mid-1990s, scholars such as James Valentine (708–9), Arran Stibbe (2004) and John Maher (2010) have demonstrated how most of these narratives have been slow to challenge medical models or hearing accounts that marginalize the deaf and Deaf culture as "other." Whereas many early Japanese television dramas and films managed to avoid the heavy-handed hearing perspective of many of their international counterparts—such as ascribing Deaf characters with "special," superhuman, artistic characteristics or understanding (Valentine 2001, 719)—many nonetheless reinforced the hearing and medical-model stereotypes. Stibbe identifies five aspects found in a medical-model script in such dramas. They revolve around the expectation that disabled characters should change in order "to achieve a more 'normal' life by: a) being cured; b) stoically putting up with the disadvantages caused by barriers; c) battling to overcome barriers; d) psychologically adjusting to disability; and e) submitting to the protection of a non-disabled person" (2004, 27). The Deaf were schematized as strong-willed (*gaman-zuyoi*) characters who were scripted to overcome obstacles through willpower, and as "interesting" types who engaged in "out-of-the-ordinary" activities that did not involve any of the banal concerns of daily (Deaf) life (Nakano 1998 in Maher 2010, 148). As Valentine (708) and Maher (148) have suggested, many dramas also emphasized sentimental story lines that provoked one-sided sympathy for the hearing-impaired characters. They further overemployed deafness as a dramatic device, relied on Signed Japanese instead of Japanese Sign Language (JSL) and the accepted (written, spoken, and nonverbal) language of the Deaf community. As Valentine points out, Japanese Sign Language (JSL) is different from spoken Japanese "in word order and form of expression" (715), and many dramas disregarded Deaf linguistic preferences. In other words, most film neglected to convey the Deaf community in a balanced or nondisabled way.

Although the Japanese Deaf community rejects the idea of Deafness as even a subcategory of disability, many films continued to treat deaf people as "special." Despite the Deaf community's self-identification as bilingual and bicultural, Deaf characters were usually portrayed as solitary individuals operating within hearing culture rather than within broader Deaf culture or operating equally between the two cultures (Valentine 2001, 723). Deafness was, then, often foregrounded in dramas as a disability and the concept of Deaf culture was not well represented.

Nevertheless, some later disability romance films raised awareness of the need for egalitarianism for people with disabilities, especially following the movement known as "bariafurī," "barrier free," or working towards a barrier-free society. According to Stibbe (23), few Japanese people understood the term "bariafurī" until the 2000 television drama *Beautiful Life* (Byūtifuru raifu), about a romance between a female wheelchair user and an able-bodied male hairdresser. In contrast with previous representations of romantic relationships between hearing-impaired and hearing people such as the aforementioned *Heaven's Coins,* the 1999 collaboration between two directors, hearing and deaf, *I Love You* (Ai rabu yu), demonstrated better awareness (Maher, 148). Despite an apparent move away from a medical model of disability towards new constructions of impairment as a social rather than individual concern, however, most romance dramas continued to reinforce both gender stereotypes and conservative models of disability (Stibbe, 21). Such stereotypes become particularly visible in romance scenes between young hearing and hearing-impaired characters, especially through cognizance of the mental activities of their characters.

The gendered and disability communication patterns, perspectives, and strategies found in Japanese disability-romance scripts have not only developed through social discourse, media, and previous narratives, but can also reflect how cognitive activity operates in self-development. A typical "disability romance script" is, for instance, one in which a poor (but beautiful) disabled character overcomes difficulties, then either lives happily ever after or, as particularly pertinent to the Japanese situation, perseveres through continuing trials and tribulations. While watching a film with a Deaf romance script in particular, viewers' communicative expectations and mental activity will be highly charged during the miscommunication scenes and will be modified according to whether predictions (internal schemas and scripts) are met or rejected as the narrative progresses.

A Silent Voice is an example of a mainstream anime that operates with such preexisting scripts and audience expectations by heightening viewers' cognitive activity. Its narrative deviations encourage engagement with characters, their theory of mind (ToM), and different linguistic and cultural mores to help address some of the oversights of earlier Japanese dramas. Preceding dramas have often been less self-reflexively critical of institutionalized or paternalistic attitudes, thus reinforcing hearing perspectives and the medical model of Deafness as a disability.

Just as live-action television and films have the potential to reflect, construct and affect social attitudes about Deaf culture, so does anime. Indeed, because anime is at an even further remove from reality than live-action fictional dramas with real actors (or documentaries), it relies on narrative devices that encourage even higher-level imaginative strategies in the understanding of why characters act in certain ways. Documentaries, for instance, explicate rather than encourage imaginative engagement with what a character may be thinking or hiding from another character, so they require less theory of mind. In anime, characters' facial expressions, for instance, are usually less expressive and thus less conventionally "readable." In other words, as Roberta Silva (2013, 161) suggests about fictional narratives, more interpretive mental work is needed to decode the symbols built up around the mental model of any given character. Further, the hearing characters in *A Silent Voice* (and its audiences) are encouraged to interpret JSL through the projection of meaning onto unexplained signing or to characters' actions, feelings, and expressions. A simple example of this is the sign for friend/ship that is repeated many times throughout, thus negating the need for translation, but also encouraging active linguistic and cultural acquisition of the sign. (In response to the anime, many YouTube lessons that reference the film have now become available on JSL for both Japanese and non-Japanese-background language learners.)

By reflecting and activating theory of mind strategies in (mis-)communication scenes that require multiple characters to be understood simultaneously, *A Silent Voice* encourages reflection on Deafness as a social issue rather than as the hearing-impaired individual's problem. When, for example, the male protagonist, Shōya, bullies the deaf Shōko when she comes as a transfer student to his elementary school, and classmates go along with his merciless pranks, the focus is on their constant failure to read Shōko's feelings. Shōko makes continuous (heart-rending) efforts at communicating through voicing and notebooks that, together with the sequencing and focalization techniques, give pause for reflection upon her needs, but also upon the need for effort by more than one party for successful communication. As Maher (143) notes, a reliance on Deaf peoples' lip-reading or voicing skills has in the past been institutionalized in schools across Japan and has resulted in lowered literacy levels for Deaf students. Polyphonic visions of the hearing characters' selfishness through shot-reverse-shot sequencing encourage reflection on their insensitivity and lack of empathy for Shōko's position. During the newly created daily (three minute) sign language classes by a specialist teacher (at 00:10:32), for example, several students steadfastly refuse to try to learn and communicate through signing. Close-up shots of Shōko's impassive face and quiet humiliation are juxtaposed against the sign teacher's defense of Shōko's position and their usual class teacher's visual

Figure 9.1. Shot-reverse-shot sequencing of morning sign class: at 00:10:39; 00:10:5; 00:10:56; 00:10:59; and 00:11:08. *Koe no Katachi* [A Silent Voice]. Directed by Yamada Naoko. Japan: Kyoto Animation, Shochiku, 2016.

disgust (from the sidelines of the class) at the students' attitudes (see Figure 9.1). Shōko's classmates' failure at "hearing," "listening" or understanding her needs prompts abhorrence for their cruelty and unfair ostracism of Shōko, thus empathy with her. Viewing alignment with Shōko not only provokes distaste for their failure to understand her feelings, but also awareness of the need for their cooperation for her linguistic and social efforts to be effective. The juxtapositioning of these scenes against a series of scenes of Shōya bullying Shōko also provokes consideration of Shōya's (and other hearing characters') failure of theory of mind. It encourages thought about how the real "communication" problems do not lie with Shōko's deafness but with those who have "other-ed" her as disabled. Such scenes thus interrogate conventional schemas of monolingualism, monoculturalism and Deafness as a disablement and challenge the idea that communication with a Deaf subject is that unitary subject's problem.

Moreover, these visuals stimulate cognitive alignment with Shōko's feelings of rejection by fostering imaginative hurt or disappointment for her pain. Despite

her minimal facial or voiced expression, Shōko's silent stoicism against others' continuing negativity encourage cognitive questioning of her attitude, of her *tatemae* "face" versus her *honne*, or "true," inner feelings. The attribution of theory of mind to Shōko's constant equilibrium incites deductions about how she must feel under such duress. (Any inklings are confirmed when she later attempts suicide, which shows that much of her equilibrium must have been a show of "face.") Although she is stoic, viewers may *wonder* how she can continue to put up with all the ostracism and ignorance from others, especially that of Shōya who she has so often tried to befriend. If Shōko's potential feelings of isolation or embarrassment at not being able to communicate her feelings and words to others are recognized, it will arouse affective indignation for her or anger with others on her behalf. In other words, the visuals urge empathy with her underlying pain through neural mirroring and the cognitive capacity to deduce how she *must* be experiencing her classmates' ignorance of her efforts and to *feel* her pain with her.

Figure 9.2. Shōya pulls out Shōko's hearing aids. 00:14:18; 00:14:30. *Koe no Katachi* [A Silent Voice]. Directed by Yamada Naoko. Japan: Kyoto Animation, Shochiku, 2016.

Similar neural mirroring has the capacity to prompt viewer empathy with Shōko in other scenes. In one shocking early scene for instance, after Shōya has violently tugged Shōko's hearing aids out, blood pours from her ears (see Figure 9.2). Shots of Shōko's downcast face and body, blood dripping, are interspersed with those of Shōya's own shock and limp excuses for his viciousness. Affective horror at Shōya's callousness and lack of empathy, his failure of theory of mind, arouses both criticism of Shōya and bodily alignment with Shōko's feelings. The sequencing of events after this incident further prompts affective neural engagement with Shōko's sense of dejection as she transfers to another school soon after. This empathy contrasts with the initial lack of sympathy inspired for Shōya when he is subsequently ostracized by his classmates. The ability to see, to read the signs (and between the lines), and to feel for others thus becomes a more significant pointer to understanding others than does the physical capacity to hear.

Metaphors of hearing and listening also challenge the disability model and hearing perspective by provoking engagement with characters' theory of mind to perceive how it can be much more important to understanding than physical "hearing." According to conceptual metaphor theory, the general metaphor IDEAS ARE PERCEPTIONS enables more specific metaphors in which perception stands for deeper processes of understanding, in this case UNDERSTANDING IS HEARING. Because hearing is a metaphor for understanding, particularly in a hearing world, and it is Shōya who has the capacity to hear but fails to understand, rather than deaf Shōko, audiences are engaged in a bodily or mental inquiry into how physical deafness may not be the real disability, but that lack of theory of mind may be. Shōya's early failures at listening and perception engage viewers in attendance to other signs. Reflection upon his lack of comprehension is encouraged, for example, through metafictional crosses that appear over the faces of Shōya's acquaintances when he begins his first term at junior high school (after he has also attempted suicide). (See Figure 9.3.) His continual downward gaze works with the crosses to encourage reflection upon both his remorse and his inability to communicate. The crosses on their faces indicate his inability to see or understand others and this postulation is confirmed as he holds his hands to his ears to block out sound. He cannot look at or listen to his peers anymore (especially after he realizes he is being avoided when he overhears two boys disparaging him and asking why he is still alive). Given that he has tried to commit suicide, and that this scene comes after scenes of his mother making Shōya promise not to make another attempt, his lack of ability to communicate is conceptually tied to death and the meaning of life. Cognitive deductions connect the crosses to Shōya's new realization that he is now irrelevant to his classmates, and that he has never fully understood what it means to truly communicate as a friend. Shōya's lack of communication, particularly with Shōko, is metaphoric not only of his inability to interact with others, but also of his own inner pain. It is through his pain that thoughts about the values of friendship and communication arise, and that the capacity to listen, see and perceive is postulated as a more reliable indicator for understanding the feelings of others.

Further mind-reading strategies are needed to understand particular communication problems when narrative explanations are omitted or delayed in the film. Such narrative structuring stimulates reflection on events as they happen and in retrospect. Reasons as to why events are happening or why characters

Figure 9.3. Crosses representing the consequences of Shōya's inability to communicate (00:30:26 and 00:30:26). *Koe no Katachi* [A Silent Voice]. Directed by Yamada Naoko. Japan: Kyoto Animation, Shochiku, 2016.

may have acted in certain ways are left hanging or postponed, leaving potential answers open for contemplation and questioning before any cause is revealed. For instance, when Shōya seeks out Shōko at her new school to apologize to her for his earlier bullying, it is only later that the audience learns, through Shōya's self-reflective voiceover, that for him to confront Shōko has been "the most difficult thing he'd ever done" (at 00:28:09 in the film). It also transpires that Shōya has decided to make amends because he is about to commit suicide (something that has been flagged visually at the outset of the story, without explication, by images of him crossing off days to one "final day" (*saigo no hi*) on his calendar). As his visit to Shōko intimates, by this stage he has accepted responsibility for intimidating Shōko, but the reasons for the visit remain unclear until later.

The characters themselves also display delayed reactions to particular situations. While it is in this visit to Shōko that Shōya uses sign language for the first time, Shōko's realization of his new signing skill is belated. Her sudden awareness and questioning of him contrast with his understated response, "I've learned" (*oboeta*), to inspire wonder about how and why he has attained these newfound linguistic (signing) skills. The unexplained time lapse until this meeting also urges consideration of why he has abruptly visited her and what his new self/other awareness might be about. A bit later during the same meeting Shōya suddenly realizes that his request to become friends is the same as Shōko's earlier signing to him. Together with the minimal and delayed narrative explication, such character realizations encourage reflection upon previous communication errors, but particularly upon Shōya's earlier insensitivity and ignorance. His new efforts at trying to make friends and the results they bear on his life after failing in his suicide attempt foster further speculation about his newfound questioning of the concept of friendship. Moreover, Shōya's retrospective self-acknowledged stupidity in not knowing the simplest of signs (for "friendship," see Figure 9.4) and the contrast with those who continue to refuse to learn to sign or support Shōko help interrogate the hearing community's lack of awareness or neglect of Deaf culture and language. The cognitive interactions required to understand this nexus highlight the difficulties of integration—of any minority into mainstream (school) culture—and thereby encourage cognizance of communication and understanding as complex and multi-faceted, and thereby the recognition that true understanding cannot be achieved without the cooperative perception of other social participants besides the marginalized themselves.

Because of the building questions and tensions around the relationship between Shōya and Shōko, audience mental activity is further heightened during (imminent or failed) "romance" scenes between them. The Deaf romance script works with narrative gaps in these (mis-)communication scenes to arouse (and dampen) expectations, predictions and neural mirroring of the characters' mental processes, feelings, and attitudes. The script relies on a standard of ironic miscommunication between a pair who are mutually attracted to each other, but one of them (usually the male in a heterosexual attraction script) humorously avoids realization of how the other feels. The audience, however, is aware of the (mutual) attraction, thus potentially amused or frustrated by characters' mis-readings of signs. Indeed, Shōya's continual failure to comprehend Shōko prompts audience reflection upon the basis of their misunderstandings.

Figure 9.4. Signing of "friendship" to Shōya (00:10:10), and his later sudden acknowledgment of meaning (00:25:09; 00:25:13). *Koe no Katachi* [A Silent Voice]. Directed by Yamada Naoko. Japan: Kyoto Animation, Shochiku, 2016.

The differences between their cognitive capacities activate viewers' mental processing about, for instance, how and where each of the protagonists may be going wrong, and how such problems may be corrected. In other words, narrative expectations are set up for the audience to accept, reject or mentally create excuses for these characters as they fail to communicate their thoughts and feelings to each other. While theory of mind makes Shōko's affection for Shōya obvious to the audience, her interest and desires remain imperceptible to Shōya himself. He is frustratingly unaware of his own attraction to Shōko despite his continual efforts to see her (often with her younger sister, Yuzu who, aware of her sister's attraction to him, initially tries to subvert Shōya's efforts at seeing Shōko).

One scene of heightened audience mind-reading demonstrates how theory of mind operates and how it is Shōya's lack of theory of mind, which is the basis of his misunderstanding rather than Shōko's failed communication or pronunciation skills. Audience understanding is situated in Shōya's mis-comprehension of the near homonyms *suki*, which means "like," and "*tsuki*," which means "moon" (see Figure 9.5). After Shōko has been practicing voicing (instead of signing) with her sister, in a scene with Shōya she uses her voice and gives him a gift. Whereas the audience is led to understand that she is making a huge effort to express her emotions and to voice the word *suki*, Shōya hears the word but searches in vain for understanding. After looking up at the moon, he has an "aha" moment, ironically misinterpreting her repeated voicing of "*suki*," a spoken form of (*Anata ga*) *suki desu*, (I "like" you), as (*Tsuki ga*) *suki desu* (I "like" the moon). (While Japanese language often omits subjects and pronouns, spoken Japanese frequently omits particles, so, besides the

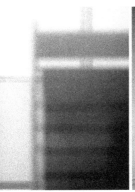

near homonyms, the object of "like" could be unclear to either a hearing or hearing-impaired person.) Feeling as if he has "got it," he comments on how beautiful the faint crescent moon above is and remains uncomprehending when Shōko flees in disappointment. Whereas the audience sees and understands their mutual attraction and exactly what Shōko is saying, Shōya fails to comprehend that which appears obvious—that Shōko likes him and that he is denying his own attraction to her. Shōya is not only insensitive to her feelings but also to his own. This failure increases audience frustration with Shōya's lack of depth of awareness. Understanding of his lack of perceptive skills may be further enhanced by the ironic connection between his mention of the beauty of the moon and the recollection of moon symbolism as per novelist Natsume Sōseki's famous 1800s translation of "I love you" from English into Japanese as a statement about the moon's splendor.

The application of theory of mind and affect to this aspect of the film's romance script is perhaps best demonstrated by the experience of a young male viewer in the theatre where I first saw this film. The young man became visibly and audibly frustrated at Shōya's failure to understand "suki" as "like." He began yelling at Shōya and groaning, hands to his head, and calling him a fool, in apparent psychological pain, frustration or annoyance (and suspension of disbelief). His motor reactions (yelling, groaning, and cringing) at Shōya's ignorance and stupidity indicate his cognitive understanding of the implications of the romantic scenario, but also an affective empathy for Shōko's position, if not her feelings. Although there are gendered implications in this and other potential romance scenes, it is Shōya's lack of theory of mind that the young man in the audience seemed to be frustrated with. He was evidently

Figure 9.5. Shōya's misunderstanding of "like" as "moon" 01:06:55; 01:07:04; and 01:07:09.

berating Shōya because he understood what Shōya was failing to see, hear, and understand. The example shows how affect can help drive a narrative towards comprehension of misunderstandings. Whereas viewers can readily apply theory of mind to ascertain, feel and understand Shōko's words and feelings for Shōya, Shōya fails completely in this. Even Shōko's sister quickly sums up this situation when Shōya later tells her about not being able to comprehend Shōko's voiced "*suki/tsuki*." His almost willful misinterpretation (as he seems to refuse to believe she *could* like him) of Shōko's "*suki*" thus engages the audience in the wry humor and frustration of Shōya's failure of theory of mind.

Because Shōko's and Shōya's romantic attraction is not resolved by the end of the film, audience anticipation continues as expectations are heightened then thwarted. The miscommunication script between the pair continues to the film's closure, leaving their romance open-ended for audience contemplation. Shōya has failed to ascertain not only Shōko's feelings for him but also the standard romance script whereby friendship and outings usually evolve into dating. Expectations of a resolution to Shōya's obliviousness to Shōko's romantic feelings interpellate the audience into affective support for their romance to blossom. Such support ultimately makes Shōko's deafness irrelevant. In other words, feelings of frustration with Shōya's lack of awareness and the open ending help subvert the disability romance script by encouraging viewers to want Shōya to understand Shōko as a fully fledged social participant rather than as a deaf subject to feel sorry for.

Whereas *A Silent Voice* may be more progressive than many previous films in interrogating and raising awareness of Deaf culture and communication issues, gendering remains a less questioned aspect of its disability romance script. While standard romance schemas and scripts gender heterosexual

romantic relationships in terms of female passivity, for instance, the Deaf romance script emphasizes notions of female silence, stoicism, isolation, vulnerability, and self-blame. In contrast, masculine uncertainty or silence can be interpreted as an enigmatic and attractive masculine surliness or restrained emotional "strength," even as the protagonist often fails, like Shōya, to know his own mind. The differing gender models for males and females are often dependent upon which counterpart is Deaf, the male or the female. Whereas a common romance script revolves around a hearing male and nonhearing female who is stereotyped as disabled, as Stibbe indicates, it is usually female characters who "display [more] admirable *gaman*" (31), or perseverance. For the female, the disability characteristics are often in exaggerated form and can include a stronger sense of abandonment, isolation, or passive acceptance of her fate. Such gender conventions are borne out in the anime.

A cognitive perspective similarly operates through audience interaction with the film's gendered scripts of miscommunication. Not only do these scripts affect interpretations of the protagonists' subjectivities, but the similarity of patterning to that in earlier cultural representations has an effect on how the characters are perceived. For example, although Shōya eventually develops affection and respect for Shōko, his continued failure to realize her regard for him propagates ideas of Shōko as passively accepting and vulnerable. Shōko's silence can be taken as *gaman* perseverance and stoicism, and her ability to understand others—her higher theory of mind—is cast and potentially reinforced as typical feminine and disability traits. Shōko is more attuned to the emotions of others even though (or because) she cannot physically hear. These skills underline a stereotypical gendered bias (about female "intuition" and potentially special Deaf communication skills). Whereas Shōko's apparent passivity is displayed through her continual (and ironic) apologies for her inability to understand Shōya (and others), Shōya ignores most of her efforts and follows the pattern of a masculine lack of communication skills, of being unable to listen or "read the signs." Even though Shōko occupies a central role, she is more stoic, silent, and introspective against Shōya's loud and boisterous masculinity. His ignorance, solipsism, and failure to notice (see/listen to) Shōko's pain and hurt may be construed as masculinized enigmatic naïvete, especially in relation to the romantic encounters. Contrasts in Shōya's earlier and later behavior towards Shōko also help instantiate his highly masculine subjectivity through his early lack of remorse, self-reflection, and failures at understanding Shōko in particular. Cast against his later "enlightenment," however, which implicates the audience in his more internal pattern of development, his masculinity takes a sensitive turn that, together with his lack of sexual awareness, is more like the recent phenomenon of the gentle Japanese herbivore, which Morioka (2013) describes as a male who lacks "manly" interest in romantic relationships. Some scenes nevertheless imbricate both the hearing and nonhearing into similar social and personal problems without, for example, the stereotypical need for an able-bodied savior for the disabled partner. For example, even though Shōya saves Shōko from a suicide jump in a later scene, it is he who falls and she who ultimately rescues him. The romance script is nonetheless highly gendered in that it follows stereotypical gendered behaviors and ideas that reinforce rather than interrogate gendered divisions of disablement.

The narrative ultimately goes against the usual medical model or hearing perspective, however, through miscommunication exchanges that encourage more cognitive engagement with the characters. It is the romantic situations in particular that show the potential of theory of mind through the way they interpellate audiences into an affective experience of how ToM is more important to communication than "hearing." Narrative misunderstandings that involve Shōya's failures to reflect on how Shōko feels about him drive the story by prompting interpretations of his behavior and motivations through the application of ToM to his (and her) actions. This mental activity also enhances empathy for stoic and silent Shōko, for her continual efforts to communicate and become friendly with Shōya as he constantly misreads situations. Further, the anime's use of JSL throughout not only coheres with the Japanese Deaf community's preference (over Signed Japanese), but also challenges expectations of reliance on lip reading (*kowa*) or "voicing." The movie's encouragement of cognitive interaction with both the Deaf and hearing characters provides a critique of ignorance about such expectations and an interrogative model of how it may *feel* to communicate with or live as a Deaf person.

NOTES

1. My translation. For a list of television dramas and films by separate types of disability, see: https://ja.m.wikipedia.org/wiki/障害を扱った作品の一覧#テレビドラマ; and https://ja.m.wikipedia.org/wiki/障害を扱った作品の一覧#映画.

2. The anime was adapted from the 2011 manga of the same name by Yoshitoki Ouima and can be translated more literally as "the shape of the voice." All names are given in Japanese order, family name then given name, and translations are my own.

CHAPTER 10

Sociopolitical Contexts for the Representation of Deaf Youth in Contemporary South Korean Film

—Sung-Ae Lee

In *Memento Mori* (1999), the second film of the highly successful South Korean *Whispering Corridors* series, Si-Eun, a talented athlete at a girls' boarding school, has been partially deafened by a blow she received from a violent male teacher. She is thus rendered imperfect in a society that equates deafness with disability, stigmatizes those who are not "normal," and "[assures] the non-disabled world that normal is right, to be desired and aspired to" (Morris, 28). When all the girls are subjected to an annual physical evaluation, one of them helps Si-Eun to fake the hearing test and satisfy that criterion for normality. This example defines some of the key social attributes that media representations of deafness reproduce or campaign against: assumptions about normality and even perfection; a patriarchal, Confucian society that tolerates the abuse of women and the disabled; and a legal system that privileges the rich and powerful and habitually prevents the abused from finding justice. However, as *Memento Mori* illustrates, films or television series produced in South Korea rarely thematize deafness but rather incorporate it so that deaf or hard of hearing characters have a plot function, are secondary to hearing characters, or function as a metaphor of society's deficiencies and failings.

The four films examined in this chapter illustrate the range of such representations of deafness. *Dogani* (*Crucible*, directed by Hwang Dong-Hyeok,[1] 2011; subtitled version released as *Silenced*) is a traumatic fictionalized account of the sexual and physical abuse of young deaf students by members of staff at Gwangju Inhwa School for the Hearing-Impaired, the struggle of a new teacher to expose the scandal, and the corrupt legal system that subsequently imposed trivial penalties on the perpetrators. A film with an activist purpose, *Dogani* prompted a political and legal uproar, leading to a reopening of the case and the passing of stronger legislation in late 2011 that abolished the statute of limitations for sex crimes against minors and the disabled. Like *Dogani*, *Glove* (directed by Kang Wu-Seok, 2011) strives to make a difference by revisiting actual events. A sports drama film, it recounts the determination of a baseball team from Sacred Heart (*Seongsim*) School, a live-in high school for deaf children, to be competitive in a national tournament. While deaf characters in each of these films must to varying degrees deal with stigmatization because of their deafness, the overcoming of stigmatization is overtly thematized in *Glove*.

In contrast, the most overt thematization of deafness appears in the made-for-television film *Bling Bling Sounds* (directed by Park Yeong-Hun, 2018). The title in Korean—*Banjjak Banjjak Deullineun* (Twinkle Twinkle Sound)—appears to be an ideophone coinciding with the hip-hop slang term "bling bling," which denotes diamond-accented ornamentation, shiny cosmetic jewelry, glitzy clothing, or ostentatious displays of wealth. It thus seems to be an ironic comment on sound and speech from a nonhearing perspective, referenced early in the film by a comment that, "Seeing with your eyes is as good as listening." The film centers on high school senior Ju Hyeon-Seong and his relationship with a beautiful classmate Su-A, who has ulterior motives for wanting to befriend him. *Bling Bling Sounds* has an expressed educative intention that sets it apart from the three other films discussed in this chapter, although none is without some intent to convey information about deafness. This well-made film is the tenth in a drama series that aims to further understanding of disability. The series was designed, funded, and executed by ROK Department of Education, the Disabled First Campaign Headquarters, and Samsung Fire & Marine Insurance. Apart from its first TV screening on National Disabled Persons Day, 2018, the film is intended to be distributed to high schools.[2]

A deaf/hearing relationship is also portrayed in the romantic comedy *Like for Likes* (directed by Park Hyeon-Jin, 2016), a breezy narrative about the life and love tribulations of three couples. The problem facing the youngest couple, twenty-somethings Lee Su-Ho and Jang Na-Yeon, is that Su-Ho is profoundly deaf, having lost his hearing as a young adult and his loss has made him withdrawn and lacking in confidence. Like Hyeon-Seong in *Bling Bling Sounds*, he has retained excellent vocalization and relies on speechreading and social media for communication, but often struggles to pick up inferences and implications. Miscommunication is thus a source both of emotional angst, of humor, and of some viewer education, as when Su-Ho reminds a friend that he can't be understood if he has a mouth full of food when he is speaking.

Of these four films, *Dogani* has made the greatest public impact. This powerful film thus supports Miriam Nathan Lerner's observation that "films shape and reflect cultural attitudes and can serve as a potent force in influencing the attitudes and assumptions of those members of the hearing world who have had few, if any, encounters with deaf people" ("Introduction"), but its purpose is not to contribute much to a wider understanding of deafness itself. The film does, however, interrogate the assumption widely held in Korea that deafness is a disability and that it is concomitant with other disabilities, especially muteness and intellectual disability.

LEARNING LESSONS ABOUT DEAFNESS: *BLING BLING SOUNDS* AND *LIKE FOR LIKES*

The deaf characters in these films are postlingually deaf and live within hearing communities. Hyeon-Seong (*Bling Bling Sounds*) lost his hearing when in primary school, but is being mainstream educated, the only deaf student in his class. Unable to use a hearing aid because acoustic feedback rendered human voices as a painful cacophony, and with his mother the only person in his circle who knows Korean Sign Language (KSL), he depends on speechreading for communication, while he himself has retained excellent vocalization and does not obviously present as deaf. Challenges associated with speechreading are thus core motifs in the film, in particular people who speak to Hyeon-Seong without looking at him, people who speak too fast, and people who speak with minimal lip movement. The filmmakers seek to draw these issues to the attention of the film's audiences. When Su-A, unaware that Hyeon-Seong is deaf, first tries to talk with him, her speech is so fast he has no idea what she is saying. The film conveys this miscommunication by overlaying the screen image with a meaningless string of characters and symbols emanating from her mouth and passing unregistered through the head of bewildered Hyeon-Seong (see Figure 10.1). The incident has a key plot function in setting Su-A on a learning path relating to deafness, but it also conveys an important understanding to the audience about the practicalities of speechreading (see Lander and Capek, 600–601) and the need to dismantle negative representations of disability and disabled people.

The plot of *Bling Bling Sounds* pivots on a falling-out of Su-A and Elle, two members of the Girl Band featured in the film. The presence of this band is a further aspect of the film's audience appeal, as it parodies the often extreme or absurd behavior of such a group's fan-base. Rumors have spread that Su-A

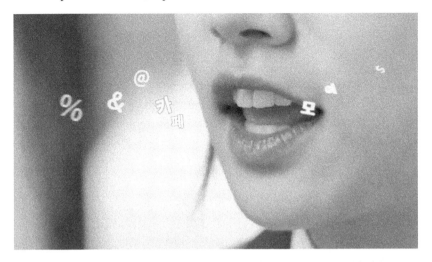

Figure 10.1. *Bling Bling Sounds*. Importance of pace and clear articulation for speechreading. *Bling Bling Sounds* (*Banjjak Banjjak Deullineun*). Directed by Park Yeong-Hun. Korea: Gomaun Media, 2018.

is arrogant, and though younger than Elle considers herself superior. It later emerges that a representative of another agency is trying to break up the group and head-hunt Su-A, and in order to sow discord instigates an attack upon Su-A by Elle's fans, who dress in a rather comical uniform and pelt her with raw eggs. Hyeon-Seong is coincidentally a passer-by at the scene, absorbed in practicing his ten-pin bowling action, and pays little attention to the attack on Su-A. It is here hinted that his deafness tends to isolate him from events in the world around him. Su-A, however, assuming he was somehow involved, decided to befriend him in order to find out who was behind the attack. The main function of this melodramatic plot is to introduce the theme of deaf/hearing relationships, here further complicated by the celebrity status of the hearing character. Su-A must not only learn how to relate to a speechreading deaf person but must also learn to accept that Hyeon-Seong is complete as he is. The friendship ends when he speechreads a comment she makes to her manager about him: "He is nothing. And he also cannot hear anything. He is a disabled person." When Hyeon-Seong confronts Su-A about her motives he invokes the issues of stigmatized inferiority and pity:

> **H:** Do you think deaf people don't have any feelings? That you can behave however you like towards them? . . . Don't pity me.
> **S:** This is not pity.
> **H:** Then what? Friendship? There has been no such thing from the beginning.
> **S:** I had my personal reasons.
> **H:** If I were your friend, you would have told me everything because you trusted me.
> **S:** I couldn't trust you. How could I, since you were there that day?
> **H:** You don't have to trust me anymore. We are no longer friends.

Another egg-throwing episode, which I will come to later, will be needed to recuperate the friendship.

The deaf/hearing relationship portrayed in *Like for Likes* thematizes the situation in which a deaf person may be cut off from the surrounding community, even when living within it (South Korea does not have a developed Deaf community), and a challenge for cinematic representation is to find a balance between supercrip characters who successfully shape their lives and characters who are in some way saved by hearing characters. The outcome in *Like for Likes* is of the latter type. Su-Ho is a composer who, after losing his hearing, is switching his career to song-writing, but his shyness is delaying his maturation: on hearing one of his songs, not identified as his, Na-Yeon, his love interest, is unwittingly cruel in dismissing the lyrics as written by someone who has no experience of love and loss. Su-Ho eventually attempts to end the relationship because he feels inadequate, and it is only because Na-Yeon pushes him—sometimes forcefully, sometimes playfully—that they stay together and move on. In their penultimate scene she asks him to sing to her, pushing against his self-limitation, and threatens to kiss and cuddle him until he gives in (see Figure 10.2). The moment is romantic, playful and comedic,

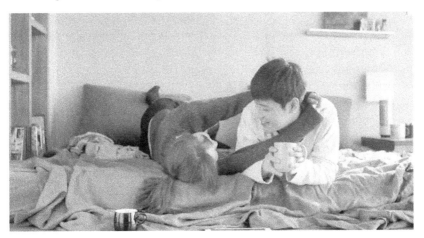

Figure 10.2. *Like for Likes.* Na-Yeon, "Sing for me … I'm going to bother you until you do." *Like for Likes (Joahaejwo)*. Directed by Park Hyeon-Jin. Korea: Liyang Film & JK Film, 2016.

but its implication is that the disabled person will remain emotionally isolated unless an emotional mentor takes control.

DEAFNESS AS STIGMA: THE SPORT FILM *GLOVE*

As previously remarked, the stigma associated with deafness in South Korea is directly addressed in *Glove*. The association of deafness with stigma has been extensively discussed (Brown 2013 [1997]; Erlich 2012; Foss 2014a, 2014b; Hindhede 2012). Foss points out that in the USA, for example, hearing loss is becoming more prevalent and that media representations are too narrow, such that entertainment media, news, and children's books medicalize deafness, framing it as a disability to be treated ("(De)stigmatizing" 890). Like *Bling Bling Sounds*, *Glove* dramatizes how fictional storylines about hearing loss could help to destigmatize the condition, with the possibility of improving the educational, occupational, and social opportunities of deaf members of the community (889). Brown's argument that "Stigma represents a view of life; a set of personal and social constructs; a set of social relations and social relationships; a form of social reality" (147) encapsulates a situation early in *Glove* where young adult Cha Myeong-Jae is introduced. The depiction of Myeong-Jae, a day student at Sacred Heart who has recently lost his hearing after he contracted meningitis, draws sensitively upon common adult responses to hearing loss, such as resentment, isolation, social withdrawal, and depression. According to Kaland and Salvatore, "Some of the more commonly noted secondary aspects of hearing loss [amongst young people] include communication and behavioral problems, self-esteem and image problems, and depression and introversion" (4). In this episode, Myeong-Jae exhibits hyperactivity and aggression, behaviors that can be the outward expression of such emotional difficulties.

The episode functions to establish the social reality that the hearing populace is apt to stigmatize deafness. Myeong-Jae is treated as an object of ridicule by a group of teens who regard his deafness as a stigma. He is practicing shooting baskets, quickly throwing ball after ball, when a girl leaves the group and attempts to flirt with him. He is aware of her presence and her intention but concentrates on his repeated throwing, and of course does not respond to her voice. The three boys in the group find the situation very funny and, laughing, inform the girl that "He's deaf," as the camera moves to an extreme close-up on the speaker's mouth (a technique often used in these films in association with a character who speechreads). Brown cites several studies that conclude that stigma appears to be a process whereby people are treated categorically rather than individually, and in the process are devalued. The girl is further told that Myeong-Jae "goes to Sacred Heart School," thereby erasing his individuality while asserting his difference. The girl's attitude shifts from her initial approach—"I think you are cute"—to embarrassment that she tried to flirt with a boy who is deaf.

In this shift it is apparent how the only attributes of the stigmatized person made relevant are those that fit the stereotype that enables the stigma. As Brown observes, this kind of social categorization entails that stigmatized people are not expected to be attractive or intelligent (152), so Myeong-Jae's attractiveness suddenly dissipates. He then walks over to confront the mocking boy, who cringes away from him in accordance with the affective component of stigma that generates fear or dislike (Brown, 150). Myeong-Jae simply tells him to look at his face when he speaks to him and turns away. Here one of the other boys attempts to taunt Myeong-Jae further, shouting that he is not just deaf but dumb too, and slaps the back of his head. Myeong-Jae's response is to vigorously punch the offender and then (off-screen) beat up the other two boys, an act of rough justice that reflects his resentment and frustration but also affirms his physical capability.

Myeong-Jae's stigmatization is taken further when his participation in the school team is opposed by his mother, who does not want him to mix with the other deaf children, or to use KSL to communicate, as she believes both carry a stigma and hence entail loss of respect. She takes an oralist stance because, she argues, if he uses only speechreading he can pass as hearing: "you can live like a normal person," she asserts. Attempting to "pass" and derogating others like themselves are two ways in which stigmatized people effectively accept the society's negative perceptions of their stigma (Brown, 152). Unlike the deaf protagonists in *Bling Bling Sounds* and *Like for Likes*, however, Myeong-Jae is depicted with an obvious voice impairment consistent with severe hearing loss: his delivery is slow, and voice pitch and volume are anomalous and unstable (see Sellek and Sataloff, 688–90). The mother is presented to audiences as a negative example because of her audist assumption that someone who can hear or simulate the behavior of a hearing person is intrinsically superior to a deaf person. Within this group of films she contrasts with Hyeon-Seong's mother (*Bling Bling Sounds*), who will be seen by audiences as a model parent, happy to communicate by whichever mode Hyeon-Seong chooses, including a mixture of oral and signing.

People who acquire a stigma may also experience downward mobility and thus lose their place in their social hierarchy. Such stigmatization happens to Kim Sang-Nam, the new coach of the baseball team. Once a star pitcher in the Korean League, he has developed a reputation for drunken and violent behavior, and following a recent incident fans have rejected him. Like most people, he thus wants to maintain respect and not slip into a stigmatized minority, but, as also demonstrated by Myeong-Jae's mother, this need leads to stigmatization of others to maintain position in the superior/inferior dynamic that underpins stigma (Brown, 149). Kim Sang-Nam is thus unwilling to coach the deaf team and disrespects them at their first meeting. Where the boys have a lot to achieve if they are to become competent players, Sang-Nam has much to learn about respect and altruism if he is to become a decent human being and win back the respect he has lost.

At the outset of the film both the temporary coach and the team members are thus in need of respect. The thematic configuration acquires a third component when the team's pitcher withdraws because of the other players' incompetence and is replaced by Cha Myeong-Jae, who had been a star pitcher before his illness. Myeong-Jae is desperate to pitch again, clearly in the hope he will regain self-respect and the respect of others. A significant narrative theme in films about sport is the process of winning respect (Whannel, 195), an issue that is exacerbated in the case of the deaf participants, who may not only be lacking in confidence but are also hampered in regular team sports, which depend on verbal communication among players during a match. Thus, *Bling Bling Sounds* opens with Hyeon-Seong deciding to give up playing basketball because his deafness hinders the team, and the boys in *Glove* are shown at the outset to be in poor physical and mental shape and to lack basic playing skills. They also lack basic coaching expertise, as this responsibility has fallen to Na Ju-Won, a female music teacher who cares deeply for the boys but assumes they will never play competitively. In this regard she reproduces a general low expectation shared by the hearing teachers for the students that prevails in the school and underscores their stigmatized status. A filmic representation of a boarding school in which young people or children are effectively confined is a heterotopical metaphor for a view of society at large and "[projects] representations of how individuals fit into a nation's social and political landscape" (Safran, 223). An institution whose pupils are deemed to be disabled renders those pupils even more vulnerable to neglect and abuse. As Carol A. Padden argues, a deaf school can, on the one hand, be a place where children meet others like themselves and teach one another sign language but, on the other hand, "deaf schools are places of overbearing management of children's bodies, which, sadly, leads often to physical and sexual abuse" (510). Depictions of live-in schools in films may also foreground the mental or psychological abuse pupils can be subjected to, whether knowingly or inadvertently because of educational ideology or misassumptions.

As Whannel suggests (197), a sport contest has an implicit narrative structure in that it is rule-governed and proceeds to an outcome. A sport film generally aligns audience sentiment with one team, usually the underdog, and hence the possible outcomes of win, lose or draw deliver a strong affect in accord with that alignment. Two baseball games are presented in *Glove*, both between Sacred Heart School and the Gunsan Commercial High School team (a school in reality renowned for its baseball team). These games function as embedded narratives with a *mise en abyme* effect, in that they blur the line between a baseball game and a sport contest as a microcosm of everyday life and mirror the film's overarching progression from lack of (self-)respect to respect. The first game is an informal contest arranged so the Sacred Heart boys can experience what it is like to compete. However, their skills are very inferior and the Gunsan team does not take the game seriously. Sang-Nam calls a pause and harangues the Gunsan team, asking them to play to their full ability. He points out his team's disadvantages—they can't hear when the ball is hit; they can't coordinate play by calling to one another—but asserts that to show them pity is to disrespect them. That pity is an inappropriate response to disability is a thematic insight expressed in all the films discussed here. People identified as disabled are at least implicitly stigmatized, with the possible consequence of lowered self-esteem and diminished self-concept (Crocker and Major, 609). In *Glove* the Gunsan team apologizes and responds as Sang-Nam asks, consequently crushing Sacred Heart 32–0. The result is that the deaf players strengthen their resolve and engage with determination in the sustained training program Sang-Nam devises to increase their physical fitness and speed, and in doing so develop confidence in their own bodies and embark on the road to respect.

The transformation in the boys has a wider effect within the school. The girls at Sacred Heart decide to form a cheer leader squad, and the teaching nuns observe that the children "have become brighter" because of the baseball team—that is, the students have begun to develop a sense of community and purpose and are beginning to function as a Deaf community grounded on self-respect and respect of others. As individuals accumulate valued social roles, the sense that life has meaning and purpose increases, leading to improved well-being (Hartwell and Benson, 333). In parallel with the students' developing self-respect, Sang-Nam undergoes his own transformation. As the boys gain his respect, his attitude changes, to the extent that he intrudes upon a meeting of the School Board to defend the boys' aspirations for agency and fuller social engagement via participation in the tournament:

> What do you think [those boys have] been thinking about? When living life, sometimes others' decisions can overpower their own desires, so they can't always do the things that they want to do. They don't know that yet, but you want to teach them that now. There's nothing positive about it, but you want to give them a taste of that. If this is education, then damn it.

The Board is swayed, and the boys go to the tournament, where they again face the Gunsan team, who now find them unexpectedly competitive. Only a miscommunication between catcher and pitcher in the final moment of the game prevents them from winning. Whannel comments that "the concept of 'respect' grows out of the need to manage the ideological tension between winning and losing. You cannot necessarily or plausibly win, but you can win respect" (202). Underdog sport films do sometimes allow the improbable outcome, but *Glove* instead shows that winning is not essential to repudiate a stigma based on difference and to earn respect. Immediately after their defeat the Sacred Heart team stands disconsolate on the field but are shaken out of their sorrow when they become aware that the Gunsan team has lined up and is applauding them to demonstrate respect and peer acknowledgment (see Figure 10.3). The boys in turn bow to their opponents and are revitalized.

The sport film centered on underdogs who are also deaf, largely separated from society, and are conscious that they are not expected to achieve very much reflects a script that recurs across the four films, all of which resist its assumed outcomes. In his "Introduction" to a forum in *American Quarterly* (2000) on disability and self-representation, G. Thomas Couser remarks that the marketplace admits disability narratives "only on the condition that the narrative take the form of a story of 'triumph'" (308). The protagonist(s) must achieve "heroic status" (Maples, Arndt, and White, 78). Couser refers to this

Figure 10.3. *Glove.* The Gunsan team affirms that the Sacred Heart team has won their respect (above), while the SH team show their respect by bowing (below). *Glove.* Directed by Gang Wu-Seok. Korea: Cinema Service, 2011.

restrictive paradigm as "the tyranny of the comic plot" (308). Actual comedy may be employed to present the paradigm in a more tongue-in-cheek fashion as happens in *Bling Bling Sounds* when Hyeon-Seong (as supercrip knight errant) rescues Su-A (damsel in distress) after he had ended their friendship. Hyeon-Seong is accomplished in ten-pin bowling, as several scenes in the film illustrate. The episode begins when Hyeon-Seong sees another assembly of Elle's fan group intent on more mischief. When their leader talks on his mobile phone, Hyeon-Seong speechreads the location of a meeting with the ANC representative behind the plot (speechreader as supercrip!) and quickly runs there, where he uses his phone to record their conversation and the passing of a payment. When the representative challenges him, Hyeon-Seong proves he is deaf and could not have heard anything. He then sends the recording to his friend Yong-Jun who transcribes it and tells him what was said and where

Figure 10.4. *Bling Bling Sounds.* Hyeon-Seong skittles Su-A's assailants. *Bling Bling Sounds* (*Banjjak Banjjak Deullineun*). Directed by Park Yeong-Hun. Korea: Gomaun Media, 2018.

the next attack will occur. The egg-pelting has already begun when he arrives, but he intervenes first to shelter Su-A with his own body and then to use his bowling ball to skittle all eight assailants at once by means of a perfect strike that ricochets across the line of throwers (see Figure 10.4), just as a ball ricochets across the pins in a bowling alley. By now the deaf character occupies the high moral ground and can advise Su-A to confront her resentment of Elle, who has been a lifelong friend, and become reconciled. They then commission Hyeon-Seong to write a song for their next performance, where his career as a song writer is triumphantly launched.

DEAFNESS AND SOCIAL JUSTICE: *DOGANI (CRUCIBLE)*

As remarked above, in *Dogani* the physical, psychological, and sexual abuse of children in a live-in school for deaf children functions as a metaphor for society's deficiencies and failings. In narrative fiction deafness may function as a symbolic commentary on society, as Miriam Nathan Lerner argues, "The inability to hear and/or speak can represent the more generalized powerlessness that a culture or a society's disenfranchised experience." *Dogani* is a highly symbolic film in which events and visual images function metonymically. For example, at the end of the body of the film, there occurs a mass rally, which includes many deaf citizens, to protest against the corrupt judicial system that imposed ridiculously light sentences on teachers and school administrators convicted of abusing and raping deaf children. Confronted by riot police, they are warned by megaphone that they must disperse. The police commander realizes that they cannot hear the warning, but they are nevertheless attacked with water cannon and riot batons. In-Ho, the teacher who initiated the investigation, walks into the melee holding the funerary photograph of Min-Su, the tragic hero of this story, and declaiming, "This child cannot hear or speak. His name is Min-Su." In-Ho is also hit with water cannon, knocked to the ground and assaulted, while the photograph is crushed under a policeman's boot (see Figure 10.5). This segment is both self-contained and has a plenitude of metonymic significance as part of larger whole (see Stephens 1992, 249). Its mode is metonymic in the sense that the violent suppression of the protest has immediate narrative significance but also represents (is metonymic of) the corruption and violence that those who control South Korea have endemically inflicted upon the people in the preceding half century. The smashed photograph of the deaf child likewise stands for all stigmatized and marginalized people crushed by societal disregard.

Min-Su had died when he attempted to seek justice by attacking teacher Park, who had repeatedly raped and beaten him and his brother (who had suicided). Min-Su stabbed the teacher as he walked home along a railway track, and when they scuffled and fell on the track he held him there in the path of an oncoming train, thereby sacrificing his life to gain the justice denied by the legal system. He thus exemplifies a particular type of represented disability, the tragic victim who triumphs against the odds. Drawing on Martin Norden's work (1994), Maples, Arndt and White derive four schemas (my term) for representations of disability identified by Norden and which in some ways continue in more recent films: the "sweet innocent," the "comic misadventurer," the "heroic disabled person" or "supercrip," and the "tragic victim" (Norden, 20–33; Maples, Arndt, and White, 78). There have been ideological shifts in

Figure 10.5. *Dogani.* Top: "This child cannot hear or speak." Bottom: the smashed photograph of Min-Su. *Dogani* (*Crucible, aka Silenced*). Directed by Hwang Dong-Hyeok. Korea: Samgeori Pictures, 2011.

attitude since the films Norden describes, so that the comic misadventurer is now a marginal story schema, but the other three persist and can be seen in Korean films that thematize deafness. Naïve and vulnerable Lee Su-Ho (*Like for Likes*) is a "sweet innocent," whereas Hyeon-Seong (*Bling Bling Sounds*) is a supercrip, as I have shown.

Dogani, however, is the only film to include all three schemas, which it identifies among the deaf children as they rise above or succumb to their stigmatization and consequent abuse. Teacher Park informs In-Ho that the children are "not normal": "a disability in body leads to an impairment in mentality," and he thus considers them less than human. When In-Ho looks through the children's files, he finds that they are described in terms of disadvantage: they are orphans, abandoned, or defined as mentally impaired, and thus lack rights or protection. As stated, Min-Su is the tragic victim: targeted by Park; he is brutally beaten and sexually abused. He sees a glimmer of hope when his abusers are brought to trial but is distraught when his grandmother accepts a monetary settlement and the perpetrators are given suspended sentences and are free to resume their positions subsequently. His attack on Park and self-sacrifice are the culmination of his victimhood and mark his refusal to die as a victim. In contrast, thirteen-year-old Yeon-Du is the supercrip: she is observant, intelligent, shows promise of artistic talent, and makes a crucial contribution to gathering evidence against the perpetrators. She has a moment of triumph during the trial when asked to distinguish the Principal, her abuser, from his identical twin brother (the School Manager), which she does by inducing him to respond to KSL, which only he knows. Such a use of sign language is a filmic motif that Lerner calls "sign language as 'hero.'" Third, Yu-Ri is the sweet innocent: very attached to Yeon-Du, she has been psychologically and emotionally damaged by extended neglect and abuse and is known for binge eating, presumably a response to stress, anger, or distress. In the eyes of her peers, her eating aligns her with the "comic misadventurer," as when she laps from a bowl and covers her face with food, but surfaces with a happy smile. In an epilogue set a year after the trial, Yeon-Du is described as flourishing in a new environment and nurturing an ambition to become an art teacher, while Yu-Ri is responding positively to psychological treatment and is teaching KSL to the human-rights activist who helped In-Ho expose the abuse and subsequently helped care for the abused children. The epilogue also reports that the children now affirm that they are precious human beings, which they had not known during their time at the school.

The film's symbolic quality is established in the opening scene, in which In-Ho is driving through dense fog to start his new job in Mujin as an art teacher at Benevolence Academy (*Ja-Ae Hagwon*) for deaf and hard of hearing children. Fog can be used in film to establish an ominous mood because of the reduced visibility, because of how the fog seems to swallow everything and makes noise and sight unfamiliar, and because of the difficulty of driving in thick fog. Fog initially problematizes viewers' genre expectations—is it a natural or supernatural phenomenon? As a supernatural event, fog may imply the opening of a portal or gateway between our world and another that might contain things alien to our experience. However, while Mujin may seem like another world, and viewers might hope it is, it is the everyday Korean dystopia with its everyday corruption. In the fog, In-Ho hits a deer on the road, but initially thinks he has seen and hit a child. The damage his car sustains is narratively the source of his meeting with Seo Yu-Jin, a local human rights activist who will play a key role in future events, but the episode foreshadows a story about damaged children. The first children In-Ho meets at the school flee when he signs "Hello." In his first class, he finds that the children are unresponsive to positive comments on their artwork. It is easy to assume that their deafness has cut them off emotionally, but the incident foreshadows a later disclosure that they assume a compliment is a prelude to sexual abuse.

The deep corruption that prevails in Mujin is signaled in In-Ho's first meeting with the Principal and Manager, who immediately demand a fifty-thousand-dollar bribe if he wants to keep the job, so endemic corruption instantly becomes part of the school context. It is also evident in the wider community and legal system, in that police, prosecutors and churches strive to prevent justice, but also the very structure of the legal system promotes corruption. Three key elements that militate against the possibility of justice for the deaf children are: "privileges of former post" (*jeon-gwan y-eu*), which guarantees that a former judge now practicing as an attorney will win his first case; a system that allows any relative of a victim to agree to a monetary settlement and absolve the perpetrator, even if that relative is ignorant of the case or of the law or is mentally disabled; and rampant bribery of judges and prosecutors. In a legal system that denies justice to the stigmatized, the marginalized, and the economically disadvantaged, where prosecutor, defense lawyer, and judge collude to bring about minimal and suspended sentences, perpetrators will triumph over their victims. When In-Ho arrived at the court to hear the judgment, the camera moved to close-up on the judicial-system motto on the front of the building: "Liberty, Equality, and Justice." This ironical effect quietly asks the audience if there is any possibility of justice in Korea.

South Korean films with principal characters who are deaf appear in a range of genres, illustrated in this chapter by romantic comedy, high school melodrama, sport film, and social critique. Within these genres appear some common deaf character schemas—the sweet innocent, the supercrip, and the tragic victim. It is rare for deafness to be the core focus of a film, and of the films discussed here only *Bling Bling Sounds* can be said to be principally *about* deafness. In the other films, deafness has a plot function—for example, Lee Su-Ho's deafness is a temporary impediment to his romance with Jang Na-Yeon (*Like for Likes*), and in *Glove* the lead character is Kim Sang-Nam, while the roles of the most prominent deaf character, Cha Myeong-Jae, and the other members of the team are essentially secondary to the story of Sang-Nam's character development. The motivation for the making of *Dogani* was lead actor Gong Yu's determination to adapt Gong Ji-Yeong's novel *Dogani* for the screen to draw attention to the abuse of vulnerable children. As a work of activism and advocacy its main focus was on the deficiency and corruption within society and the campaign by teacher Gang In-Ho and human rights activist Seo Yu-Jin to achieve justice for the abused children.

Bling Bling Sounds also aims to educate its audience, with special reference to the dynamics of classrooms that include deaf students and the procedures and support networks appropriate to the situation where a deaf student depends on speechreading for communication. Its many close-up shots of speaking mouths emphasize the huge effort of concentration necessary for speechreading. The film draws attention to other issues associated with speechreading, such as people who speak too quickly or look away while speaking. The four films represent the two familiar deaf populations: prelingually deaf subjects who use sign language as their primary communication mode; and postlingually deaf subjects who can speak fluently and rely on speechreading as their main communication mode, especially with hearing people, most of whom are nonsigners. According to Suh et al., none of the postlingually deaf subjects in the Korean sample they studied acquired sign language. This is the cohort represented in *Bling Bling Sounds* and *Like for Likes*. The young people in *Glove* and *Dogani* are prelingually deaf and did not acquire speech.

An important theme dealt with in the films, and notably in *Glove*, is the common assumption that deafness carries a stigma that imputes inferiority to the deaf and defines them as objects of pity. Both attitudes are rejected, and a way to challenge this assumption in *Glove* and *Dogani* is to envisage a nascent Deaf community. South Korea has not yet developed a Deaf community, and while KSL has been in use since the late nineteenth century, it was only legally declared an official Korean language in 2016, and thus such important reforms as mandated signed interpretation in courts postdate both films. The sense of purpose that galvanizes the children in *Glove* and a glimpse of a utopian community in the epilogue of *Dogani* foreshadow such a development. All of the films represent a desire to destigmatize deafness and accept it as part of everyday culture.

NOTES

1. Korean names follow the general East Asian convention of placing family name before given name, and that has been followed here throughout.

2. All participants in the making of the film, including those in the lead roles, freely donated their talent and gave the film a solid core of well-known performers. The first generation of viewers will thus see some popular faces. The lead couple is played by pop idols Lee Hong-Bin from the boy band *VIIX* and Ahn Solbin from the girl band *Laboum*. The girl band that featured in the film was made up of Solbin and three other members of *Laboum*. Small or cameo roles were also played by other film and television celebrities.

CHAPTER 11

Local Hawai'i Children's Literature

Revitalizing Hawai'i Sign Language at the Edge of Extinction

—Nina Benegas, Stuart Ching, and Jann Pataray-Ching

University of Hawai'i linguists recognized Hawai'i Sign Language (HSL) in 2013 when Hawaiian-Chinese HSL user Linda Lambrecht demonstrated it at an endangered languages conference. Furthermore, tracing HSL's history, linguist Barbara Earth cites an 1821 letter from Reverend Hiram Bingham to Thomas Hopkins Gallaudet that describes deaf islanders using a sign language unique to Hawai'i (McAvoy 2013; Tanigawa 2016; Perlin 2016). Some of the signs described in the 1821 letter remain in the HSL lexicon, which according to linguists evidences HSL's distinct origin (Perlin 2016). Although HSL's discovery has excited linguists, this excitement is additionally characterized by concern for HSL's potential extinction. Linguists estimate that currently there are approximately forty or fewer HSL users, most of whom are elderly (McAvoy 2013; Tanigawa 2016; Perlin 2016).

Current revitalization efforts include publication of an HSL dictionary and textbooks as well as HSL documentation on YouTube and in academia. However, no one has explored the potential contribution of local Hawai'i children's literature. This article does this, first by framing the emergence and endangerment of HSL within Hawai'i's colonial and postcolonial contexts; second, by interpreting the ways in which recent YouTube media, within a postcolonial globalized electronic space, imbues HSL with a sense of place and the *local* Hawai'i body (specifically, the HSL user as a *kupuna*, or respected elder and bearer of knowledge for posterity); and third, by analyzing how Hawai'i children's literature might support HSL's revitalization through connections among language, place, community, and body.

Children's picture books have the potential to play an active role in the revitalization of HSL, just as they have already contributed to a renaissance of Hawai'i Creole English. In recent years, the large number of picture books engaging with various aspects of childhood deafness have included books that give a central position to American Sign Language, British Sign Language, or Auslan.[1] For example, *Hands and Hearts: With 15 Words in American Sign Language* (2014), by Donna Jo Napoli and Amy Bates, is an exquisite depiction of a day a deaf girl spends at the beach with her mother. The brief text is poetic, and each opening includes a panel with diagrams showing the ASL sign for a key word in the text. A book of this kind, both educational and inspirational, suggests a model for a next step Hawai'i picture books might take from the affirmation of HCE vocabulary and grammar as evident in, for instance, Sandi Takayama's *The Musubi Man*, to an affirmation of HSL.

INTERSECTING LINGUISTIC HISTORIES: HAWAI'I SIGN LANGUAGE (HSL) AND AMERICAN SIGN LANGUAGE (ASL)

The 2013 announcement of the official documentation of Hawaiian Sign Language (HSL) as a unique language prompts investigation into the relationship between HSL and the dominant signed language of the United States, American Sign Language (ASL). The history of ASL's creation and development in America spans over two hundred years, and the story of its conception runs parallel to the economic and social developments of the early twentieth century. Likewise, it is reasonable to assume that HSL would emerge and develop along the corresponding developments occurring in Hawai'i, but the recent focus on HSL as a "newly discovered" language reveals the relative lack of information contextualizing it. This section presents two timelines: the development of ASL and the acceptance of sign language education in the continental United States, and the information currently available concerning the use of HSL in Hawai'i and the acceptance of that language throughout the islands. The intersection between these two timelines occurs at the start of WWII, though the conditions of that intersection are, at the time of this research, circumstantial.

Thomas Hopkins Gallaudet traveled to London in 1815 to research educational practices for deaf students after growing frustrated with the absence of schools for the deaf in the United States (Smith). His transportation plans derailed, he was redirected by a Mr. Laurent Clerc to a deaf school in Paris, and this coincidental meeting affected the course of deaf education and language development in the United States (Padden and Humphries 2005, 16–17). At the Parisian Royal Institute for the Deaf (and unlike at the British Braidwood School) students studied and conducted all business exclusively in sign language. Gallaudet became Clerc's student and convinced Clerc to return with him to America, bringing both his manual educational philosophy and his French Sign Language in tow.

The educators returned to a United States fully immersed in the Industrial Revolution. As urban populations exploded, increased diversity prompted panic over the potential loss of a central American culture. That fear inspired assimilation initiatives and eventually the creation of public education (Burch 2002, 7). This educational enterprise highlighted the situation of students in need of specialized educational methods (for example, those with physical disabilities). Addressing this context of deaf students in otherwise hearing communities, philanthropic educators and other interested parties founded and built asylums and institutions specifically for deaf children (Padden and Humphries 2005, 12). Gallaudet and Clerc founded the first deaf school in Hartford, Connecticut, in 1817, and the American School for the Deaf used the French method of sign-language-based teaching, in which teachers would use the signs to construct meaning rather than teach the signs through spoken French language. This method of deaf education would be dominant in deaf schools across the country until the late 1860s (Burch 2002, 2). Clerc's influence reached beyond pedagogical philosophy and into the development of an American sign language itself. The title "American Sign Language" would not be coined until 1965, but the sign language unique to American deaf schools was developed from Clerc's French Sign Language, combined with home signs[2] brought by deaf students to American deaf schools, and structured within the context of an English grammatical system. ASL today is a unique language reflective of its French and American influences.

With the establishment of deaf schools segregated from the hearing population and insulated with a common language, the concept of a unique and proud Deaf Culture began to develop in the United States. By the 1850s, Deaf individuals found accessible faith in Deaf churches, relevant news in Deaf publications, and even discussion of a Deaf-only state in Western territories (which never came to fruition) (Burch 2002, 3). Indeed, sign language and Deaf culture enjoyed a "golden age" until the 1880 Milan Congress introduced the stigmatization of sign language and Deaf identity (Baker and Battison 1980, 222). The Second International Conference on Deaf Education, commonly referred to as the "Milan Congress," ruled definitively in favor of oral over manual methods of educating the deaf. Just one month earlier, in August, Deaf advocates founded the National Association of the Deaf (NAD), an organization dedicated to the rights of deaf people relating to language use, civil liberties, and national representation ("About Us"). But despite the best efforts of the NAD to advocate for sign language education (also referred to as the manual method), the movement for oral education became more organized and visible. By the end of the nineteenth century, there existed eighty-seven deaf schools in the United States, with nearly 40 percent of deaf students educated orally (Padden and Humphries 2005, 39, 47). With the majority of deaf students still learning sign language, newly heterogeneous deaf schools became segregated by teaching method, with oral and manual students in different classes and often different social circles. The turn of the century brought a new generation of teachers of the deaf who viewed sign language as "primitive" and "clannish" and its proponents as antiquated and resistant to modernization (Padden and Humphries 2005, 39, 73).

But explicit bias against sign language was not the only factor affecting the Deaf community in the early 1900s. An increased national interest in scientific disciplines motivated administrators and teachers in both hearing and deaf schools to seek a new type of education, one that would prepare students for life outside of the classroom through practical activities and lessons. In addition, the intense national campaign to Americanize immigrant communities extended to the deaf (Burch 2002, 3, 10, 12). The creation and maintenance of an independent Deaf community, complete with language, schools, and clubs and organizations, threatened the sensibilities of assimilationists, even though deaf individuals more often than not were raised in hearing families and had been born and raised on US soil. Ironically, this marginalization of deaf persons based on their independence resulted in the creation of more Deaf associations, such as clubs and sporting leagues. By the 1930s most American immigrant groups had either fully assimilated or at least established permanent communities in US cities, but members of the Deaf community remained isolated largely due to communication barriers with the hearing population (Burch 2002, 97, 110).

By 1920, 80 percent of all schools for the deaf had implemented the oral method as their primary means of instruction. The NAD remained active in legislative discourse, campaigning against the Nebraska State Legislature, for example, and its attempt to require oral education for all students at the Nebraska School for the Deaf (NSD). The NAD's efforts were unsuccessful both in 1913 and in 1915 (Padden and Humphries 2005, 59). During this same conflict, Deaf community leader George Veditz performed in the NAD's film project for the preservation of sign language. His signed presentation, entitled "The Preservation of Sign Language," provided a detailed and impassioned appeal for the necessity of signed language in relation to deaf people, and is still widely used today as an invaluable cultural artifact in the Deaf community.

By 1939 and the start of WWII, hearing society's requirement that deaf people assimilate into hearing culture conflicted with the simultaneous exclusion of deaf people from places of employment. Deaf men who had tried to enlist during the First World War were rejected even with strong lip-reading skills, and, citing safety hazards, employers conflated the deaf and other disabled groups out of fear of incapacitated workers endangering others (Burch 2002, 104). Stigmas resulting from this "Safety First" movement of the early 1900s would affect deaf employment well into the twentieth century until clarification of the definition of "total deafness" in 1940 finally expanded employment opportunities for deaf workers (Burch 2002). Aside from prejudices concerning physical capabilities of deaf workers, the Deaf community also contended with the perception of their mental health. Deaf individuals with or without other linguistic impairments were often misdiagnosed as mentally retarded or mentally ill; the effects of these misdiagnoses in terms of education, health care, and employment would not be addressed or resolved for decades (Burch 2002, 138).

During the 1940s and amid the throes of WWII the known timelines of ASL and HSL intersected. Though written documentation confirms HSL's existence in 1821, information about HSL's origins and history is scant up until WWII. Even in the period after the war, the language was largely undocumented and rarely, if ever, discussed on a national or even state-wide scale until the 2013 announcement by linguists at the University of Hawai'i at Mānoa. In 1914, the School for the Deaf in Honolulu was founded, but the school had an oralist philosophy not unlike its counterparts on the mainland. In 1941, the United States joined WWII after the bombing of Pearl Harbor, at which time Alden C. Ravn, a graduate of Gallaudet University, served as a dorm supervisor at the Diamond Head School for the Deaf in Oahu ("Deaf People + World War II"). Deaf people were not allowed to teach at deaf schools as outlined by the Hawaiian Public Education System, but when the school closed indefinitely on December 7, 1941 (it would remain closed until February of 1942), deaf students from other islands could not return home, so they stayed in the home of Ravn and his wife ("Aldin Charles Ravn" 2009). The war provided positive outcomes for deaf individuals, however, in terms of employment. Deaf individuals, along with women, helped to fill the void in manpower caused by the wartime draft, and deaf citizens worked in war production plants and contributed to the war effort financially through war bonds and the sale of Victory Stamps ("Deaf People + World War II").

The start of the US's involvement in the war aligns with the phasing out of HSL in favor of ASL (Friedman and Botelho 2013). By the 1950s, ASL existed as the dominant language, "gradually superimposing itself on the indigenous Hawai'i Sign Language that predated it" (University of Hawai'i at Mānoa

2013). But what is unclear in the information readily available today is how exactly that transition happened or why ASL emerged on the islands at all. The ideological and political milieu pervading both the US and the islands provides a context: (1) During the late 1800s, Hawaiʻiʻs entrenched American business community believed that linguistic assimilation would signify loyalty to the US and would move Hawaiʻi closer to gaining admission into the Union (Kawamoto 1993, 199). (2) After WWI, the "One Hundred Percent American" ideology directed against foreigners spread rapidly across the US (Kawamoto 1993, 203). Furthermore, this mood would have reached Hawaiʻi through the American oligarchy that had risen to power (Kawamoto 1993, 203). (3) During the early 1900s, English Standard schools were created discriminatorily in Hawaiʻi to favor Caucasians and exclude *locals* (Kawamoto 1993, 201–2). (4) Finally, the United States' entrance into WWII started an even more fierce "speak American" propaganda movement (Hazama and Komeiji 1986, 147–48). This propaganda, along with long-standing US nationalistic ideologies that pushed Hawaiʻi toward becoming a US territory and then a state, significantly shaped Hawaiʻiʻs language ideologies and policies. Thus ASL's rise over HSL would have followed this institutionally endorsed pattern of Americanization that inextricably connected language and race.

Linda Lambrecht, the Deaf Hawaiian woman who spearheaded the research grant that resulted in the official documentation of HSL, learned HSL from her older siblings, who were also Deaf, and she commented to *Hawaiʻi News Now* that before the 2013 University of Hawaiʻi announcement, people who encountered HSL considered it nothing more than a pidgin language, somehow derivative of or otherwise related to the highly visible ASL (Gutierrez 2013). HSL was only "discovered" in 2013, but the language has long been known to its users and their affiliates. The missing component, and what likely kept the language off the radar of the national linguistic community, was its lack of identification as a unique language (University of Hawaiʻi at Mānoa 2013).

PARALLEL ORAL LINGUISTIC HISTORY: THE EMERGENCE AND DEVELOPMENT OF HAWAIʻI PIDGIN AND CREOLE ENGLISHES

The histories of Hawaiʻi Pidgin and Creole Englishes (HPE and HCE, respectively) inform both our understanding of the endangered status of Hawaiʻi Sign Language *and* the potential contribution of local Hawaiʻi children's literature to HSL's revival. Documenting this oral linguistic history, scholars call attention to the early *hapa haole* (or half foreign) English that preceded HPE and HCE and that enabled communication between Hawaiians and foreign English-speakers who arrived in the islands because of three kinds of trans-Pacific trade. Between approximately 1790 and 1810, vessels of the fur trade between China and the US west coast used Hawai'i as a stopover. Between 1810 and 1830, the sandalwood trade brought more vessels commanded by English-speaking crews. Between 1820 and 1880, the whaling industry necessitated additional cross-linguistic communication. Although this *hapa haole lingua franca* integrated parts of Hawaiian and English, no real pidgin had yet formed (Kawamoto 1993, 194; Romaine 1994, 530; Sakoda and Siegel 2003, 3–4).

Scholars differentiate this *hapa haole* English from the pidgins and creole that emerged later on the Hawaiian sugar plantations. (a) Pidgin Hawaiian consisted of the dominant language (or lexifier) Hawaiian and other languages' pronunciations, diction, and derivations. (b) Reflecting the shifting economic and political climate, Hawai'i Pidgin English (HPE) consisted of the lexifier English and pronunciations, word meanings, and derivations from Hawaiian and other languages. Although Pidgin Hawaiian and Hawai'i Pidgin English included different lexifiers, they similarly were fluid languages of geopolitical/cultural contact. (c) In contrast, Hawai'i Creole English (HCE), also informally called "Pidgin," became the grammar-governed language of the descendants of first-generation plantation laborers, and it has been the language of local identity to the present (Sakoda and Siegel 2003, 6–18; Romaine 1994, 530).

Negative attitudes toward HCE speakers—i.e., HCE's association with the back-breaking labor of the Hawai'i sugar plantation and its use by the working class that was exploited and controlled by the plantation oligarchy—shaped discriminatory educational policies and created prejudicial attitudes in commerce. Between 1924 and 1948, this discrimination motivated the formation of English Standard schools, which segregated speakers of Standard English (SE) and HCE (Kawamoto 1993, 202). According to Romaine, these English Standard schools legalized "racial discrimination along linguistic lines" (1994, 531). Moreover, the public discourses from the early 1900s to present have associated HCE with "low social status" (Romaine 1994, 531), cast HCE as a "liability on the job market" (Romaine 1994, 531), characterized HCE as "illiteracy" and "backward thinking" (Sato, "Sociolinguistic," 1991, 654), and portrayed HCE as a "broken" language (Sato, "Language Change," 1993, 132). One 1994 *Honolulu Advertiser* editorial even equated HCE with "garbage" (quoted in Young 2004, 113).

Just as Americanization discourses likely systemized the decline of Hawai'i Sign Language and the emergence of American Sign Language, so they also shaped institutional structures that favored SE and discriminated against HCE. Moreover, according to Sato, these attitudes have likely influenced HCE's decreolization, or HCE's increasing alignment with its English lexifier ("Language

Change" 1993, 122). However, Sato also notes that decreolization signifies only one pathway of language change when a creole community faces discrimination ("Language Change" 1993, 132–38). As researchers have shown, negative stigma toward HCE has also created paths of resistance, preservation, and even resurgence and renaissance (Sato, "Sociolinguistic," 1991, 654; Sakoda and Siegel 2003, 18–20; Romaine 1994, 531–32; Young 2004, 135–40).

One path of resurgence has been the formation of a local literature that within a colonial Western metanarrative has recovered the temporarily unnoticed and empowering relationship among three *local* elements: local body, local language, and local place. In 1978, local writers convened in Honolulu at the landmark Talk Story Conference, which intended to mobilize and assert the agency of local Hawaiʻi authors. Also in 1978, Eric Chock and Darrell Lum, who founded Bamboo Ridge Press, released the first issue of *Bamboo Ridge: The Hawaiʻi Writer's Quarterly*. Both the press and journal have since energized the production of local literature (Romaine 1994, 532–33; Morales 1998, 109–12).[3] This literary reinscription of both the local body and language into the place that is Hawaiʻi pervades the imagery and plots of local literature. For example, John Dominis Holt's story "The Pool" takes place near a lagoon linked to the ocean by "underground arteries" and a "volcanic umbilical cord" (1987, 30). In Lois-Ann Yamanaka's poem "Name Me Is," the characters carve their names into a tree "for infinity" (1993, 221) and into their skins "all the way inside" (1993, 240). In Stuart Ching's story "Way Back to Pālolo," the grandmother of the character Mrs. Chun works on a sugar plantation until she grows "old and worn and withered" and becomes the "dust of those fields" (1998, 186). These are just a few examples of this shared theme composing local literature. Perhaps the title of Milton Murayama's novel set in the early 1900 Maui sugar plantations best embodies this collective cry: the character Tosh is caught in economic bondage within the plantation hierarchy—a system of indentured servitude—and he desires most to determine the future of his own body on the land that he has become. Hence the title: *All I Asking for Is My Body* (1988).

REPRESENTATIONS OF THE HSL USER IN DIGITAL YOUTUBE SPACE: LINDA LAMBRECHT AS KUPUNA, OR BEARER AND PRESERVER OF KNOWLEDGE FOR THE CHILDREN

In a March 1, 2013, Honolulu KITV news feature posted on YouTube, newscaster Paula Akana and field journalist Cam Tran report on HSL's origins and its documentation by University of Hawaiʻi researchers. In one segment of the story, HSL user Linda Lambrecht and an ASL user stand side-by-side while signing the same English words and phrases. In that segment, linguist James Woodward explains HSL's distinctness in (1) lexicon and (2) syntax (which follows a subject-object-verb order that contrasts with the verb-subject-object order of the Hawaiian language) (KITV 2013). The story ends with Lambrecht signing to the camera as an interpreter translates orally, conveying Lambrecht's inflections and emotion:

> Over the years, it has been a concern as speakers of the language have passed away, my very close friends, I have talked to them repeatedly about the need to preserve this language, and so I was very determined, and I worked very hard over the years to do what I could, and I've seen the fruitage of my work today, and so I'm very happy. (KITV 2013)

Speaking from the position of respected elder who bears and preserves knowledge for the children, Lambrecht concludes, "Oh, yes, yes. It is my dream for the future that the senior citizens here in Hawai'i will be able to share their knowledge of Hawai'i Sign Language with the young . . . the younger generation" (KITV 2013).

In a CCTV *Americas Now* short documentary, Lambrecht is cast in the same role of knowledge bearer, or *kupuna*, as are the small group of aging senior citizens gathering with her and University of Hawai'i linguists at a public event to encourage support for HSL's preservation. Here the newscaster quotes William O'Grady, professor in the Department of Linguistics at the University of Hawai'i at Mānoa. O'Grady insists that preserving HSL is tantamount to "the preservation of historical treasure." As O'Grady says in the interview, "There will never be another opportunity to study Hawai'i Sign Language or what it tells about [the] human condition" (CCTV 2013).

The short documentary, which includes interwoven images of the majestic Ko'olau mountain range, rural and urban Hawai'i, and island beaches and shorelines, conveys a powerful connection among the land, the people, and language. In this context, HSL becomes a binding linguistic thread. Ninety-two-year-old HSL signer Betty Tatsuda expresses her happiness regarding efforts to revive the language. In a voiced translation, she calls HSL "a language . . . that defines her identity and evolution" (CCTV 2013). And the story ends poignantly with Linda Lambrecht signing a marriage proposal the way it may have been done years before in old Hawai'i. Movingly, an interpreter translates in a voice bearing traces in sound and syntax of the HCE dialect: "We been together two years now. I love you. We get married?" (CCTV 2013).

LOCAL BODY AND PLACE: THE POTENTIAL OF LOCAL HAWAI'I CHILDREN'S LITERATURE IN PRESERVING AND SUSTAINING HAWAI'I SIGN LANGUAGE

Connections among place, body, and language in Hawai'i children's literature may enrich HSL's revitalization. This literature comprises three primary perspectives: indigenous, pan-ethnic local, and touristic/paradisiacal (Ching and Pataray-Ching 2018, 289–98). Because of the sociolinguistic parallels between HCE and HSL, we focus primarily on the pan-ethnic local perspective and make some reference to the indigenous. We exclude the touristic/paradisiacal perspective, since historically it has threatened both local and indigenous identities.

Ching and Pataray-Ching describe how children's authors Sandi Takayama and Lisa Matsumoto compellingly join language, body, and place in picture books. Takayama's work delightfully blends traditional Western children's stories with local culture. In *The Musubi Man*, an adaptation of the Gingerbread Man, a *musubi* (or Japanese rice ball), bears *limu* (fresh seaweed) hair, a *nori* (dried seaweed) jacket, *takuan* (or pickled radish) eyes, an *ebi* (dried shrimp) nose, and an *umeboshi* (or pickled plum) heart. The landscape opens on a weathered plantation-style house, a wet taro field, papaya and coconut trees, beaches, and the ocean. Across this landscape the characters—a little old local man and woman, a poi (mixed-breed) dog, a mongoose, and a mynah bird—chase the runaway *musubi*. All the while, the *musubi* teases, "Run, run, fast you as you can! You no can catch me. I'm one musubi man!" But the *musubi* man befriends a surfer, and together they escape into the sea, where they surf all day (2018, 293). Takayama's other stories also adapt Western fairytale to local sensibilities, traditions, and tastes: In *The Musubi Man's New Friend*, the lonely *musubi* man falls in love with a beautiful *musubi* that bears a heart of spam (or spiced ham), which is a favorite local food. *Sumorella*, a Cinderella adaptation, playfully honors Hawai'i's extraordinary athletes who have ranked among the best sumo wrestlers in Japan. In *The Prince and the Li Hing Mui*, a princess seeking marriage recognizes her true prince when the tiny crack seed (a favorite playground snack) tucked secretly beneath twenty featherbeds and twenty mattresses disrupts his sleep (2018, 293).

Similarly, Ching and Pataray-Ching note that the protagonists of Lisa Matsumoto's picture books *How the B-52 Cockroach Learned to Fly*, *The Christmas Gift of Aloha*, and *Beyond 'Ōhi'a Valley: Adventures in a Hawaiian Rainforest* continue to enchant Hawai'i's children through locally adapted "fairytale and high-fantasy plots of initiation, adventure, struggle, maturation, and return" (2018, 293). These stories prominently convey Hawai'i's local sensibility and imagination: gigantic flying cockroaches, local-style box lunches, sandmen, *menehune*, and Hawaiian rainforests of indigenous flora, insects, and animals (2018, 293).

Other picture books focus on the geographic place of Hawai'i: *The Sleeping Giant: A Tale from Kaua'i* tells the story of Kaua'i's legendary Nounou mountain range that resembles an enormous slumbering figure. *Naupaka* tells the folkloric love story explaining why the *naupaka kahakai* flower grows near the ocean and why its counterpart *naupaka kuahiwi* grows in the mountains. Furthermore, *'Ai'ai: A Bilingual Hawaiian Story* tells the legend of the giant eel that becomes the stone rock formation that contrasts with the surrounding landscape in Hana, Maui (Ching and Pataray-Ching 2018, 292).

Current HSL revitalization efforts primarily target adults through university instruction. However, in order for HSL to thrive, this audience eventually must include children. Connecting HSL to a larger renaissance would strengthen this necessary expansion. Furthermore, the sociopolitical parallels that we have drawn between HCE and HSL suggest that the renaissance of Hawai'i's local literary art creates a space and marks an historical time in which HSL may enter and flourish within such a larger community. In 1999, a group calling itself Da Pidgin Coup comprising community members as well as faculty and graduate students of the University of Hawai'i at Mānoa responded to negative comments directed toward HCE by the state's Board of Education.[4] At that critical historical moment, Da Pidgin Coup's position paper, "Pidgin and Education," validated HCE as a first language:

> Pidgin is a language just as English is a language. Children whose first language is Pidgin come to school with a language. That language should be respected and never denigrated.... While teachers should teach standard forms of English at school, in no way should English replace Pidgin. (1999, 19)

As HCE reclamation efforts have gained traction through literary art, HSL may do so now by forming allegiances with this continuing movement. In this context, the local children's literature of Hawai'i may weave a sustainable pattern within a larger tapestry of language, place, body, and identity.

Two theatrical organizations in Hawai'i may potentially augment this integration. Kumu Kahua Theatre, which specifically supports original plays and adaptations by Hawai'i's artists and about its cultures, holds significant potential for future collaboration. Honolulu Theatre for Youth—Hawai'i's prominent children's theatre—in 2016 mounted a bilingual play *Can You Hear My Hands Speak*, which was described as a "whole new type of fusion theatre" comprising visual spectacle, musical vibration, and signed and spoken language (Staff Reviews, Youth). Thus, Hawai'i's local children's literature, along with the digital technology noted previously and Hawai'i's rich history of local theatre, compose an infrastructure with significant potential to further HSL's reclamation and sustain its preservation.

CONCLUSION

In this chapter, we have drawn parallels between HSL's and HCE's development within Hawai'i's colonial history. Doing so, we have argued that HCE continues to exist because it affirms a local identity resistant to colonial forces that threaten local culture. We have also underscored the importance of local Hawai'i literature regarding HCE's preservation. We have extended this argument, drawing a connection between HCE's literary renaissance and, within this movement, local Hawai'i children's literature's potential to advance the development of Hawai'i Sign Language.

But this argument does not arise without its own internal hierarchy. Noticeably, HCE's resurgence has largely excluded Hawai'i's Deaf community until now. In fact, there is a common HCE expression, "deaf ear," which is spoken by both adults and children and which turns deafness into vulgarity. The saying connotes stupidity or stubbornness. When people clearly hear something but cannot understand or refuse to respond, others might say to them: "What you mean you no can hear? You deaf ear or what?" As Stephen Sumida states in his landmark analysis of local literature:

> Regarding the silence where a voice falls dead because it is utterly unheard,
> many-voiced Rap Reiplinger in his first solo comedy album, the revolutionary *Poi
> Dog*, uses a local term to characterize the obtuseness of people who will not hear:
> they are "deaf ear." "I was deaf ear; I never like listen," moans one such character,
> crooning a farewell ballad to his beloved "Fate Yanagi," a takeoff from "Tell Laura
> I Love Her." (1991, 236)

Upon its release, *Poi Dog* was immediately adored by both adults and children and became a marker of *local* identity. Through the late 1970s and through the early 1980s, "Fate Yanagi" played over and over on local radio stations. Children memorized and sang its lyrics in the school yard. However, the Deaf community was largely absent from this collective *local* body.

At this critical junction, we close with an exhortation: the reclamation of Hawai'i Sign Language creates an historical moment when we can reverse such uncritically checked negative attitudes and when we can reclaim the story of Hawai'i's Deaf community and inscribe it—move it from absence to presence, from periphery to center, from vulgar representations of silence to empowering representation imbued with the whole humanness of experience and the memory and wisdom of our elders—into the ongoing history of Hawaiʻi's linguistic renaissance.

NOTES

1. Some examples are Myron Uhlberg and Ted Papoulas, *The Sound of All Things*, 2016 (ASL); Ava, Lilli, and Nick Beese and Romina Marti, *Proud to be Deaf*, 2017 (BSL); James Kerwin and Marie Kerwin, *My Friend is Deaf*, book and DVD set, 2015 (Auslan).

2. "Home Signs" refer to gestures used by a deaf child raised in a hearing household and community who has no meaningful linguistic or cultural connection to other deaf sign language users. The hearing family members and friends often adopt and contribute to this collection of signs (not a fully fledged sign language) to aid communication with the deaf child.

3. Our treatment of HCE agrees with scholars and writers who recognize the dual and contradictory sociopolitical functions of *local* identity. In one sense, comprising non-Western plantation immigrants, their descendants, and Native Hawaiians, a *local* identity has historically signified pan-ethnic solidarity and resistance against colonialism. In another sense, paradoxically and simultaneously within this pan-ethnic solidarity, local identity has also enabled settler colonization—that is, Asian descendants of plantation workers emerging into positions of economic and political power that disfranchise Native Hawaiians (see Morales 1998; Fujikane and Okamura 2008). Nevertheless, researchers largely agree that at different times in Hawaiʻi's history, HCE has been a language of protest and resistance against colonialism for both pan-ethnic locals and Native Hawaiians. For an accurate representation of HCE's complex and rich history, see *Pidgin: The Voice of Hawaiʻi*. Film trailers are also available for viewing on YouTube.

4. Da Pidgin Coup's membership and full position paper, "Pidgin and Education," is located on the University of Hawaiʻi's website on the homepage of the Charlene Junko Sato Center for Pidgin, Creole, and Dialect Studies: www.hawaii.edu/satocenter/?page_id=195.

PART 3

Deafness and Cultural Difference

CHAPTER 12

Intersections of Deaf and Queer Embodiment in Fiction for Young People

"Able-Bodied Sexual Subjects"

—Josh Simpson

Compulsory able-bodiedness is the perception of an able body as the natural, default condition, an ideology first identified by McRuer (2013) and linked by him to compulsory heterosexuality. Compulsory heterosexuality is the perception of heterosexuality as the default identity from which all other sexual identities are seen as alternatives (Rich 1983). These socially prescribed norms render all other identities (that is, queer and disabled) abnormal and compulsory in a society where everyone wants to be normal (McRuer, 370–71). A key element is that the existence of one system is dependent on the other: to perform heterosexuality, one must be able-bodied, and vice versa. Because able-bodied heterosexuality depends on a disabled and queer existence "that can never be quite contained," the hegemony of able-bodied heterosexuality is always at risk of disruption (375).

This chapter focuses on the literary containment of disabled, queer sexuality in three novels for young people: *Stick* by Andrew Smith, *St. Nacho's* by Z. A. Maxfield, and *War Boy* by Kief Hillsbery. Through representations of d/Deaf and queer identities, these novels operate at the nexus of able-bodied, heterosexual compulsion, making them appropriate for analysis through McRuer's (2006) work. An essential perspective of that work is the understanding that "able-bodiedness, even more than heterosexuality, still largely masquerades as a nonidentity, as the natural order of things" (1). With that understanding, my analyses focus on the ways in which fictional narratives facilitate and make visible able-bodied heterosexuality.

Each novel is categorized as either YA or New Adult (NA). NA, which includes *St. Nacho's*, is a term coined by St. Martin's Press in 2009 (Strickland, 143; Brookover, Burns, and Jensen, 42). While the definition remains unsettled, there have been attempts to pin it down. For example, Margo Lipschitz, while a senior editor at Harlequin, defined NA as "a romance subgenre revolving around college-age and early twenties protagonists" (Cart, 144; see also Brookover, Burns, and Jensen, 42). According to Michael Cart, examples of this category include Rainbow Rowell's *Fangirl* and Aidan Chambers' *This Is All* (145). On the other hand, YA novels, which include *Stick* and *War Boy*, feature teen protagonists and are "aimed at middle school and high school students" (Brookover, Burns, and Jensen, 41). YA novels depict the emotional preparation necessary for a journey toward adulthood, while NA is about the actual journey, after which the protagonist becomes "situated within the adult realm" (or not) by the end of the narrative (43).

According to Amy Pattee (2017), another factor distinguishing YA from NA is that YA rarely features "the type of erotic content found in new adult literature" (222) and, while both types employ "immediate-engaging-first-person narration," in NA it is used "to describe, in mildly erotic terms, the sexual experiences that contribute to its protagonists' coming of age as adults" (221–22). Pattee, however, does not define "erotic terms" or provide examples, nor does she consider YA novels that violate this purported rule. Consider, for example, *Release* by Patrick Ness (2017), a YA novel containing detailed scenes of sexual intimacy between two teenagers, including a description of the protagonist's first time naked beneath a young man while fully erect and penetrated anally (134–36). Pattee's definition also ignores the possibility that metaphor, and even abstinence, rather than explicit sexual acts in YA novels can indeed be considered erotic, such as in Stephanie Meyer's *Twilight* series or any other vampire novel. The complicated, often sexual lives of YA protagonists thus blur the YA/NA boundary of these novels and their intended audiences.

THE INTERSECTION OF D/DEAFNESS
AND QUEERNESS IN *STICK*

Angel Daniel Matos (2016) notes that d/Deaf and queer identities share many parallels and experiences, including a history of medicalization, oppression, and injustice (see also Healy; McRuer *Crip Theory*; Sandahl). Both communities also share a history of activism. Healy (2007) compares, for example, the 1969

Stonewall riots, and launch of the gay civil rights movement, with the 1987–88 Gallaudet University protests and Deaf President Now movement, which saw the appointment of the first Deaf president at the university and the beginning of the Deaf-pride movement. Another parallel is that most deaf people are born to hearing parents (Chen, 3; Peters, 36; Skelton and Valentine, 85) and the "vast majority of sexual minority youth are born to heterosexual parents" (Katz-Wise et al., 1014). Those children may feel alienated due to being unable to identify fully with their families (Glickman, 58, 63; Katz-Wise, Rosario, and Tsappis, 1014; Peters, 36; Yadegarfard, Meinhold-Bergmann, and Ho, 348).

The intersection of d/Deafness and queerness is represented through two characters in *Stick*: Stick, the eponymous first-person narrator, who is a thirteen-year-old with anotia, and his older brother Bosten, who is gay. Stick describes anotia as having "what looks like the outline of a normal boy's ear, but it's pressed down into the flesh, squashed like potter's clay. No hole—a canal, they call it" (Smith, 6). Stick and Bosten are physically and mentally abused by their parents; they are also sexually abused by their father, which their mother is aware of but does nothing about. The abuse escalates until Bosten flees, eventually ending up in another city, where he engages in prostitution and drug use. Ultimately, he is saved by Stick, who finds Bosten and brings him to their aunt's home, where Stick and Bosten are soon able to live permanently away from their parents.

The narrative's trajectory is toward able-bodiedness, with disability portrayed as shameful. Stick often reveals his shame while imagining what people think of him. For example, when people remark on his unusual name, he believes they must really mean to say, "Look at that poor deformed boy" (5); when people stare, it must be "on account of [his] missing ear" (5); and his mother is "sad" and "horrified" at his very existence (7). Stick's shame is further revealed by a wish to hide his condition, although he is unable to do so, at least initially, because his father will not allow him to grow his hair or wear a hat indoors.

A balm for Stick's discomfort is his friend Emily. After seeing sexually explicit photographs of people bathing together, he asks Emily if she would ever bathe with another person. This leads to her suggesting that they bathe with each other. Stick agrees and, having removed his underwear, feels unashamed, "totally comfortable and relaxed" in front of Emily (56). His comfort in being naked with her is in sharp contrast to his desire to hide his condition, suggesting that the heterosexual relationship he and Emily share acts as a quasi-treatment relieving his shame. That suggestion, in turn, emphasizes the medical model of disability as an individual (rather than societal) problem that should be treated for correction (see Harlan Lane, "Construction of Deafness"). Because the "treatment" is effective, Stick's shame for his anotia is validated and compulsory able-bodiedness is even further reified.

Another key aspect of the bath scene is that it lacks eroticism. That is, the scene ultimately is rather platonic, which Stick realizes: "It didn't feel sexy or nasty or anything else, because Emily was my friend, and that's all there was to it" (56). Emily washes Stick's hair, after which they dry off and have lunch. Stick has several awkward erections throughout the novel, indicating he is aware of and does experience erotic desire, yet his scene with Emily is devoid of any such response, as though disabled people are able to dream of, but never actually enact, their own sexual agency.

Even in moments that are more physically intimate, the narrative still manages to contain Stick's sexuality by reasserting his self-perceived "ugliness" (that is, his disability). The first time he is kissed by Kim, a new friend in California, he wonders how someone "so beautiful" fails to realize "how goddamned ugly" he is (139). When they kiss again, "their "tongues all over in each other's mouths," Kim whispers, "I think you're brave" (264). Why she thinks of Stick as brave is unclear, however. He has not yet decided how to help Bosten, so it is unlikely that Kim is referring to that matter. Is she suggesting, then, that he is brave to love her, an abled-bodied woman? Or is he brave simply for living with his condition? While the answer is unclear, Stick's response is to run from her, to feel dirty and ugly (265). His reaction is caused by his belief that, by kissing Kim, he is "stealing something" from her (265). That thought suggests he continues to see himself as unworthy of love, that a kiss would never willing be given to someone like him (that is, someone who is disabled). In the moments that Stick seems about to experience a sexual awakening, his disabled sexuality is suddenly and safely contained.

Aside from an able-bodied trajectory, the narrative also works toward heterosexuality. After stealing the family car to save Bosten, Stick recites to himself:

I drive at night
I blow things up
I French-kiss older girls
when nobody's looking
I take baths
and go to bed
with Emily Lohman
because I love her
I love her
I love her
and I steal cars
two days before turning fourteen

so I can drive to California
and stop my brother
from falling
over the edge. (189–90)

The act of reciting this at the beginning of the trip suggests that Stick is drawing on his (apparently platonic) love for Emily as motivation and courage. The visual presentation of his thoughts even resembles a romantic poem, with the sharp juxtaposition of contrasting images (blowing things up and kissing older girls), line breaks, and repeated emphasis on Stick's love, the "I" voice centering his emotions.

For Bosten, same-sex eroticism is depicted as shameful, even ultimately destructive. Their father repeatedly rapes him and sexually assaults Stick. Bosten is then caught having sex with his friend Paul, spurring a series of events that begin with his father calling him a "goddamned faggot" (173) and beating him, and end with Bosten becoming homeless, selling his body, and using drugs. Because same-sex eroticism is associated with rape and assault, it is portrayed as a destructive force in Bosten's life that results in even more tragedy: prostitution, drug use, and homelessness. In Paul's case, gay sex is literally destructive, driving him to attempt suicide "with a pair of sewing scissors" (285).

In contrast, Bosten now embodies his queerness: his arms are covered in marks "made by all the uncareful needles that boys on the streets spent their money on and traded their bodies for . . . one of the needle marks [oozing] pus" (Smith, 285–86). His queerness is now marked upon his body for all to see. He does not, as Stick says, "continue very well" (292), reifying heterosexuality as the natural desired state.

Yet the novel also resists compulsions of dominant norms through its very form, making deafness and queerness visible in the structure through the use of space "inserted *between* the letters and words of a text" to produce silence visually (Davis 1995, 116–17) and represent how anotia is experienced, such as in this passage:

The world sounds different to me than it does to anyone else.
    Pretty much all of the time, it   *sounds like*
                                                        this.
                        Half my head is quiet. (Smith, 6)

As first person narrator, Stick addresses the reader directly to explain the purpose of the format:

> *You see what I'm doing, don't you? I   am   making*
> *you hear me*
> *The way   I   hear the   world.*
> *But I won't do it too much, I   promise.*
> *I know what it can do to you.*
> *I know what it can do to you to not have that hole there.*
> *Humans need that hole, so things can get out.*
> *Things get into my head and they bounce around and*
> *around until they   find a way out.* (6–7)

Matos (2016) argues that these experiences are "odd, eccentric, and perplexing" (221), meant to "control and limit how one perceives" language (237). Additionally, through odd experiences, the novel embodies queerness, marked by its own unique format: its centering of silence through visual emphasis (that is, the use of gaps and spaces where words would be found in a typical novel) resists conventional structures and norms. Line breaks are also a prominent feature, causing the narrative, at times, to resemble poetry, as in this example:

> *The first sounds*
> *were things being broken.*
> *Big things.*
> *That nobody would ever fix.*
> *It sounded*
> *like the house itself was coming apart.*
> *I heard some words.*
> *Goddamn*
> *Faggot*
> *Queer* (174)

The mix of prose and poetry, of words and space, is a structure not typically seen in novels, queering the reading experience.

Another innovative use is that of section titles. The novel is broken into three parts: "First: saint fillan's room"; "Next: california"; and "Last: bosten." The first two sections are places, locations, while the last is the name of Stick's brother. The placement of his name alongside physical locations suggests that Stick finds some part of himself in Bosten, that he can locate himself in his brother. That deep connection completes them: the queer (Bosten) complements the disabled (Stick), suggesting that neither identity is complete or whole on its own.

DEAFNESS AS A NARRATIVE PROSTHESIS: *ST. NACHO'S*

In *Narrative Prosthesis* (2001), David T. Mitchell and Sharon L. Snyder argue that "the socially 'forbidden' nature of the topic [of disability] has compelled many writers to deploy disability as an explicitly complicating feature of their representational universes" (2). A consequence of this strategy of complication is that where differently abled characters are depicted, they are apt to function as secondary and are thus, to borrow a key term from Mitchell and Snyder, a form of narrative prosthesis, a supporting device that allows the narrative to develop a new direction. In the NA novel *St. Nacho's*, this direction is the intersection of queerness and deafness. The novel portrays a developing romance between two gay men in their twenties: first person narrator Cooper, who is hearing, and has been kicked out of Julliard, and Shawn, who is a college student and deaf. Ultimately, Shawn and Cooper end up in a committed relationship with each other after being pushed apart by Cooper's ex-boyfriend. The story begins with Cooper stopping in a local restaurant called St. Nacho's, a "sleepy little dive" in a "tiny seaside town" (chapter 1, sec. 1, para. 2) that turns out to be a gay bar. When Cooper mentions he's looking for a place to stay, he is offered the studio above the bar and eventually accepts a job there.

When Cooper first sees Shawn, he notices his "beautiful hand" and "beautifully tapered fingers" (chapter 1, sec. 1, para. 20). He describes his face as young, "dazzling in its vitality" with "golden brown" eyes—in all, a "lovely boy" (chapter 1, sec. 1, para. 20). The only communication between the two men is when Cooper nods his head yes for a coffee refill. In their second encounter, Cooper accidentally bumps into Shawn before recognizing him as "the beautiful golden-eyed boy" (chapter 2, sec. 1, para. 4). Again, the interaction is minimal, with Cooper murmuring an apology. Through its descriptions of Shawn, the narrative emphasizes physical appeal, rendering him as desirable and desired before revealing that he is deaf. One might argue that physical attraction is often the first spark in sexual relationships; however, the deferral of any substantive communication suggests that the author is using the "reveal" of Shawn's deafness as a plot twist or a means of characterization. The use of disability superficially in storylines is an aspect of narrative prosthesis.

Deafness as a narrative prosthesis is further suggested by Shawn's position as a secondary character[1] and the static portrayal of his experiences. For example, Shawn is postlingually deaf, having contracted bacterial meningitis at the age of four. Knowledgeable readers might assume that he had, by that age, a reasonable language proficiency. As Shawn says: "I can remember talking, and it was something I could work on with teachers" (chapter 3, sec. 1, para. 34). The limited purpose of this information appears to be to explain why Shawn can easily communicate with the other characters rather than to render him as his own fully developed character. The lack of a background story, coupled with the lack of any real agency for Shawn, marks deafness as his defining characteristic, one that the author seems to want to compensate for by giving him a golden beauty that dazzles. The emphasis on his physical beauty continues even after the literal containment of deafness when Cooper is penetrated anally by Shawn. After finishing, Cooper looks at Shawn's "high cheekbones" and "wet dream" of a mouth (chapter 3, sec. 1, para. 84), as though seeking justification for his attraction to someone who is deaf.

In contrast, compulsions of able-bodiedness are resisted through visual representations of communication between Cooper and Shaw. In its Position Statement on American Sign Language (ASL), The Alexander Graham Bell Association for the Deaf and Hard of Hearing (AG Bell) emphasizes the importance of different modes of communication in addition to ASL ("American Sign Language" 2008). Those modes include listening, spoken language, cued speech/language, and Total Communication. Total Communication consists of "finger spelling, speech reading, speaking, and the use of amplification" ("Communications Options" 2008). The form of the novel provides an opportunity to portray these various modes.

In *St. Nacho's*, when Cooper and Shawn first talk to each other, Shawn uses his voice to say hello and then signs his name while repeating it. Cooper makes a "c" with his hand when saying his own name. It's unclear in this scene, however, whether Cooper actually knows sign language and Shawn is, in fact, using his sign name, whether Cooper just assumes that this is what Shawn is signing, or whether Shawn is actually finger spelling like Cooper. These distinctions are lost, undermining sign as a complete and separate language. Moreover, rather than depicting the signs and gestures used, they are described, as is this example:

> "I saw the people when you played." Shawn came up behind me [Cooper] and jumped up to sit. As he'd done before, he faced the opposite direction so he could study my face as we talked . . . "They looked really impressed. Are you that good?"
>
> *Probably*, I texted him . . .
>
> "Do you ever go see plays?" he asked.
>
> "I have," I said, carefully nodding.
>
> "I have tickets for a play next Friday night in Santa Barbara. Will you come with me?" He grinned.
>
> *Are you asking me out on a date?* I used the phone for that . . .
>
> "Yup."
>
> Thumb, thumb, thumb. *Can I think about it?* (chapter 5, sec. 1, para. 4–18)

This hybrid of oral and visual communication decenters hearing and speaking through the use of technology. As Pray and Jordan (2010) note, advances in technology benefit many deaf people who use smartphones, messaging, email, flashing lights, and other devices to communicate (177). Not all technology, however, is valued universally by deaf people, especially cochlear implants for children (180) who are deemed unable to consent legally to such a procedure. *St. Nacho's* does not, however, engage with these issues and it is unlikely the author was even aware of them when first writing the story.

Lack of awareness may also be responsible for the ways in which the use of sign fails to resist compulsory able-bodiedness. When characters sign, the words are written in English rather than in actual sign, such as in these examples: "'Liar,' he said, but made the international sign L on his forehead for loser" (chapter 3, sec. 1, para. 5); "his friends signed in agreement" (chapter 3, sec. 1, para. 56); and "his friends began to interpret the lyrics in American Sign Language, but more, they danced the words" (chapter 3, sec. 1, para. 60). The issue is that the author appears to believe sign is a literal interpretation of English, describing Shawn as signing "the English translation" of the song La Habanera. The misrepresentation of sign undermines it as a distinct language rather than a mere translation. As Supalla, Cripps, and Byrne (2017) argue, English is the wrong language to represent sign in print (540–41). Their underlying premise is that "reading is treated as synonymous with spoken language out of convenience, which is both erroneous and antiquated in terms of what is understood about human languages" (549).

An alternative is ASL gloss, through which reading in the signed language becomes possible (549) "thanks to the matching of signing and print" (546). ASL gloss is text written by rearranging English words or roots to conform to ASL grammar and ensure that ASL is represented adequately on paper (e.g., underline used to show a topicalized sentence). In other words, ASL gloss involves a manipulation of the English text to represent the signed language (Supalla and Crips, "Universal Design," 4).

> One way this is accomplished is through the "ASL-phabet," a system made up of thirty-two graphemes, which represent the three phonological parameters of handshape, location, and movement (which underline the formation of all signs). Each sign must be written with the handshape information that it possesses, then followed with its location and, finally, movement. Up to eight graphemes may be necessary to write a word in ASL. For example, the sign WORK requires the use of two hands; thus, two handshape graphemes are written. (Supalla, Crips, and Byrne, 544)

A benefit of ASL in written form is that it gives d/Deaf students the "experience of reading based on the language they know," resulting in greater confidence as readers (546). ASL gloss is thus positioned as an answer to the call of Bauman and Murray to reconfigure "our understanding of language, in all its complexities" (216). By not understanding this complexity and representing sign language as merely a translation, the author of *St. Nacho's* participates in the compulsions of able-bodiedness.

The potential use of ASL gloss in fiction, however, has yet to be realized. This may be because one would first need knowledge of ASL gloss in order to understand a novel written in it, reducing the readership and marketability of such books, although such books are not entirely absent from the market. One example is *Islay*, by Douglas Bullard (1986). Though that novel does not use graphemes, it combines English with ASL grammar to form a hybrid of both languages.

"I'M TELLING THE STORY": THE DEAF, QUEER NARRATOR OF KIEF HILLSBERY'S *WAR BOY*

In the YA novel *War Boy* (2013), one character—Rad, the fourteen-year-old protagonist—embodies both d/Deafness and queerness, putting both experiences center stage. He is deaf, does not speak vocally, Black, and just beginning to discover his queer sexuality. He takes charge from the novel's very first page: "I'm Rad I'm deaf I don't talk I'm fourteen I'm telling the story" (Hillsbery, 1). Rad's story begins when his friend, Jonnyboy, tries to protect him by tackling Rad's father, who then ends up bleeding and unconscious. Frightened, Rad and Jonnyboy decide to run away. Along their journey, Rad discovers not just his sexuality but also drugs, nightclubs, and even environmental terrorism (which results in Jonnyboy's death).

Compulsory able-bodiedness is threaded throughout the narrative. Consider, for example, the scene in which Rad realizes someone has broken into the apartment where he was showering alone. As he searches for the intruder, his fear gives way to anger:

> [Getting mad] is something you can't help when you're different like me. The way you feel about people taking advantage. Because in some wayz it's the story of your life and always will be. And it's why lots of deaf boyz just live silent days silent nights with no hearing friends and hardly anything to do with hearing people. They just don't trust them. They'd rather be around someone they don't have anything in common with who's deaf than their fucking soulmate who's

hearing. Plenty kweerboyz are like that too actually and it's stupid and it's wrong but I understand how it happens. You always wonder what normals REALLY think and what they're REALLY saying about you to each other and it's just too much feel the weight crushing down on your face so you turn away and never turn back. (169)

This passage indicates that Rad is aware of Deaf communities but refuses to be a part of them, seemingly in the belief that such communities exist out of fear so that no one can take advantage of them. His opinion is ironic, given that he himself takes advantage of others. As he describes it:

So maybe you're thinking I must be at least a little retarded which is a common reaction that comes from misunderstanding the expression deaf and dumb. I don't mind really since it gives me a little edge. When you're deaf and you don't say anything it makes hearing people nervous at first and sometimes you get special attention that bites if you're shy but once the novelty is gone you might as well be the Invisible Man. And the end result is you get to find out a lot of things that nobody realizes you know because they either forget about you or don't even notice you in the first place. (25–26)

These negative portrayals of d/Deafness reify able-bodiedness as the preference, the norm by which all other experiences are measured.

And yet, at times, the novel oscillates toward representing d/Deaf experiences as another way of being in the world instead of a lesser alternative to hearing. The positive representations are accomplished primarily through innovative forms used to visually represent difference, similar to how St. Nacho's incorporates different ways of communicating. Rad, for example, often uses a notebook, and Jonnyboy even keeps a pencil stub in the piercing of his left ear for this purpose. These conversations are written in bold, with Rad's responses italicized, as in this brief conversation:

U know what i think? we should go down south.
   Kewl with a k. (14)

But writing is not the only way Rad communicates: he also spells letters in the air, such as "K" for kewl to show his agreement with something (14), and he can lip-read. One of the secondary characters, Ula, also knows sign language, which allows sign to be incorporated, though it is done through description rather than actual visual representation of sign. The following passage demonstrates this. It occurs in a scene where Rad is bothered by the way men stare at Ula:

Ula just shrugs.

> – I'm used to it. Men always look at me that way.
> *You mean everybody? All the time? Like the checkout clerk at the market?*
> *Dewds at gas stations?*
> – Yes. (99)

At other times, Rad is described simply as "signing back" his responses, such as in this example: "I sign back that whether she knows it or not she's a punk rocker" (100). Ula's knowledge of ASL may be questionable, however: since she is from Sweden, she presumably learned Swedish Sign Language, not American. This implausible depiction of signing could perhaps be understood as authorial license, or perhaps the author is aware that users of different sign languages are at times also able to make apt assumptions about meaning based on context:

> In ASL and many European sign languages, for example, there is a constellation of semantically related words having to do with mental processes. . . . As a result, speakers of these languages can intuit, at least roughly, what someone making a sign in the vicinity of the head might be trying to convey. (Fox 2007, 82)

Perhaps this is the case with Ula and Rad, or maybe they use International Sign, "a form of cross-national communication that emerges when signers from different signed languages come into contact" (Bauman and Murray, 220). Without more detail, however, the novel risks misrepresenting sign as one uniform language, pushing it back toward the compulsion of able-bodiedness.

Heterosexuality in *War Boy* is, at times, reinforced by gender norms. Ula, a registered nurse, takes on a maternal role, caring for the other characters through food and nursing them through recovery after a drug binge. Rad and Jonnyboy, meanwhile, are steeped in skate culture, punk life, and "skinz," as they call themselves (121). Jonnyboy "was in all the sk8 mags and won a million contests" (12), which emphasizes his physical ability. But such portrayals are relatively limited when compared to the resistance of heterosexual identity. Ula is the only central character attracted to the opposite sex and same-sex relationships are not represented as destructive. In fact, one of the more intimate moments between Rad and Jonnyboy is a scene that occurs after Rad covertly (or so he thinks) watches Jonnyboy having sex with a mutual friend and finds himself unable to pull away (echoing the scene in *Stick* where Stick seems compelled to watch his brother kissing another man). Later on, Jonnyboy admits that he knew Rad had been watching:

i wanted U 2 know Because it was the best time ever 4 me. it was really making love . . . and i wanted U 2 know I'm glad U were there. 2 see me like that & feel that love. 2 know it. U being there makes it more real 2 me. i'll never look back & wonder if it was just a dream. it wasn't. it was love, true love. (77)

Eventually Rad moves in with Jason, a man he has fallen in love with, fully embracing his queer sexuality and finding some measure of happiness. Jason's attitude toward Rad's deafness is never explicitly revealed but it was his idea that Rad "really could become a DJ. As in fuck that weak deaf-boy shit" (322). Though the perception of d/Deafness as a weakness is not attributed directly to Jason, one wonders whether that is the case or if it ("weak deaf-boy shit") is just another example of Rad's own self-flagellating attitude. The nature of their relationship is thus left ambiguous.

CONCLUSION

Novels for young people have the potential to promote cultural awareness of marginalized identities and to celebrate d/Deaf and queer experiences. This potential is significant. According to Peters (2000), many deaf people born to hearing parents "feel a need to 'achieve' an identity. They must go out into the world and join with other deaf people to learn what it means to be a Deaf American" (37). But going "out into the world" is not always an option, particularly for younger people who are dependent on their families. Youth literature may offer hope to these young people by providing access to identities they might not otherwise encounter, allowing them "to engage with different roles at an imaginative level" (Hopper, 114).

And this is not merely conjecture: while there currently is little to no research on young readers who are d/Deaf and the role literature plays in their lives, similar research has been undertaken with young readers who identify as queer. In one such study, participants reported using various media sources, including fiction, to avoid isolation and to find people, even if fictional, that they could relate to and learn from (Kivel et al.). Literature, then, is vital to opening up other worlds and futures. Yet as *Stick*, *St. Nacho's*, and *War Boy* reveal, literary mechanisms continue to render beauty, youth, and ability as compulsory and even as compensatory for perceived weakness and imperfections, limiting the potential significance of these works in the lives of young people.

NOTE

1. Positioning deaf characters as secondary is par for the course in the few YA and NA novels depicting both queer and deaf characters. For examples other than those discussed here, see *A Really Nice Prom Mess* by Brian Sloan and *My Most Excellent Year* by Steve Kluger.

CHAPTER 13

Didacticism or Seeking Harmony with Nature

Contrasting Presentations of Deafness in Contemporary Chinese Children's Literature

—Lijun Bi and Xiangshu Fang

My dream is quite small
With my mouth, I could talk
Sing our national anthem and call mum
So I wouldn't be a deaf-mute child any more
—Liu Jinying (A deaf-mute child)[1]

Written by a a deaf child who does not speak vocally, the above short poem reflects both the author's longing for acceptance and inclusion, as well as the social expectations of children with hearing and speaking disabilities: to conform, politically, morally, and physically. In China, the two disabilities of deafness and muteness are often correlated through the commonly used term *longya* (deaf-mute). On the one hand, Chinese society has always had a sympathetic attitude toward people with disabilities; on the other hand, the dominant Confucian ideology emphasizes an established social order, and thus people with disabilities have traditionally been placed at the bottom of the hierarchical ladder of Chinese society (Deng and Harris, "Meeting the Needs," 196). In this position, vocational education has always been emphasized in Chinese special schools—such as painting and carpentry for students with hearing and speaking disabilities, massage and weaving for students with visual disability, and sewing for those with mental retardation (Deng and Manset, "Analysis Learning," 129). In 1951, the Chinese government stated that special schools for the deaf and blind should be established at all levels. However, the development of such special education did not truly start until the late 1970s when China "cast off the shadow of the Cultural Revolution" (Yang and Huang, 96). China's new policy of "Reform and Open Door" coincided with a worldwide trend of recognizing the education of children with disabilities as an area of policy in itself, for example with the US legislation, *Education of All Handicapped Children Act of 1975* (Yang and Huang, 96). Nonetheless, China is largely an agricultural country, where physical labor is the primary work; it does not require a high level of literacy, and therefore many children with disabilities still may not attend school in rural and remote areas (Kritzer, 59).

On the whole, traditional Confucianism still dominates practices in health, care and welfare in China. Confucius stressed the importance of a social order, focusing on the individual behaving in accordance with the ancient concept of a cosmological order consisting of Heaven, the earth, and other human beings. Confucianism fundamentally conceives people to be members of social groups in the order of the family, the clan, the community, and the state, with life fulfillment being achieved through associating with others. This is as opposed to people being autonomous individuals, as commonly perceived in the West (Fang and Bi, 134–35). Consequently, this family-oriented notion considers the family as the provider of health care and well-being to people with disabilities such as those with hearing and speaking disabilities, providing an alternative to the Western model of the Welfare State. Arguably, this approach places the burden of care too much upon the family, with Chinese families having to draw heavily upon their own financial resources when caring for members with disabilities. From this, it can be deemed that Chinese society as a whole fails to take responsibility for its citizens with disabilities by failing to account for a family's limitations to both save and care for a family member affected by a disability. In this context, the purpose of educating a deaf child is usually closely linked to the aim of lessening the financial burden on the family. Indeed, this emphasis is such that some Chinese scholars have claimed that too much emphasis has been placed on vocational training at the expense of proper moral education (Li 2011, online; Wang 2010, online). They further assert that this issue of moral education becomes particularly urgent because "serious physical and mental injuries have often made deaf-mute children develop negative solitary, selfish, narrow-minded and impulsive personalities, which make them go morally astray very easily" (Jiaqiang 2017, online). It was in this void that Chinese children's literature began to touch the subject of children having a disability in general, and deafness in particular, toward the end of last century.

However, the body of literature dealing with children who are deaf must be placed in the broader context of Chinese children's literature. In spite of a venerable history of literature in China that can be traced back four thousand years, children's literature, as an independent and identifiable branch, emerged less than a century ago, when China faced a number of national humiliations on the international stage. In the midst of this crisis, youth represented a new vigor for a revitalized China, and children gained a symbolic status—that of the future. Attempting to strengthen China's global position, Chinese leading intellectual figures advocated a Western child-centered pedagogy, which recognized children as independent human beings, entitled to their own rights and thoughts. This movement was in reaction to what was regarded as a spiritual lethargy, a remainder from the Confucian cult of ritualized subordination. In Mao's China after the Communist victory in 1949, children were no longer viewed as heirs to the family, but rather to the new socialist motherland and the proletarian revolutionary cause. Children's literature was developed on the conviction that its task was to train a new generation, who would ultimately advance society. Furthermore, after Mao's death, a new ideological system of Neo-Confucianism began to take shape, filling in the vacuum left by the decline of faith in Marxism in China. Since books had been used to convey the moral principles necessary for social stability for thousands of years in China, the general public was accustomed to the idea of the leading role of the literati in society. Consequently, it was considered "normal" that modern writers advocated a kind of modern ideology in modern children's literature, educating them for the purpose of social progress. In this context, explicit ideological messages in children's literature would be considered natural and rational. As a result, didacticism in children's books could not be said to be as obvious to the Chinese eye as compared to third parties watching China from the West (Bi, "China's Patriotic Exposé," 33). Analysis of such didacticism in the context of literary works dealing with disabilities offers an insight into Chinese society, as well as Chinese children's literature as a moral education tool.

THE JOURNEY TO FIND THE WAY HOME

Cheng Yi's novel *The Journey to Find the Way Home* (*Huijia de lu* 1998) is one of a very small number of the early crop of Chinese children's literary works touching the theme of disability published in the late 1990s and early 2000s. Written in the genre of social realism, these works reflect, and indeed, critique the treatment of disabled children in society. While most of the early works are in the genre of short stories, this novel is a substantial piece of work, comprising sixty-one chapters. The protagonist is a a deaf boy who does not vocalize, Taiyang, whose silent observations and personal thoughts are narrated in first-person throughout the novel.

Taiyang was born deaf in a rural village, to a happy and loving family consisting of a grandmother, a mother, a father and two elder sisters. Being the only male child in the family, he became the center of attention and affection in the family. His family also protected him by not sending him to school, in fear of the potential bullying he might suffer due to his disability. Despite the frequent warnings from his grandmother, Taiyang did not understand that his disability and consequent lack of education could have profound repercussions. Indeed, the problem of his illiteracy becomes devastating, when he is lost in a nearby town where he was seeing his sister off at the bus station. The story turns to one of survival, as it takes the then only thirteen-year-old Taiyang eight years to return home, during which he suffers hunger, illness, bullying, prejudice, discrimination, deception, humiliation, and isolation. The plot of the novel reminds readers of a carefully controlled laboratory experiment, the goal of which is to observe what happens when an illiterate deaf boy, without spoken language and with little experience communicating with people other than his own family, is placed in a totally unfamiliar location in Chinese society, and to find out if or how he survives. Thus, it is a story of constructing the character of determination as well as exposing the lack of societal empathy for the disabled.

The novel follows the trend of social realism in modern Chinese children's literature, which emerged in the early twentieth century in an attempt to improve society through the study and reflection of its problems. This strategy, argues Jerome Grieder, is based upon "the assumption that society, or a culture, can be dismantled piece by piece, its components scrutinized to determine whether they remain useful or must be discarded, and then the whole slowly reassembled, piece by piece" (268). In light of this compartmental analysis of social realism, it is important to note that the author portrays four types of adults in the course of the story, representing the four "typical" attitudes in society towards disability at the time. The first group of people are the "sympathizers" who usually offer Taiyang food, drink, sometimes shelter and even money. The example of this type can be found in the workers mending the highway. When they see Taiyang, a sick child lying on the side of the road, they take him back to their hut, demonstrating even greater compassion when they find that the sick boy is deaf and cannot speak.

The second group of people are simply "ordinary people" who are a lot less sympathetic towards the deaf boy. Some are depicted as polite and others as rude. They are busy with their own schedule of life and work and cannot care less for other people. They represent the indifferent majority of the population in Chinese society towards people with disabilities—a population of Chinese people who feel that the issue has nothing to do with them. Their attitude towards Taiyang is to simply ask him to "go away," often without a "please." Then, there are "villains," who are negatively portrayed as taking advantage of Taiyang, even going so far as to abuse him as a slave laborer. The fat man and the fat woman, owners of a small restaurant, are such nasty people in the story. They make Taiyang wash dishes and clean up the kitchen, but only let him eat the food left over by the patrons. To make matters worse, they even lock Taiyang up in the courtyard to prevent him from escaping. Then, the final group are the "heroes." The best of them is a woman, who the deaf boy calls "Mama" in his mind. Mama has a strong sense of righteousness and possesses a maternal instinct. She treats the homeless Taiyang as one of her own, providing all the care and support that a mother would do to her own child. Taiyang stays in her family for years, learning how to make straw hats to earn a living. He is shown to thrive with this new skill in the friendly environment of Mama's home. It is with the help from her and from the people around her that he finally finds his way back own home after the long, eight-year separation. It is then revealed to the protagonist that his own family never stopped searching for him. The characterization of this welcoming, caring, generous and noble role-model of Mama, however, is a cliché in Chinese children's literature.

The portrayal of children in this novel reinforces the categories of people that author, Cheng Yi, creates in the adults. Sympathizers are a very small minority: there are only two in the whole story, who go to get water for the thirsty homeless Taiyang. There are no shortages of bullies with Taiyang being a prime candidate for their abuse. However, the majority of children are simply depicted as curious watchers. Having never encountered a deaf child, they follow Taiyang as if he is some kind of circus. According to Rosemarie Garland-Thomson, "Disabled people have variously been objects of scorn, terror, delight, inspiration, pity, laughter, or fascination—but they have always been stared at" (56). The protagonist's first-person narration provides access to his inner pain: he feels deeply humiliated and horribly isolated among the laughing mob of children, who do not intentionally mean to harm him. Subsequently, Taiyang often tries to conceal his disability when encountering other children. He blames himself and hopelessly feels as though his fate is sealed: "I feel so ill-fated to be born deaf-mute. So many things are so easy to others, but terribly difficult to me . . . I am destined to run up against a stone wall everywhere, forever (*sichu bengbi, yongyuan sichu bengbi*)" (144) The depiction of the protagonist's feeling of despair reflects the common characterization of disabled people as "ill," "dependent" and "infantilized" (Darke, 104) and reinforces their representation as "outsiders" of "alienation and social isolation" (Brittain), making this novel well "situated within a discourse of pity," which "articulates disability as a problem of social, physical and emotional confinement" (Hayes and Black, 114).

In the first half of the twentieth century, one of the important themes in Chinese children's literature was to tackle the social ills that the authors regarded as the root of the nation's weakness. Ye Shengtao's "Scarecrow" (*Daocao ren* 1923) is an example of this patriotic exposé. It was the first major work of modern Chinese children's literature to depict a scarecrow as a creature with human motivations and the ability to reason. Focusing on the destitute lives of peasant women, Ye Shengtao uses the figure of the scarecrow to express his frustration about the enormity of this issue. The genre of social realism in stories like "Scarecrow" was aimed at exposing the harsher realities of life. The goal was not to amuse, but to show the young reader the evils caused by poverty, immorality, and war in China. Ye Shengtao's primary concern was the question of how to change the social environment so that the oppressed women could be treated more humanely and thus they could ultimately regain their dignity. In 1921, he wrote "Pity for the weak is the most universal emotion of artists" (32). Similarly, the author, Cheng Yi, implies his frustration about the enormity of the mistreatment of those with a disability in China. From the beginning of the story, the family decides not to send Taiyang to school because of the widespread antidisability prejudice. The treatment of the deaf child in the novel is an example of how China treats children or people with a disability more broadly. Through the mental monologues of the main character over the course of the novel, the reader is reminded again and again of the obstacles that an individual with a disability encounters in society. Indeed, the novel portrays an entire community lacking in empathy, acceptance, and inclusion, instead being full of prejudice and discrimination. Thus, through his writing, Cheng Yi protests against how people with a disability are treated: without respect or dignity. But this protest is moderate, and the critique is very mild, as compared to the early works of exposé written in the first half of the twentieth century.

In contemporary China, the ideological apparatus has shifted and nowadays most children's books attempt to reinforce positive feelings for the nation by emphasizing its great achievements. Ostensibly, *The Journey to Find the Way Home* is, in many ways, a fairytale with a happy ending. However, upon a deeper reading, the main character's fate relies entirely on the kind-heartedness of one single woman and simply his good luck, instead of the exercising of his civil rights, and thus the book offers a more truthful glimpse into the lives of people with a disability in Chinese society. Furthermore, stories like this usually portray characters with disabilities as final victors over their respective situations, so that the disability is seen as an adversity to be overcome, as Alison Callaway discovers that in China "deafness" is regularly designated an "illness" (*bing*) "for which a cure should be sought" (cited in Dauncey 78). Thus, stories like *The Journey to Find the Way Home* do not encourage understanding of alternative embodiments and abilities, but reinforce the "normal" body as the body to be aspired towards. As a result, young readers are tacitly encouraged to patronize and pity those with disabilities, without questioning "how disability is socially created and managed by a domineering notion of 'normal' embodiment" (Kunze, 306).

As an educational tool, the didacticism of the novel lies in its descriptive nature, instead of prescribing a remedy. It describes and even tries to analyze society for the young readers, but ultimately remains at the level of arousing pity in its readers—a common trope in children's literature—for the deaf boy, without increasing their understanding of how to create systemic change against the maltreatment of people with a disability in the Chinese community. These young readers might as well be "the laughing mob of children" who curiously follow the deaf boy, merely as spectators at the circus. Even though the reader could be a sympathizer, or even a hero, they are but the minority and a mere individual who cannot change broader society's prejudice against the disabled. These youngsters need to be transformed. The first-person narrative provides access to the protagonist's inner injuries, and this intimacy draws the readers very close to the perspectives of a child with a disability.

IF I WERE HELEN

Confucians believe that children are able to reach their full potential—an innate sense of benevolence—by following the proper deportment of their elders, or role models in books. This ancient Chinese emphasis on the moral educability of youth has persisted to the present and continues to inspire both writers and the state to pursue the fulfillment of this education (Bi, "Politics and Ethics," 39–40). Countless role models have been created in Chinese children's literature, but protagonists with a disability as role models are still rare and relatively new. As such, *If I Were Helen* (*Jiaru woshi Hailun* 2005) is indeed a rare gem: this autobiographical novel is written by a very young writer, Zhang Xini, who herself has hearing and speaking disabilities. Zhang Xini started writing the book at the age of thirteen and, when it was published by the most prestigious literature publishing house in China, *Remin wenxuechubanshe* (People's literature publishing house), she had reached the mere age of fifteen. At that time, she was already a prolific writer, with over two hundred published works to her name, including an extensive novel of one hundred chapters, set in an exhilarating period of Chinese history, the fragmented period of the Three

Kingdoms (220–280 CE). The author states her purpose for writing her own story on the second page of *If I Were Helen*: an experienced specialist who had treated many children with hearing and speaking disabilities told her that many patients and their parents were extremely depressed about these disabilities. The doctor asked Zhang Xini if she could write her own story to demonstrate that deafness itself is not frightening, thus educating and giving hope to people, to believe in their potential to conquer even the most unimaginable adversity (2).

Because the content of this book is based on a true story, it opens a unique window for scholars to look at disability, and particularly deafness, in China. Deafness, viewed as a limitation by the author herself, her family, her educational institutions, and her society, eventually becomes Zhang Xini's main source of pride, and it is this transformation that forms the backbone of the book. Narrated in the first person, the reader follows her journey from (mis)diagnosis, to seeking treatment, facing the cruel reality of her condition, to eventually fighting back and triumphing in gaining social recognition as a high achiever. Whilst her deafness causes obstacles, it motivates the family and the protagonist to be victorious against the difficult odds.

It is important to note, however, that in the publisher's preface, the book is referred to as an autobiographical novel (*zizhuanti changpian xiaoshu*)—a categorization that reveals the clash between complete honesty and the license to dramatize for the purpose of moral education: "This work has recorded the fighting process and robust mentality of a new generation of the disabled against their cruel fate. And it has created an image of a brave and self-confident deaf girl, who loves study and loves life" (1). Despite this emotive language in the publisher's prologue, the author emphasizes her fidelity to the truth. Again, this indicates the concealed tension between her honest writing style, which she calls *suibi* (informal, casual), and the publisher's intention to champion a new role model who embodies the uplifting national spirit, so as to encourage millions of youngsters, disabled or otherwise, to follow suit.

The title of the book *If I Were Helen* unmistakably points to the author's main source of inspiration: Helen Keller, the most celebrated woman with disability in American history. Almost a half century since her death in 1968, Keller continues to be popular and relevant to children's literature as a didactic tool, not only in the United States, but now in China as well. However, Zhang Xini draws upon other inspirations, mentioning other notables such as Beethoven, Picasso, Bill Gates, Van Gogh, James Joyce, Darwin, Rousseau, Nietzsche, Fabre, Stevenson, Shakespeare, Bunin, Homeric Hymns and Stiglitz, a contemporary American economist. Rabindranath Tagore appears to be one of the author's favorite writers, as his short poems, as well as Goethe's *Faust*, are quoted quite a few times in the book. One of the most frequently used terms in the book is *Shangdi* (God), which can easily be read as an equivalent to "fate." Whilst Zhang Xini mentions that she has read *The Bible*, there is little evidence in the book to suggest a Christian faith. In terms of Chinese influences, Zhang Xini draws mostly upon fields of literature, philosophy, and history, from antiquity to the present. The feeling that this teenaged author is extremely well read and exceptionally intelligent is immediately apparent. Thus, it is not a huge surprise when it is revealed that she is from a very well-educated family: her mother is a trained lawyer, and her father has authored books in the fields of philosophy and economics. However, both gave up their careers and moved to the South of China where the treatment of hearing and speaking disabilities is most advanced in China, when Zhang Xini, an only child, became deaf after an illness at the age of three.

Zhang Xini writes at length about her mother's experiences, which are intertwined with the author's experience of deafness. Her mother is lonely. Her husband is out most of the time, working hard to earn enough for the costly medical treatment and much needed equipment, such as imported hearing aids, computer software and books, as well as covering their living expenses. Zhang Xini's mother lives in isolation in a totally strange city after the family had moved to Shenzhen. However, not all is lost: this new isolation is a source of relief as well, saving her from the Chinese notion of "losing face"—a sense of shame from having a disabled daughter. Furthermore, here in Shenzhen, no one knows about her past, of which she is very proud. Apart from loneliness, her mother is naturally overwhelmed by constant worry: "My mum is worried about me every minute: What will her future be like? How about her schooling, her job and her life? Oh, who will love her, like her own parents, tolerant and patient?" (40). She almost breaks down entirely when her daughter's "irreversible deafness" was first confirmed, described as "a thunderbolt out of a clear blue sky" to her (45).

Zhang Xini's mother's resilience is highlighted when she takes her daughter's education into her own hands. First, she refuses to allow her daughter to go to the school for the deaf, where a statue of two hands looms over the entrance, symbolizing the segregation of deaf people from society in their ability to only communicate in sign language—described by Zhang Xini as difficult as *tianshu* (illegible like celestial writing) to those not trained in it. Because of this difficulty in communication, the future of deaf people was traditionally very bleak, as they were reduced to menial jobs requiring low communication skills, such as carpentry, painting, sewing or straw hat making. Believing that her daughter could do better, Zhang Xini's mother enrolls her in a special training center that promises to teach Zhang Xini how to speak. This turns out to be a nightmare: deaf children, boys and girls, were forced to have their heads shaved (it is not explained why) and sit in a dimly lit room, listening to the beating of a drum to get a sense of rhythm, chanting words entirely irrelevant to their life. Soon, they discover that these so-called teachers have no teaching qualifications, let alone qualifications for special education. Instead, most of them only had a junior high school certificate and were employed on a temporary basis only.

And so Zhang Xini's mother decides to educate Zhang Xini to speak herself, but first, to make her daughter China's Keller, she has to train herself to be like Keller's mentor and teacher, Anne Sullivan. Books about Helen Keller and Anne Sullivan become her (and her daughter's) spiritual, emotional and educational support. She also reads volumes of books in the field of deaf education and Chinese phonetics, leading her to conduct five hours of lessons a day in the efforts to teach her daughter how to speak. It is not easy: the tones of the Chinese language are a real challenge. Believing in her daughter's abilities, she resorts to all and every possible means to push Zhang Xini, including occasional corporal punishment. Feeling extremely frustrated, this qualified lawyer sometimes even locked her deaf daughter out of the house as a punishment! Nonetheless, in overcoming her own personal worry and loneliness, and despite her sometimes-unconventional methods, Zhang Xini's mother is portrayed as having devotion, determination and wisdom.

With the help of the expensive imported hearing aids and assiduous work, Zhang Xini feels confident and ready for "normal" school. However, local schools only offer very limited places to children of migrant workers, let alone children with a disability. Zhang Xini's hearing aids were instantly noticed, and her candidacy was rejected even before the rigorous testing began. Again, her mother's determination was called upon.

> My enrolment was rejected, and the principal was very impatient, "Look, so many normal children can't get enrolled into the school, and how could I give a place to a kid like . . ."
>
> So, I am not a "normal child!" When we got home, my heart was broken.
>
> My mum said to me, "Xini, mum will teach you at home, okay?" (160)

The concept to prevent "ableism" appears alien to this highly competitive society, especially in its educational system. Ironically, for the protagonist, her exclusion from school and subsequent home schooling turn out to be much more beneficial, with the flexibility that home schooling allows. Zhang Xini's mother manages to purchase the whole syllabus of textbooks, and her daughter studies according to her interests, skipping what is too easy. One year later, when another school had places to offer, mother and daughter went to an interview together with the principal, this time hiding Zhang Xini's hearing aids and, of course, her disability as well. She was placed in the second grade. She writes: "The restoration of my real social statues started on this day. I was very happy, feeling that I was a 'child' not different from other children" (178).

Alas, Zhang Xini soon discovered school life to be extremely boring and tiring. In a very rigidly controlled classroom, repetitive reading and copying characters numerous times until memorized were the main learning methods for children, who started school at 6:00 in the morning and finished at 5:30 in the evening. A huge amount of homework was prescribed, usually taking hours until midnight to finish, and this pattern went on day after day. Zhang Xini found that she was miles ahead of her peers in reading and writing, which now were her crucial communication revenues acquired through her mother's home schooling. When other children were learning to read, she was already reading to learn from her mother and father's collection of books. However, no matter how torturous school life was, Zhang Xini had to remain in the system. Throughout the book, what she and her family fight for is a spot in the educational system, to compete with other "able-bodied" students, ultimately for one of the most prized, but limited places in a good university. This tradition can be traced back to two thousand years ago, when the Chinese imperial civil service examination system started. The competition to go to university had always been vigorous and ruthless, but it was especially so for the one-child generation. To graduate from a renowned university would guarantee a secure job, which in turn comes with better pay, respect, and the ability to provide better support to one's parents when they are old—like care for the disabled, aged care is also a family responsibility in China. Childhood consequently becomes a preparation phase for this future battle, known as *gaokao* (higher education entrance examination). The book reveals that in this competitive environment, no individual help to students with special needs is available. Besides, large class sizes, typically between forty and seventy-five students, make it impossible to individualize instruction for those students who need it (Kritzer, 59–60).

As an autobiography, *If I Were Helen* features the journey of the author's personal triumphs over the slimmest of odds. It also clearly confronts the obstructions that society places in the way of deaf children like her. Whilst Zhang Xini often expresses her frustration, she also demonstrates an understanding of the insufficiently funded system. Further, the ideological apparatus of China now asserts that Zhang Xini's book is an achievement of the system and holds her up as a role model who embodies the unwavering qualities of willpower and self-reliance. It attempts to demonstrate Zhang Xini's extraordinary individual strength over collective political action in conquering difficulty in the educational system, the community, and society. This very young author, however, seems to be fully aware of the potential danger of her work being taken as inspirational discourse by the ideological apparatus, with her status as a hero potentially causing alienation, frustration, and even resentment among members of the disabled community. Zhang Xini emphasizes at the very beginning of the book that she does not intend to show off, maintaining that she is no hero but just an ordinary girl talking about the troubles in her life, just like every ordinary person dealing with all kinds of trouble in their life. She further states that deafness is a part of life to a broad range of people like Helen Keller and Beethoven, but also to millions of children in China's rural areas, who live in poverty and desperation without any hope, thus implying that not everyone can become a Helen Keller or a Beethoven. Indeed, deaf children like the main character in the previously discussed novel *The Journey to Find the Way Home* may never have even heard the names of Helen Keller or Beethoven.

CONCLUDING COMMENTS

In China, there is a long history of joining artistic creativity to moral education in the field of literature. In the more recent past, literature was used as a weapon to unite people to fight against foreign threats, and as an educational tool to train socialist constructers. Didacticism is hence well established in Chinese children's literature. In a modern society concerned with equality and opportunity for the disabled, one would naturally expect didactic works of children's literature representing disability to focus on unjust discrimination, as well as the need for social conditions to change. From the late 1970s to the present, following decades of extensive reform and substantial development in lawmaking in regard to education of the disabled, China has become more aware of the issue of social justice. However, today's China, although greatly modernized, is still in many ways a developing nation. For example, the cost of funding special schools for children with disabilities is still regarded as too expensive even in relatively affluent places like Shenzhen, let alone in poor rural areas, where most of the Chinese people live. In depicting the life of children with hearing and speaking disabilities in such a setting, the two books discussed in this chapter rely chiefly on realism, which helps the young understand the realities of life for deaf children. *The Journey to Find the Way Home*, however, has its less realistic moments, such as its fairytale ending of happy family reunion. Contrastingly, *If I Were Helen* depicts the transition phase of the protagonist from the restricted family space to a broad arena of society, thus realistically reflecting upon the traditional forces in Chinese society and culture that run counter to the adequate provision of state-funded support to people with disabilities. Both books reveal that there is a severe lack of diagnostic technology and experienced professionals, both in the fields of education and medicine. However, they differ in that *The Journey to Find the Way Home* is more concerned with the notion of "charity," whereas *If I Were Helen* places a stronger emphasis on the struggle for civil rights for the disabled. But ultimately, it should be noted that in both books, the main characters achieve their personal goals through their own individual efforts rather than social change. Have these two books made a strong case for celebrating difference and inclusivity? No, they haven't, but they have contributed towards a more enhanced awareness of disability among young Chinese readers.

NOTE

1. http://work.kids21.cn/dfcz/cqsdfcz/201401/t20140121_257009.htm. Accessed on 20 December 2017.

CHAPTER 14

Examining Deaf Culture
in Coming-of-Age Novels within
a Multicultural Framework

—Angela Schill

Stories of deafness in young adult (YA) fiction have the potential to portray the intricacies and complexities of Deaf Culture in a unique way that can provide insight into deafness as a cultural phenomenon. Lynn McElfresh's *Strong Deaf* (2012) and Esty Schachter's *Waiting for a Sign* (2014) are two YA coming-of-age novels that explore some of the intricacies of Deaf Culture from an adolescent perspective and an engagement with "strong Deaf" characters, a term used within Deaf Culture to refer to people who fully embody the values embraced and advocated by the Culture. Thus McElfresh both adopts the term as the title of her novel and depicts a family that is completely immersed in Deaf society, strong in their views of cultural Deafness and acknowledged by other Deaf people as "a strong Deaf family" (26). *Waiting for a Sign* portrays a mainly hearing family that supports their Deaf son/brother and respects his ties to the Deaf community. Both books address emotional aspects of their adolescent protagonists' experiences as they navigate complexities often related to living in both the Deaf and hearing cultures. The settings, themes and narrative structures of these coming-of-age stories allow for a melding of d/Deafness and multiculturalism. A key element in the representation of the nexus between multiculturalism and d/Deafness is the treatment of stereotypes within these texts and the implications for how adolescents might view d/Deaf individuals—that is, whether stereotypical views are perpetuated or disrupted.

A priority of multiculturalism is to advocate the dissolution of biases and prejudices informed by stereotypes. In a consideration of the impact of stereotypes on adolescent readers who are in various stages of cognitive formation, a disruption of stereotypical views, as John Stephens suggests, "[enhances] understanding of relationships between selfhood and otherness and [informs] . . . social action designed to foster equity and social justice" (2011, 34). Such a potential outcome is ideal from a multicultural and Deaf culture standpoint. Of course, the multicultural analysis of these stories requires that I also address possible stereotypes of d/Deafness in the novels that might lead to negative social behaviors fueled by prejudice.

In this analysis, I additionally consider the political, cultural, familial, and other ideologies that are, as described by Karen Coats, attributed to children, whether conscious or unconscious, and how "it becomes important for those who study child literature to examine how ideologies appear and are reinforced in youth literature" (2017, 10). Application of this ideological examination to YA fiction with culturally Deaf characters provides a rich opportunity to explore the cultural diversity of Deafness. Such an ideological investigation is essentially multicultural and enables examination of the imbalance of power that results when a mainstream culture enacts power over a minority culture (Gopalkrishnan 2010, 5). Viewed as such a minority culture, Deafness can then be analyzed in terms of this examination of power.

DEAF CULTURE, COMMUNICATION, AND LANGUAGE

Deaf individuals, with their own language and unique customs, have deemed themselves to be members of a Deaf community and culture (see Gregory, 1992, 184–85). Being Deaf "is not simply a camaraderie with others who have a similar physical condition, but is, like many other cultures in the traditional sense of the term, historically created and actively transmitted across generations" (Padden and Humphries 1988, 2). Of course, the characteristics of deafness can be as varied as the people who experience deafness, yet there are also commonalities that are distilled when considering deafness from a culturally Deaf perspective. In this vein of thought, deafness is regarded as a characteristic of a person rather than a disability. It also signifies a cultural distinction complete with its own language and norms (see Lane, 1995, 171). This culture is one in which being Deaf is viewed with pride. This pride can sometimes even lead to segregation from, and a rejection of, the hearing community (see Padden and Humphries, 2009, 35–36). There are also many other complexities surrounding the cultural perspective of deafness. Deaf culture, as an aspect of multiculturalism, can then be explored in relation to these many complexities in a way that can increase understanding and appreciation of Deaf society amongst the greater community and particularly amongst adolescents.

The narrative strategy in *Strong Deaf* is one in which two sisters, aged fourteen and twelve, are alternating narrators within the story. Jade is the younger, hearing sister and Marla, the elder, is deaf. The alternation of perspective between the two characters offers an insightful duality between Deaf and hearing points of view. Firstly, as Perry Nodelman proposes, alternating narratives "invite and accommodate the expression of a specific subset of the concerns and values that texts for young people more generally express" and it also allows for multiple ideologies to be disseminated (Nodelman 2017, 144). Additionally, this approach has the potential to instill appreciation for diversity through the representation of a story told in two voices. Yet in considering the insight such a narrative structure can provide, there is also an issue of the reliability of narrators that must be taken into consideration.

The chapters alternate between these characters, and the narration by Marla is written in a style that evokes American Sign Language (ASL) gloss. ASL gloss is a means whereby American Sign Language is represented or translated in writing with English words and accompanying symbols. It does not follow the grammatical structure of English and is often used as a bridge to help individuals, either deaf or hearing, transition between both languages (see Buisson, 2007, 332–33; and Supalla, Cripps, and Byrne, 2017, 541). Brenda Jo Brueggeman describes sign language gloss as being "not smooth or articulate" (2005, 24). In this text, the representation of ASL in English varies from gloss in that it mostly represents unsigned communication and thought. Utilizing this gloss could be a unique way to illustrate the nuances and differences in language and grammatical structure between English and sign language. However, when translating one language to another, care is required to extract the exact meaning and essence of what is being stated in the original language and then finding as much accuracy as possible to transmit that meaning into the translated language (Hickey 1998). This shows a respect for the message and allows readers to access the ideas as fluently as if it were written in his or her own language. There is also much more to translation than simply achieving the correct grammatical structure: "Whatever translation is in its entirety, it seems to involve semiotic, linguistic, textual, lexical, social, sociological, cultural and psychological aspects or elements" (Hickey 1998, 1). However, the representation of communication in ASL within this text does not achieve such fluency or clarity. and thus the use of an in-between language constructs Marla as an unreliable narrator in terms of narratorial discourse. Dan Shen defines narrator unreliability in this way: "If a narrator misreports, (mis)interprets or (mis)evaluates, or if she/he underreports, underinterprets or underevaluates, this narrator is unreliable or untrustworthy" (para. 2). A comparable effect occurs with Marla's discourse in that its representation seems to be underinterpreted, that is, there are too many gaps that readers cannot fill confidently. While gloss, even applied loosely, can be used as a means of written translation, it is not fluid or thorough. The use of this technique to represent Marla's signed language, her internal thoughts, and her focalization arguably simplifies the character's mental processes and thus creates an impression that she "underreports, underinterprets or underevaluates." There is a feeling of lack here that may negatively impact readers' perceptions of Deaf individuals. While it might be common in some multicultural books to represent those speaking a foreign language in ungrammatical English (for books written in English), the thoughts of an individual are usually rendered in standard English, reflecting the fluency of the character's thoughts and allowing readers to have access to this fluency regardless of what the native language of the character may be. This does not occur in Marla's communication, however. Rather than applying a makeshift gloss in what would normally be spoken text, as a way of representing sign language and then giving readers access to a more fluent and realistic depiction of Marla's linguistic abilities and intelligence, the text provides no differentiation amongst the possible scenarios for communication. She is represented one-dimensionally and quite simply. This can be illustrated in Marla's rendition of her arrival home from boarding school as she shifts from mental reflection to focalizing:

Open car door, climb out, stretch. Home long time. All summer. No homework. No tests. No dorm inspection. Surprise. Feeling same snake touch leg. Maybe scream, but no. Turn around, Beezley greet me. Not snake. Dog tail. (McElfresh 2012, 10)

This approach is evidently intended to provide an ASL authenticity to Marla's character, but it creates difficulties by disregarding English vocabulary and syntax as well as the linguistic and grammatical elements of English needed to communicate meaning clearly (see Baker-Gibbs and Baker, 2013, para. 13–15). The focus on a limited verbal equivalent of a signed narrative has the consequence that many visual and spatial nuances of ASL, necessary to communicate meaning, have been lost. As such, the narration falls between the two languages and readers face a greater challenge to connect linguistically with Marla. Representation of focalization is a good example. A shift from narration to focalization is generally overt in chapters narrated by Jade, as in this example: "I looked at the path. It wasn't a path now. It was a stream flowing with water" (94). The usual assumption in children's literature criticism is that focalization is an aspect of perception, and so in this case "I looked" indicates that what follows is what Jade focalizes. Focalization indicated by means of ASL gloss can be more difficult to discern because of the attempt to replicate a different grammatical structure and the absence of grammatical components such as pronouns, verb tense and function words. When in the previous extract Marla's discourse shifts from free direct thought ("Home long time. All summer. No homework. No tests. No dorm inspection") to subjective perception, that is, focalization ("Surprise. Feeling same snake touch leg") the shift is harder to discern because the cognitive process for readers is more complex, in that they must decipher the meaning, the order, and then the modal shift from thought to perception. The point of "Surprise" (= something has surprised me) is the result of a perception that is described subsequently as "Feeling same snake touch leg" (= I feel the same sensation as if a snake had touched my leg). A reader patient enough to work through the process will be richly rewarded, but it is likely that more readers will perceive the ASL glossed utterance as a form of broken English and conclude that it presents Marla's ideas in a crude and halting manner in contrast to the way her sister's thoughts and communication with others are represented. McElfresh's strategy of describing the incident from Jade's perspective in the previous chapter may thus backfire so that instead of making Marla's experience more intelligible it becomes rudimentary.

This initial introduction to the text provides an opportunity to examine equality in terms of how Marla's intelligence and her language are reflected in her communications, as opposed to the intelligence and language of her hearing sister. Multicultural theory provides the tools to do this by examining the power balance between mainstream and minority cultures through access to language. The incorporation of sign language as part of the text's dialogue has the potential to highlight and support the unique qualities of the language. However, in *Strong Deaf,* the way Marla's sign language is represented highlights her inequality in comparison with her sister's better command of language. When Jade and Marla are signing to each other, their conversations are both represented in something less cohesive than fluent English (see Baker-Gibbs and Baker, para. 15). This mode of representing sign language conveys how sign language might be demoted to a crude language that only allows for the communication of the most basic of meanings. English and sign language are now compared on the page and English becomes more reliable in terms of meaning and understanding.

Although both Jade and Marla are unreliable narrators, Jade's access to and use of English creates an imbalance in the power amongst these two characters and subtly and misleadingly suggests she is more reliable as a narrator than her sister. Readers are denied access to Marla's fluency, foregoing the respect and understanding that might otherwise be transmitted. Significantly, the translation of Jade's signed communication includes English articles and verb inflections that do not exist in Marla's linguistic representations and thus offer readers more opportunities to relate to and understand Jade. Such elements continue to assign more credibility and intelligence to Jade while signaling inequality and ineptness to Marla. For example, as Jade and Marla are arguing over their latest softball game, Jade signs to her sister, "I heard you make noise. You sounded like a wild animal" (88). Marla answers: "No sound same animal" (88), which, if translated in the same vein as Jade's signing was translated (with more inclusion of fluent English features), could be: "I do not sound like an animal when I speak." The choice to attribute more English fluency to Jade's signing than to her sister's is concerning. It supports the stereotypical idea that even when using sign language, hearing individuals are competent while deaf individuals are illiterate or unintelligent. Sign language is a nuanced and complex language that, when presented to an English-speaking readership, deserves to be fully translated into English to provide accurate representations if equality is an important facet of the text. A Deaf person who uses sign language who reads the depictions of Marla's discourse in this text is also barred from understanding their full meanings due to the limited nature of the representations. Unfortunately, the way sign language is represented helps to perpetuate mainstream cultural codes that deem spoken English as superior to sign language. As Baker-Gibbs and Baker put it, "Grammatically and syntactically incorrect, simplistic, and disjointed, McElfresh's English version of Marla's ASL narration makes Marla and the story's other ASL users appear ineptly lingual" (2013, para. 15). Perhaps the use of this pseudo gloss was meant to be educational and supportive of the Deaf community, but it negates the power given to Marla to tell her story in a way that reflects her intelligence. The author's choice of this limited language supports outdated "assumptions about sign language as a simplified, inferior form of communication . . . equated with 'broken English' and, in turn, with 'broken intelligence'" (Hall 2015).

In contrast, *Waiting for a Sign* aligns Deaf culture more with multicultural aims. It also centers on a sibling relationship in which one is profoundly Deaf and the other is hearing. It offers a unique perspective through the eyes of fifteen-year-old Shelly as she navigates her relationship with her older Deaf brother, Ian, aged eighteen. The way Deafness is presented in this novel supports the concept of "Deaf-gain"—something that is here well utilized to support more of an equality framework. This idea is one in which Bauman and Murray describe a reframing of "Deaf" as a form of sensory and cognitive diversity that has the potential to contribute to the "greater good of humanity" (2013, 246). Hall describes this deaf gain as considering "Deafness [as] not a matter of hearing loss, but instead it has the enriching potential to facilitate the acquisition of a different language, a greater awareness of the nuances of tactile relations, and a shared sense of history and community" (Hall 2015, loc. 1717). In *Waiting for a Sign*, rather than painting a picture in which Deaf individuals have limited communication skills or intelligence, sign language is treated as a legitimate language that is valued. Others in the story want to learn this language and those who use it are admired. There is no sense of inequality between the hearing and Deaf worlds. While Shelly is not Deaf, her narration gives access to Ian through her dialogue with him and through her own internal representations and descriptions of Ian's and other characters' speech—as well as their actions and reactions. In addressing the signed quality of ASL, the text qualifies the dialogue from the beginning, stating that, "Since it is not possible to show the beauty and dimension of sign language in written text, I have translated into English the passages expressed in ASL" and these appear as italicized text (prefatorial note). The strategy of representing signed communication in this way avoids some of the complications related to limited comprehension that occur in *Strong Deaf.* Perhaps an authorial description of the linguistic process used in its text would have been beneficial to *Strong Deaf.* Through the means of sign language represented as English, Shelly reveals Ian's dialogue in her narration—which is clear and intelligent. Another difference from *Strong Deaf* is that Ian, the Deaf character, lacks interiority as he is not a focalizer within this novel. While having access to Ian's own insight would be even more valuable, the way Ian is portrayed through his sister's narration delivers positive outcomes for readers because of the affirmative way a hearing sibling views and reveals her Deaf sibling. This novel still contains the realities of hardships these siblings face, yet the ability to communicate by means of sign language functions constructively in overcoming these troubles. In fact, the signed communication between Ian and Shelly is the bridge that repairs the damage and misunderstanding they once had in their relationship. This connection elucidates the benefits of having access to sign language, rather than portraying such communication as crude and disjointed. Sign language is not looked down upon. It is utilized and useful. This treatment and validation of language in *Waiting for a Sign* is a powerful signal of support within a multicultural framework.

DEAF COMMUNITY AND FORMS OF BELONGING

Another important piece of the multicultural perspective is the sense of cohesion and support a minority culture experiences within their subculture in the mainstream community. Both texts include, to some degree, the role a residential Deaf school plays in the lives of the Deaf sibling. Marla, as well as her parents, continue the strong and proud Deaf tradition of attending Bradington. Marla and Jade's grandparents are also Deaf and their grandfather is the headmaster of the school. Jade describes her disappointment as a child in not being able to live in the residential school with her sister. She suffered from the exclusion—not only because she did not continue learning sign language fluently like her sister, but because there was something special about the connections she noticed her sister had with her roommates and the rest of so many Deaf members of their extended family. There is a moment Jade describes in watching Marla with her roommates as they gather at the 75th anniversary celebration of the school that reflects a unity Jade is not a part of: "I watched Marla talking with her roommates. They were standing in a tight circle signing away to each other. There seemed to be a bubble of light around them. A special energy. I stood there for a minute, staring" (20). While there are plenty of moments in the text in which Jade seems to elevate English above sign language, this scene offers the perspective that she admires and feels excluded from the Deaf community to which her sister and many extended family members belong. She recognizes a unity of which she is not a part. From a multicultural perspective, this revelation indicates that exclusion is not unidirectional. Jade has experienced her own alienation of sorts due to her lack of Deafness. *Strong Deaf* continues from this point to explore much of the frustration between Jade and Marla, mainly highlighting cultural conflicts amongst the hearing and the Deaf, until ultimately concluding with a unity between sisters and cultures. *Waiting for a Sign* also explores similar cultural conflicts, but resolves the siblings' chasm earlier within the text, allowing for a multicultural exploration that is illustrated by a united approach between siblings.

Hawthorne, the residential Deaf school Ian attends, is being threatened with closure. Shelly, in an act of solidarity with her brother, is allowed to attend a sit-in organized to protest against the government closure of the school—which would lead to Deaf members being put into mainstreamed schools and losing the benefit of Deaf peers and teachers and being transplanted from a cohesive Deaf community to a hearing one. This protest is of great significance as Shelly is an "outsider" of sorts and her presence is tenuous until Ian and ultimately Shelly convince Deaf members of the school that she is a supporter. Shelly is confronted by Ian's friend Deyquan who wants to know why she is there. She responds that she came for herself—but as she thinks through her answer, it allows readers to comprehend a rationale that supports her brother and ultimately the Deaf community at Hawthorne in a way that also supports herself and her desires that go beyond her own interests. It forwards a multicultural awareness. She "wanted to be a part of something important" (107). Shelly's ability to interpret what administrators and teachers are discussing outside the building the students have commandeered proves to be highly valuable to the students. Their demands are met and the school is kept open—for a while longer, at least. The multicultural examination of this story highlights a unity and connection amongst the Deaf students as well as offering a bridge for unity to those in the hearing community who, motivated by empathy and a desire to support, are welcomed in.

This student protest is a particularly significant opportunity to explore multicultural aims in terms of cultural solidarity and the action taken by members of a cultural minority in response to social injustice. It mirrors real-life protests that have taken place at Gallaudet University, a predominately Deaf university in the United States and an emblem of Deaf culture. In 1988, a hearing candidate was chosen to be president of the University for the Deaf after students had been campaigning for a Deaf president. Students took over the entire campus and demanded a "Deaf President Now," a demand that was ultimately successful (see Greenwald and Weiner, 2018). Another demonstration occurred in 2006 (see Bauman, 2009). These protests, organized to combat perceived prejudice and bias, laid the groundwork for the Deaf community in terms of acting rather than being acted upon. *Waiting for a Sign* illustrates this practice of the minority culture taking matters into their own hands and convincing the mainstream community that they know what is best for their community and that they demand to be respected and understood. Given access to this protest, readers are invited to consider how the solidarity amongst the students is a celebration of Deaf culture. Both texts, with their different approaches, address the significance of Deaf residential schools as an important unifying aspect of their culture. It is a place to learn and perpetuate their language, stories, and traditions. This school setting provides an opportunity to better understand the Deaf community and some of the ways they share their common experiences. In the case of *Waiting for a Sign*, it also sheds light on how the community unites to fight against prejudice and injustice to enact change.

NEGATIVE AND POSITIVE REPRESENTATIONS OF DEAF CHARACTERISTICS

Strong Deaf and *Waiting for a Sign* also examine more specific characteristics that are often associated with Deaf culture. Some of these attempts respectfully address such characteristics and other attempts step into the realm of perpetuating harmful stereotypes. *Strong Deaf* provides access to the minds of both sisters—which provides glimpses into the frustration they share about each other, as well as their respective cultures. Jade often offers up inferior assessments of the Deaf members of her family. In an early description of her sister, Jade says: "From behind me I could hear the pop of Marla's lips as she mouthed words. She must have been excited, because as she signaled I could hear her arms windmilling. I didn't look. I didn't care what she was saying. She'd barged into my room. *I* was the one whose privacy was invaded" (5). Of course, her narration, as previously established, is unreliable and her perspectives are exaggerated because of the multifaceted nature of the rivalry and jealousy that underlie the sisters' conflicts. Marla's descriptions of Jade in their turn contain harsh judgments: "Jade run away like rat. Feel boom. Maybe Jade door . . . Want sleep . . . But sleep not happen because rude Jade" (6). However, most of Jade's descriptions of Deaf individuals engaged in signed conversations are unsettling because readers are presented with what might be their only exposure to Deaf people communicating. The characteristics connected to the communication process, as described by Jade, are usually blatantly or subtly derogatory. Jade describes Marla's vocalization as "bellowing" and as a "hoot" (13, 76, 94, 96). She also compares her voice to a "sick-cow" sound six times throughout the course of the story (13, 55, 75, 91, 96, 108). Jade's unflattering descriptions extend to other Deaf family members, such as explaining her father's reaction when she wakens him: "He sat straight up and his eyes fluttered open. He smacked his lips together a couple of times before wetting his dry lips with his tongue. His eyes had a wild, panicked look to them" (5). This description is not blatantly cruel, but it hints at a sort of childlike or at least inferior quality to her father when describing his wild, panicked, fluttering eyes and smacking lips.

On the other hand, in *Waiting for a Sign*, Shelly's description of Ian's storytelling ability explains many nuances of sign language without making signing appear to be a primitive system.

> He would tell us story after story from school, practically acting each one out at the table. He could be three characters at the same time by simply shifting his body in his chair, or changing his facial expression. I loved watching him. My parents and I always asked for more. (8)

This description supports a concept of Deaf culture that uses a complex language that lends itself to rich storytelling. Shelly's observations of Ian also help to construct the portrayal of a positive Deaf character. She observes her brother reading classic novels such as *To Kill a Mockingbird* and *The Catcher in the Rye*. Rather than being illiterate or uneducated, Ian is intelligent. Through Shelly's narration, Ian's character takes shape: he writes and performs poetry. He acts in plays. He is a leader in his school. He has a sense of humor. He is sensitive and compassionate. Such descriptions can override earlier stereotypical images of deafness perpetuated in the collective cultural subconscious, replacing them with images of diversity that can be better understood and appreciated. *Waiting for a Sign* portrays Ian as an empowered Deaf individual who is treated by his family with equity and is respected in his Deaf community. In this novel, there are other characteristics and behaviors often attributed to Deaf individuals that are represented respectfully.

Shelly, when approached by Ian's friend at Hawthorne, manages to address the bluntness that is often associated with the Deaf community in a nonjudgmental way:

> "Why are you here?" he asked abruptly. No "how's it going," no easing up to the big question. Just straight and to-the-point, which I'd come to recognize was part of Deaf culture. If your hair looked bad, you were going to hear about it. If someone wanted to know why you were the only hearing person at an all-Deaf sit-in, he'd just go ahead and ask. (106)

This approach to addressing the straightforward nature of communicating in the Deaf culture handles the topic sensitively. In *Strong Deaf*, the characterization of Deaf individuals, at least of Marla, is less favorable and at times abrasive. She is portrayed like a stubborn two-year-old. The explanation Marla gives for her return to her home in the summer highlights a maturity and intellectual gap between herself and her younger sister: "Beezley my dog. Sister Jade think Beezley her dog, because Jade live home all year. I older. I first daughter. First love of Beezley . . . Jade jealous. Now I home, Beezley sleep my bed, not Jade bed" (3). This excerpt shows Marla trying to assert her authority, thinking she knows better, but her own ideas and language portrayal suggest she is simply being patronized by others who are in the know. As Marla tells her story, the gist of the idea is there, yet there is no sophistication in her descriptions. They are basic and childlike. When the alternating narration presents an episode from two perspectives, the language of Jade's version of events is fuller and much more detailed.

The way in which Marla's character is constructed, either through Jade's descriptions or through her own point of view, portrays a deaf character who is bossy, stubborn, cruel and simple. This depiction, then, offers an interesting opportunity to examine the multicultural messages in the text. From one perspective, there is an overarching concern that the overall portrayal of Marla as a member of the Deaf community is stereotypical. However, *Strong Deaf* also provides a window into examining the cultural complexities between the deaf and hearing communities. Perhaps as a coping mechanism for dealing with the isolation she has experienced in her culturally Deaf family, Jade has elevated her hearing status so she feels superior to those Deaf members—particularly her sister. Marla, on the other end of the spectrum is tired of Jade's "rude" behavior—unable to see that her own pride in being Deaf has resulted in her own rude treatment of Jade. She refers to her as a rat and a baby, is unwilling to share the family dog, and does not realize the isolation Jade has experienced as a lone hearing person in the family. While Jade has found a way "to participate and function fully" within her culturally Deaf family (Gopalakrishnan's phrasing, 2010, 8), to truly be a multicultural family both Jade and Marla need to resolve their differences. Near the conclusion of the novel, Jade and Marla form a bond as Marla suggests to Jade that they can keep a secret between them and from their parents. This connection of trust becomes the bridge for them that crosses over the chasm between their cultural differences. Jade begins to trust Marla and Marla realizes, as she has been cared for by Jade, that she is "Lucky have hearing sister" (113). At the end of this coming-of-age novel, they both transition to a position of appreciation in which characteristics of their cultures can be seen as beneficial to one another.

The outcome of *Waiting for a Sign* is similar in that the final message is one of unity and interconnectedness amongst members of the Deaf and hearing communities. *Waiting for a Sign*, however, manages to construct a stronger positive and contributory view of Deafness and Deaf qualities and characteristics. Some of this can be explained in the way Ian is described and how he interacts with others. Even when Ian is angry, rather than describing a popping of his mouth and windmilling of his arms, which might be strange and intimidating, the focus is placed on Ian's rationale for his anger as he faces the potential closure of his school and the prospect of losing connection with the Deaf community. The text addresses Ian's potential isolation if he is no longer able to communicate with his peers and will need to rely on an interpreter for his education. His world would be greatly changed and limited compared to the freedom he has enjoyed at his Deaf school. Shelly sometimes describes Ian's physical characteristics and behaviors associated with his Deafness, but more often gives descriptions of his personality, and his thoughts and emotions revealed in his responses within their dialogue give insight into his character—of which Deafness is a part. Additionally, rather than reducing Ian's signing to a very basic form, which would simplify his personality, his full character and personality and the depth of his relationship with Shelly are more accessible to readers because communications are represented in fluent standard English. Particularly poignant is the scene where Ian comforts Shelly after the loss of her best friend: "Ian grabbed hold of my hand. *'She loved you very much'* . . . I started crying harder than I had since

I'd first heard my mother's terrible words. My chest heaved and hurt from every painful feeling that I felt in my heart. Ian cried too. He reached over and held me, and I leaned into his chest. We cried together on my bed for a long time" (56–57). Such elements of *Waiting for a Sign* encourage reader empathy as it encourages emotionally engaged reading free from stereotypical assumptions.

The text also provides numerous examples of Ian's abilities and valuable qualities rather than focusing on a caricature-like depiction of a Deaf individual. As Shelly describes Ian during a performance at his school, his character is suffused with intelligence and capability: "Ian stepped to the front of the stage. I heard my mother breathe in sharply next to me. I understood why. Ian stood tall and at ease, even with at least a hundred people in the audience. He looked so confident. He looked so grown up" (43). In addition to his self-possessed stage presence, Shelly's description of Ian's poetry performance continues in the same vein: "How can I explain how beautiful the poem was? I'd have to be a poet" (44). Shelly's narration sheds light on the beauty and emotional connection she experienced from the poetry in a foreign and visual language—indicating that she benefited and was inspired by what she saw. This scene is a transformative moment that invites understanding and a change in perspective that can supplant potential stereotypical ideas of characteristics of Deaf individuals and their community. Ian's capacity to perform, communicate, excel, comfort, and contribute are all recognized, appreciated, and celebrated.

CONCLUSION

Both *Strong Deaf* and *Waiting for a Sign,* as coming of age novels, provide a rich multicultural exploration of Deafness. I might argue that *Waiting for a Sign* conducts a more well-rounded approach to Deafness, particularly when it comes to the treatment of language and the way sign language is represented. The nonstereotypical descriptions of the Deaf community and Deaf characteristics are also presented in a manner that helps to move a reader beyond unfamiliar elements of Deafness that might exist in a reader's mainstream perspective. This multicultural work occurs as the novel outlines the way things are done in the Deaf community that a hearing person would not normally be familiar with. The narrated asides act as a guide to how things function, potentially avoiding discomfort by creating some familiarity. *Waiting for a Sign* acknowledges different nuances in the Deaf culture, but it also includes a focus on universal relationship issues and experiences that surpass potential barriers between culturally Deaf and hearing societies. While the text addresses challenges that come to Deaf individuals, families and communities as a result of cultural differences, the overall story is relatable because of the commonalities within the story that cross cultural barriers and then actually link the cultures. The fluid language representation allows for a more seamless comprehension of signed communication by the Deaf characters. Respect and appreciation for the culturally Deaf community are encouraged in the way they and their language are described. The text also invites the mainstream community to consider the challenges the Deaf community faces in a way that encourages compassion—perhaps even motivating reader cooperation to make positive changes in the mainstream community in terms of interacting with Deaf society. The absence of stereotypes within the text strengthens the multicultural goals of removing bias and prejudice that might typically be associated with Deaf culture. Where differences were once misunderstood and feared, they are now interesting and appealing. *Strong Deaf*, while perhaps not as efficient in executing the multicultural work described in *Waiting for a Sign*, still manages to consider these multicultural themes and opens the door for readers to reexamine their own assumptions as the characters within the text do the same. When considering the rapid growth taking place in the lives of adolescents as they are developing their own sense of identity and considering, and even *reconsidering*, how they view the world and the people in it, the multicultural issues raised and explored in these novels are significant.

CHAPTER 15

Coda

From Doctors' Offices to Doctor of Philosophy:
A Deaf Woman's Journey

—*Corinne Walsh*

CHILDHOOD: BLISSFULLY UNAWARE

Turns out that your daughter is deaf and will need to wear hearing aids for the rest of her life.

My parents were shocked and heartbroken. How could this be?

Four-year-old me, playing with a doll on the floor, was oblivious. Can we go home now?

This was the diagnosis delivered in a most blunt and uncaring manner by a balding male pediatrician to my Mum and Dad in April 1991.

A few months prior to this distressing appointment, my preschool teacher had suggested to my Mum that I might need my hearing tested. This teacher had been calling out to me while I was running in the other direction one day, and I had not turned around nor responded to her. In early 1991, I underwent this hearing test, which indeed revealed that I had a mild to profound (pretty serious), sensorineural (nerve-related) hearing loss in both ears.

Mum and Dad were encouraged to get my younger eighteen-month-old brother, Alexander's, hearing tested as well, which they did a few weeks after my test. In another devastating blow it was found that he too had a binaural, sensorineural hearing loss, but in the mild to moderate range.

My parents felt distraught, guilty, confused. How had they not picked this up earlier? They had noticed I was mispronouncing words—*"birdum"* for bird;

Figure 15.1. Left: seven-year-old Corinne holding a music box at Australian Hearing (10 August 1994); Right: twenty-nine-year-old Corinne holding her master's certificate at her graduation (15 February 2015) (photographs personal property of author).

"cable" for table; *"tuppa tea"* for cup of tea; *"wha wha"* for whale; *"lellow"* for yellow; *"hor-"* for horse, for instance. However, they presumed this was just cute gibberish, typical of any toddler. They also observed that I was sitting very close to the television; and that I had this bizarre habit of holding peoples' faces with my hands and gazing intently at their lips when they were speaking.

Alas, it all made sense now.

Except one thing did not make sense—when and how did not just Corinne, but Alex too, become deaf?

Doctors theorized that my and my brother's hearing loss was present at birth, and must be due to faulty genes or a mishap during pregnancy. However, written documentation suggests otherwise. Our health records show that we both passed all our baby clinic hearing tests. Mum, who was trained as a primary school teacher and is highly intuitive, stated in one letter she wrote to our GP that, as infants, her two children always seemed to respond to her voice and other sounds.

I did have a few accidents as a child, such as slipping in a wading pool and hitting my head on the concrete; as well as jumping off the bed, with my forehead colliding with the corner of the bedside table. Maybe these damaged my hearing? It did not explain my brother's hearing loss, though. Both I and my brother had suffered adverse reactions after our childhood vaccinations, especially the MMR (measles, mumps, rubella) vaccine. The MMR insert explicitly lists "nerve deafness" as a side effect. It seems very likely that this played a role, but it is not something doctors, or many people, are too willing to discuss. How and when my, and my brother's, hearing was damaged may unfortunately be a mystery that never gets solved . . .

Immediate intervention was needed. Especially for me, because 4.5 years of age is very late for a hearing loss to be detected. Because I (fortunately) had some residual hearing in the low-pitched range, and my brother's hearing was not as badly damaged, my parents decided to go for behind-the-ear hearing aids and speech therapy, rather than sign language, so their children could participate in the hearing and speaking world. I spent countless hours with health professionals—GPs, ENTs, audiologists, speech therapists. Australian Hearing at Chatswood became my second home. My parents were determined to make sure I, and my brother, did not fall behind. They regularly sat me in front of the mirror so I could learn how to speak and enunciate, and they read books to me every single night. Enid Blyton's *The Faraway Tree* was my absolute favorite. I am indebted to my Mum and Dad for their endless love, hard work, and sacrifice.

I thrived in preschool. Before and after my hearing loss was diagnosed, I keenly participated in all activities and made friends easily. I remember I had a kindergarten teacher whose name was Owen, but my faulty ears thought his name was "Orange," and so that was what I called him (though I would have pronounced it as "Owange"—I have never been able to say my "Rs" very well)! We regularly sang a jingle at kindy, too, called "Alice the Camel." Again, my poor little ears thought it was called "Alison Camel," and so I would sweetly wail at the top of my lungs: "Alison Camel had one hump!!" It was not until many years later, at my then-boyfriend's nephew's kindy concert, that I saw on the booklet that the preschoolers were going to be singing the song "Alice the Camel." I was stunned, and then amused. My whole life I had the lyrics wrong! Ha!

PRIMARY SCHOOL: HAPPY AND CAREFREE

You talk funny.

Six-year-old me felt indifferent and unaffected. All kids talk funny, right?

An insolent girl in the grade above me blurted these words out to me in the playground one day. It was like water off a duck's back at the time—I just thought she was a bit of a nincompoop, and I carried on playing. It was rare for me to receive any kind of comment about my hearing loss as a child. Most people never drew attention to it.

In primary school, I was a studious, gregarious, and popular kid, who consistently wore her hearing aids, sat at the front of the class, and wore her FM. The FM was a machine designed to amplify the teacher's voice and was humongous compared to technology these days. It looked like I was wearing a Sony Walkman—a clunky box hanging around my neck, with leads that I attached to my hearing aids. The teacher wore a similar-sized box around a belt and a microphone clipped to their shirt. The FM certainly did help me to hear what was going on; sometimes too much. Often teachers would leave the classroom, forgetting they still had the FM on, and I would hear them talking to other teachers outside, making themselves a cup of tea, sometimes using the bathroom. My classmates would ask me for reports— *"what's Ms/Mr doing now? Are they coming back yet!?"* It was a good source of entertainment. Perhaps this is why, growing up, I always said I would love to be a detective or private investigator.

My mum decided to sew an adorable pocket on the front of my school uniform to house this FM, so it did not get in my way during class. I managed to convince a few of my peers that this pocket was a holder for my morning tea snacks, and some went home and asked their mums if they could have a pocket sewed onto their uniforms too!

In primary school, I did very well academically, socially, and in sports such as hockey, softball, soccer, and swimming. I received top marks for assignments and tests; was accepted into OC classes[1] in Years 5 and 6; was a school prefect in Year 6; and gained entry into Manly Selective High School. I am fortunate to be a skilled lip reader, have sharp vision and an analytical mind, and possess a memory like an elephant. I believe these traits have helped me to function well.

As I child, I was not at all conscious of my hearing loss or my hearing aids, and never saw myself as having a disability. That changed when I got to high school.

HIGH SCHOOL: CONFUSING AND CHALLENGING

Don't worry about talking to her, she's deaf.
  I felt embarrassed, ugly, and alone. Boys will never like me, will they . . .
  Sixteen-year-old me was at a house party in 2003. These words were spoken by one dude—let's call him Richard (or Dick, for short) Head—to another (very cute) dude, who had caught my eye and was making his way over to talk to me.

Mister Head did not know I could read lips and had therefore "heard" him. I watched like a hawk as he pointed to both his ears while saying *"she's deaf."* The cute boy looked at me with hesitation and pity, then turned and walked off in the other direction.

Cruel words said about my hearing loss barely affected me as a child; but in my teenage years and adulthood, cruel words were like a white-hot knife slashing my skin, leaving deep, painful scars. In about Year 8, I was becoming a self-conscious teenager and, in an effort to fit in, I refused to wear my FM and to sit up the front of the class. As high school went on, I encountered the occasional mean comment, such as at that party in 2003, which made me feel pretty low. Thankfully, I have not experienced many incidents of discrimination, bullying and exclusion regarding my hearing loss. I have been very fortunate, too, to have many allies in my life: caring, supportive teachers and mentors, and inclusive, respectful peers and (later) work colleagues, many of whom have become dear friends. I always recall a letter my favorite primary school teacher wrote me in Year 6: that life in high school and beyond will be tough—especially having a disability—but to stay strong, rise above it and not let the world harden you.

Despite identity struggles during my teenage years, I still excelled. I attained a UAI of 95.20 in my Higher School Certificate,[2] and came first in the school in Society and Culture, Family and Community Studies and Ancient History, and second in Extension History. I was terrible at maths though! I placed third in my grade overall in Year 12. I never requested special accommodations because of my disability, such as extra time in tests, which makes me even prouder of my successes. How about that, Aristotle![3] I certainly did not fit the "deaf and dumb" stereotype.

Given my flair for the humanities and social sciences, I decided to undertake a Bachelor of Arts at Macquarie University, majoring in Anthropology and Sociology. I admit, I was slack in my undergrad years compared to primary and high school. I was more focused on my part-time job, playing soccer and softball, and going out partying. At uni, I did not visit the disability support services, nor did I tell my lecturers or tutors that I had a hearing loss. Nevertheless, I still managed to get my BA degree with a Distinction average.

My early twenties were trying years. My beloved Nan passed away when I was twenty-one, and this left a gaping hole in my life. I had a few unhealthy and unfulfilling relationships and did not see my good friends from school as much as we were all off studying and working. My support networks and comfortable routine had fallen away, and I felt quite withdrawn, lost and insecure. I found it hard to admit my deafness to new people I met, because I was frightened they might judge, ridicule, and exclude me. I hated wearing my bulky hearing aids and I wanted to be rid of them. I would often not wear them at home, in sport, and social situations. I started to notice, though, how I was struggling to follow conversations, and people were having to repeat themselves and sometimes even yell at me.

YOUNG ADULTHOOD: PAINFUL SELF-GROWTH

You need to wear your hearing aids, otherwise others will just assume you can hear like a normal person.

I felt hard reality hit me. I guess I am not normal after all, am I?

These were the firm words of advice given to me by my audiologist at Australian Hearing in 2008. I was twenty-two. I had been in denial about my disability in my teens and early twenties. By not wearing my hearing aids, I fitted in and was just like everyone else, right? Yet, I was missing so much. I soon worked out that life would be far easier if I accepted my impairment and wore my hearing aids, for my own sake and other peoples' sakes. Thankfully, technology is always evolving and hearing aids continue to become more discreet, but I am still very conscious of my now-smaller hearing aids and I still do notice when people glance at them.

After finishing my BA, I applied for and was successful in getting a place in the graduate program for the Federal Government Department of Families, Housing, Community Services, and Indigenous Affairs (FaHCSIA). This meant moving to Canberra, which I did in early 2010, at the age of twenty-three. This move changed my life for the better. I found Canberra to be a more diverse, open-minded and inclusive place than my hometown of Sydney's northern beaches, and it was much easier for me to be open and comfortable about my hearing loss. I soon met a lovely, handsome fella at a wedding, who was my boyfriend for a couple of years. He never made an issue of my disability. It did not last, mostly because I was based in Canberra and he in Sydney, but this relationship boosted my confidence and taught me a lot about myself.

It was while working in the public service that I discovered that Indigenous children in Australia and globally suffer acute and chronic middle ear infections (known as "otitis media") and consequent hearing loss. In fact, Australian Aboriginal and Torres Strait Islander people have consistently been found to have the highest rates of otitis media in the world (Burns and Thomson 2013; Leach 2016; AMA 2017:1). I felt perplexed and dismayed as to how this could be possible in a first-world country, and decided to pursue postgraduate study so that I could explore this issue further. In 2013, I started a master's in anthropology and community development at the Australian National University and secured a job as a research assistant at National Centre for Indigenous Studies at ANU at the same time. I finished my master's in September 2015 with straight High Distinction marks.

Within weeks of finishing my master's, I developed tinnitus in my left ear. When I started my PhD a few months later, my right ear started to ring. Maybe it was my body warning me to stop studying! I still have tinnitus in both ears. Some days it does not bother me, while on other days it sounds like someone high on speed is playing a xylophone inside my head. This extremely irritating condition has worsened my hearing—I can no longer hear the lower-pitched sounds I could once hear in childhood. I used to be able to have conversations at close range quite easily without my hearing aids, but I find it difficult to do this now. These days I need to wear my hearing aids in order to participate in most social situations.

ADULTHOOD: ACCEPTANCE AND ENLIGHTENMENT

You must do this PhD, Corinne. You're the person to do it, as you've got just the knowledge and the skills. I think it'll be cathartic for you too.

I felt chuffed and motivated. Finally, I'd found my path!

My work supervisor, who soon after became my PhD supervisor, imparted these words of wisdom to me in mid-2015, a few months before I was due to finish my master's. My colleagues, friends and parents further encouraged me. Feeling confident and capable, I launched into a PhD on February 1, 2016.

I spent the first few months of my PhD reading, day and night, and what struck me was how little we have heard from Indigenous people about ear infections and hearing loss, especially those who experience the conditions firsthand. It seemed logical to me to focus my PhD research on the experiences, perspectives, and aspirations of everyday Indigenous community members. After careful consultations and community agreement, the Aboriginal community of Yarrabah in Far North Queensland became my field site, and I spent the year 2017 doing fieldwork there. This was a huge push out of my comfort zone, but one of the most rewarding journeys I have undertaken in my life so far.

Ear infections of all kinds; perforated eardrums; sore, itchy, blocked ears; tinnitus and hearing loss are extremely prevalent in Yarrabah. I spoke to around 330 people who live and work in the community, and literally everyone had a story to tell about ear troubles. Apart from some health workers and teachers, no one used the term "otitis media" or knew what the term meant. Locals refer to all ear troubles as *sore bina* (*bina* being Yarrie Lingo[4] for "ear").

The vast majority of Yarrabeans[5] believe *sore bina* is caused by swimming in the creeks. The creek water, as well as the tap water, are seen by community members to be contaminated and harmful. "White people made our land and water dirty. That's why our ears are sore, why we are sick and dying," explained one young woman.

According to mainstream medical and public health experts, though, chronic ear infections are caused by bacterial overload, due to living in impoverished, unclean, overcrowded conditions, and unhealthy behaviors such as poor hygiene, smoking, and bottle-feeding. Yarrabeans I spoke to were shocked and offended that these deficit narratives are used. They tend to see the broader, colonized world—and not their individual bodies, behaviors or Aboriginal way of life—as the reason for sore, infected ears, and sickness generally.

Some Yarrabeans recognized that ear infections cause hearing loss; while others did not make a connection. They also mentioned loud music and noises; illness; physical and emotional trauma; and medical harm as causes of hearing loss. *Bina gurri* is the Yarrie Lingo term for "deaf" or "deafness."

Despite alarmism about Indigenous ear disease and hearing loss in the mainstream, many Yarrabah community members actually did not see hearing "problems" to be much of a problem. The hearing loss that results from otitis media is often mild in nature, plus nonverbal signs and gestures are part and parcel of Aboriginal communication—which means most Yarrabeans with hearing loss can easily get by, especially in their home and around the community. An Elder summed it up: "our people—if they can't hear too well—are very good at listening with their eyes."

Further, there is no word for, or concept of, "disability" in Yarrabah, or most Indigenous communities in Australia and globally. Those who are *bina gurri* are simply accepted as they are, with family and community adapting to help them. Indeed, when I was yarning[6] with Yarrabeans, they often turned to face me so I could see their faces and lips, used many gestures, and spoke louder. I found this inclusive attitude to be a welcome change from the mainstream Australian society I had grown up in, where people with disability are often constructed as an undesirable problem in need of fixing, and where the onus is on the person with disability to "do the work" and "be normal."

Yarrabeans are also not fans of hearing aids—these devices are seen, especially by young people, to be a "shame job." Being forced to comply with colonial, medical labels ("diseased," "disabled," "deaf") and interventions (like hearing aids) can be more disabling and incapacitating for Indigenous people in Yarrabah than the actual condition itself.

For the first time in a long time, it felt ok to be different and to not have to hide this difference. It felt ok to openly talk to people about what it is really like to have a hearing loss and wear hearing aids. I was around people just like me. On the cookie-cutter northern beaches, I had never really met another young person with hearing loss or hearing aids—most were elderly.

Despite the overall nonchalant attitude to both ear infections and hearing loss in Yarrabah, community members did mention that having good ears and hearing is still important, especially in highly verbal situations, such as the classroom, the meeting room and the court room.

In Yarrabah, the term *bina gurri* not only means physically unable to hear, but also symbolically "not listening" or "ignoring." Yarrabeans complained how all levels of government, and "whitefellas" generally, do not listen to them—which has been the case since the first settlers arrived over two hundred years ago. As a result, Yarrabeans will often intentionally ignore government and "whitefellas" in return. For instance, by not turning up to meetings and appointments; not heeding the advice of doctors and other authorities; not paying attention to the teacher in class. It is not just black and white who are deaf to each other; Yarrabeans all regularly complained about their own mob[7] being *bina gurri*, too. I was often told how young people do not listen to their elders. However, it is not just Yarrabah kids, but adults too, who use selective hearing. Shutting the ears off and pretending not to hear can be a strategic tool to avoid certain people, interactions, and situations. Deafness, because it is hidden, can be an easy condition to feign. A middle-aged Yarrabah woman summed up the pervasiveness of literal and metaphorical hearing issues in Yarrabah and the difficulty in distinguishing between the two: "Doesn't matter if you're deaf or not deaf, everyone here is *bina gurri!*"

I use my hearing loss to my advantage, too. I will purposely turn my hearing aids off or take them out if I do not want to "hear" or participate. I can avoid listening to the irritating drone of cicadas in summer, the overhead fan whirring monotonously, the distracting TV in the background, or family members whingeing and whining! Ah, silence really can be golden!

I uncovered many fascinating insights, stories, and suggestions in my PhD research, which I cannot do justice to in this short piece. The overarching finding is that Yarrabah community members perceive and experience ear infections and hearing loss quite differently from the mainstream. My research illustrates that there are other valid ways to view and experience the ears, hearing, the body, disability, health, sickness, and healing, and that Indigenous voices must be heard—and taken seriously—if any progress is to be made.

I submitted my PhD thesis in August 2020 and received my results three months later. All three examiners gave my thesis marks of Excellent and Exceptional. The 4.5 years of blood, sweat, and tears felt worth it! In early 2021,

I was lucky to secure a postdoc academic position at the ANU, which sees me working on Indigenous disability research, policy, and evaluation.

In my thirty-four years, my ears have certainly let me down, and often left me feeling flawed, angry, powerless, and upset. I sometimes wonder what it would be like to turn back the clock and prevent my hearing from being damaged. On other occasions, I recognize how my hearing loss has given me skills and powers that not many others have, such as exceptional senses of vision, smell, intuition, and deduction. How many people can sit in a pub and eavesdrop on others at a distance, simply by reading their lips and body language!? If I were just a "normal" Jane Doe, perhaps I would not have led such a unique, exciting, and successful life. What is "normal," anyway!? One of the most profound lessons I learned from the people of Yarrabah is that, regardless of what body part you might have "missing" or "malfunctioning," you are no less of a person; and what is important is not your so-called limitations but your strengths and capabilities.[8] When you look at it, each and every one of us—even the seemingly able-bodied—has their imperfections and limitations. I will remind myself of this valuable lesson learned in Yarrabah whenever my hearing loss tries to get me down.

Imperfection is perfection to a beautiful perspective.
—Anon

NOTES

I completed my doctor of philosophy in August 2020, and my graduation ceremony was scheduled for July 2021. Unfortunately, a COVID-19 lockdown precluded the ceremony (and photo opportunities), so a photo from my master's graduation is the next best thing!

1. "Opportunity Classes (OC), located in government primary schools, cater for academically gifted Year 5 and Year 6 students with high potential. These classes help students to learn by grouping them with students of similar ability, using specialised teaching methods and educational materials at the appropriate level" (NSW Education 2021).

2. The HSC is the twelfth and final year of secondary education in Australia. Until 2010, students in New South Wales were assigned a University Admissions Index score, which determined eligibility for entrance to tertiary programs.

3. "The Greek philosopher, Aristotle, pronounced us 'deaf and dumb,' because he felt that deaf people were incapable of being taught, of learning, and of reasoned thinking. To his way of thinking, if a person could not use his/her voice in the same way as hearing people, then there was no way that this person could develop cognitive abilities" (Gannon 1981).

4. Yarrabah's creole language. It is the first language learned and spoken by locals and is used in the home and around the community. Standard Australian English is used more in the school and in organizations/workplaces.

5. This is a colloquial term, used by a few Yarrabah community members I interviewed, to refer to a person who is local to Yarrabah. I used this term regularly in my PhD thesis to describe Yarrabah community members.

6. "Yarning" is an Indigenist research method—a uniquely Indigenous cultural form of conversation that is preferred by Indigenous people over formal, face-to-face, Q&A-style questioning. It is a dialogical encounter with Indigenous people as fellow investigators, a two-way approach that builds on the notion of reciprocal knowledge exchange between the researcher and the researched. As a research methodology, it recognises the storied ways in which Indigenous people communicate (Bond et al. 2015, 1541–42).

7. *Mob* is a colloquial term in Australian Aboriginal English used with reference to a group of people associated with a particular place or "country." Identifying who an Aboriginal person is and where they are from, *mob* can represent an extended family group, clan group, or wider Aboriginal community group.

8. The attitude of acceptance towards hearing loss (and disability generally) in Yarrabah is in fact very similar to that of the Deaf community.

Select Glossary

American Sign Language (ASL): is used predominantly in the United States and in many parts of Canada. It is not mutually intelligible with other sign languages, although it has been the basis for creole sign languages in parts of Africa and Asia. ASL is most closely related to French Sign Language (LSF, *langue des signes française*).

ASL gloss: a practice whereby signed discourse is represented in text form by transcribing sign for sign and including notations to indicate the facial and body grammar that goes with the signs. This is a process of transcription, not translation.

Audism: the "notion that one is superior based on one's ability to hear or behave in the manner of those who hear" (Tom Humphries); "the corporate institution for dealing with deaf people.... [It] is the hearing way of dominating, restructuring, and exercising authority over the deaf community" (Harlan Lane, *The Mask of Benevolence*, 43).

Auslan ("Australian Sign Language"): Auslan is related to British Sign Language and New Zealand Sign Language, which together make up the BANZSL language family. Auslan has also been influenced by Irish Sign Language, especially through the Catholic School system. Auslan was recognized by the Australian government as a "community language other than English" and the preferred language of the Deaf community in 1987.

British Sign Language (BSL): BSL is the most common form of sign language within the United Kingdom. It involves movement of the hands, body, face, and head, and its fluidity has given rise to significant regional variation. The sign languages used in Australia (Auslan) and New Zealand (New Zealand

Sign Language) substantially evolved from it in the nineteenth century and still share with it a manual alphabet, a grammar, and 82 percent of signs. There is regular communication among the three languages.

Clinical deafness: clinically deaf patients can be subdivided into two distinct populations with different clinical attributes depending on whether auditory language was acquired prior to hearing loss. Pre- or perilingually deaf (pre-LD) subjects become deaf before learning to speak; they are unable to talk, and they use sign language as their primary communication mode. On the other hand, postlingually deaf (post-LD) subjects lose hearing after complete acquisition of auditory language due to various aetiologies such as chronic otitis media, ototoxic drugs, and viral infections. These patients can speak fluently, although they cannot hear, and rely on speechreading (SR) as their main communication mode.

Cochlear implant: a cochlear implant is a small electronic device surgically inserted into the inner ear (the cochlea) that interacts with an external device to stimulate the hearing nerve and provide sound signals directly to the brain. The implant does not replace normal hearing but constitutes an alternative pathway. A high success rate is reported for prelingual children fitted with implants. While the number of people fitted with implants is steadily increasing, it is neither a universal cure nor accessed by the majority of deaf people.

CODA: the hearing child of deaf parents.

Conceptual metaphor: a concept from cognitive linguistics, conceptual metaphor is defined as a mapping between two conceptual domains, where properties from one domain (the source) are transferred onto another domain (the target). In the example, a student is a container, the student (the target domain) may be described as *"full* of knowledge," *"overflowing* with ideas," *"empty*-headed," and so on.

Deaf: is generally used to describe individuals with a severe to profound hearing loss, with little or no residual hearing. Some deaf people use a spoken language and speechreading, combined with their residual hearing and hearing aids, communication devices, and/or cochlear implants to communicate. Others use a signed language.

Deaf Culture: the culture of Deaf people based on a signed language and values, traditions, and behavior norms specific to the Deaf community. Deaf culture offers a strong sense of belonging and takes a sociocultural point of view of deafness rather than a pathological perspective. Those within the deaf community who are culturally Deaf consider themselves to be a linguistic and cultural minority, not people with a disability. A distinction is often made between "deaf"—with reference to the audiological condition of not hearing— and uppercase "Deaf" to refer to members of a Deaf culture.

Hawai'i Sign Language (HSL): a sign language unique to Hawai'i, first mentioned in written records in the 1820s. It is an indigenous language, unrelated to ASL or other signed languages. HSL is currently considered an endangered language because of its low number of signers and the wider use of **ASL** in the local Deaf community.

Home signs: gestures used by a deaf child raised in a hearing household and community who has no meaningful linguistic or cultural connection to other deaf sign language users. The hearing family members and friends often adopt and contribute to this collection of signs (not a fully fledged sign language) to aid communication with the deaf child (Benegas, Ching, and Pataray-Ching, this volume).

Indo-Pakistani Sign Language (IPSL): there are many varieties of sign language in South Asian countries, including widespread home sign and local sign languages. The urban varieties of IPSL in India and Bangladesh, Pakistan, and Nepal are related, but sufficiently distinct for scholars to consider them to be three separate languages. IPSL has not yet gained the status of a minority language, and it is not used officially in schools for teaching purposes, although few deaf and hard of hearing children attend school and illiteracy among them is almost universal.

Japanese Sign Language (JSL): sign language developed in Japan after the foundation of the first school for the deaf in Kyoto in 1878. Its fundamentals were derived from the unique home signs used by deaf students at the school to communicate with each other. Such a spontaneous, local movement was reflected in the emergence of other regional systems. However, the dominance of **oralism** in education hampered the development of JSL until after World War II. JSL forms a language group with Korean Sign Language (KSL) and Taiwanese Sign Language (TSL), both of which developed from JSL when the two countries were Japanese colonies through the first half of the twentieth century. Users of the three signed languages today have up to 60–70 percent understandability with one another.

Korean Sign Language (KSL): because of Korea's colonial history, KSL is considered part of a family with **Japanese Sign Language**. Sign language predates the Japanese occupation (1910–1945) but was heavily influenced and its grammar reshaped by teachers from Japan who established deaf schools in Korea during the occupation. KSL has been legally recognized as an official language since 2016.

Lip reading: see **speechreading**.

Manualism: a method of education of deaf students using sign language within the classroom. See **oralism**.

Milan Congress (1880): the Second International Congress on Education of the Deaf (the Milan Conference) in 1880 passed resolutions that sought to prohibit the use of sign language in the education of deaf children in favor of the oral method and thus seemed to give international approval to the banning of sign language in classrooms. The resolution had a negative impact on education for the next hundred years.

Oral deaf: is generally used to describe individuals with a severe to profound hearing loss, with little or no residual hearing. Most use speech to communicate, using their residual hearing and hearing aids, communication devices or cochlear implants, and lip reading or speech reading. Some oral deaf people (also) use a signed language to communicate.

Oralism: the education of deaf students to communicate through the spoken language by using lip reading, speech, and mimicking the mouth shapes, facial expressions, body language, and breathing patterns of speech (Flaskerud, 317). See **manualism**.

Schema: schemas are generic knowledge structures, or patterns, which provide frameworks for understanding. They shape knowledge of things and concepts, both material and abstract. In particular, schemas shape knowledge of objects (e.g., chairs), situations (e.g., birthday parties), and cultural forms (museums, sports arenas).

Script: a script is a dynamic element within our experiential repertoire; it expresses how a sequence of events or actions is expected to unfold. One does not need to be given every event in the causal chain that constitutes a script to understand it. Rather, one infers the complete script from a core element and identifies unexpressed causal links between events.

Speech reading: a communication support in which an individual watches a speaker's lips, teeth, and tongue, along with many other cues, such as facial expressions, gestures, context, and body language. When used alone, the effectiveness of speech reading varies since more than half the movements involved in sound formation occur within the mouth and cannot be detected by the eye. 40 to 60 percent of English words are homophenes (i.e., words that look identical on a speaker's face) and there is not a single sound that has a distinct lip/jaw movement/position of its own.

The term speech reading has largely replaced the term lip reading because estimates are that only 25 to 35 percent of spoken English is visible on the lips under ideal circumstances; thus, most people do not focus only on the lips of the speaker. Instead, they also gain meaning through observing facial expressions and body language and use other communication strategies for understanding the spoken message.

Spoken Language Habilitation: refers to the process(es) whereby a child who is deaf or hard of hearing develops skills related to listening, speech, and spoken language. Professionals who provide spoken language habilitation are expected to possess cross-disciplinary skills in audiology, speech-language pathology, and education of children who are deaf. The process requires a team approach that includes family members as well as audiologists, speech professionals, and teachers. How far or how quickly a child develops desired skills depends on each individual child.

Strong Deaf: a term used within Deaf Culture to refer to people who fully embody the values embraced and advocated by the Culture.

Supercrip: a trope or script that is often challenged, whether used with reference to actual life situations or textual representations in fiction, film, television, and other media. For a hearing audience this script pivots on the assumption that a person lacking sensory ability in one area may overcome it by effort or compensate for the lack by developing unusual capacity in other areas (physical or mental), which leads to achievements that are often affirmed as heroic and/or inspiring. The supercrip functions as a narrative strategy that supports upbeat or triumphant closure in fictions and celebrates a protagonist's actualized potential. On the other hand, disability scholars argue that it fails to portray the diversity and complexity of individual character traits by positioning a simplistic representation of disability at a story's center.

Total Communication: a method of education that exposes deaf children to speech, speech reading, auditory training, fingerspelling, and sign language. Total Communication (TC) is a philosophy that includes various types of sign (e.g., ASL, Signing Exact English/S.E.E., and contact languages such as Pidgin Sign English or PSE), finger spelling, speechreading, speaking, and the use of amplification. Simultaneous communication (also referred to as SimCom or SC, and, more recently, manually coded English; MCE) is TC in which speaking and signing occur at the same time. SC can include contact language (e.g., Pidgin Sign English; PSE and Conceptually Accurate Signed English; CASE), grammatical forms of English (i.e., Morphemic Sign or MSS; Signing Exact English, S.E.E.) and ungrammatical ASL and English (e.g., Signed English, Sign Supported Speech, Sign Supported English). https://www.agbell.org/Families/Communication-Options

Bibliography

PRIMARY SOURCES

Baglio, Ben M., and Paul Howard (illustrator). *Doggy Dare*. New York: Scholastic, 2000.

Barry, Lynda. *One Hundred Demons*. Montreal, Canada: Drawn and Quarterly, 2002.

Beamer, Nona, and Caren Loebel-Fried (illustrator). *Naupaka*. Honolulu: Bishop Museum Press, 2008.

Bechdel, Alison. *Fun Home: A Family Tragicomic*. Boston: Houghton Mifflin, 2006.

Beese, Ava, Lilli and Nick, and Romina Marti (illustrator). *Proud to Be Deaf*. London: Wayland, 2017.

Bell, Cece. *El Deafo*. New York: Amulet Books, 2014.

Bling Bling Sounds (Banjjak Banjjak Deullineun). Directed by Park Yeong-Hun. Korea: Gomaun Media, 2018.

Bombicino, Jim, and Gildas Chatal. *The Elephant in the Room*. Scarborough, Queensland: Small Batch Books, 2015.

Booth, Barbara D., and Jim LaMarche (illustrator). *Mandy*. New York: Lothrop, 1991.

Bray, Libba. *Beauty Queens*. New York: Scholastic, 2012.

Brown, Teri. *Read My Lips*. New York: Simon Pulse, 2008.

Bullard, Douglas. *Islay*. Washington, D. C.: Gallaudet University Press, 2013 [1986].

Canadian Cultural Society of the Deaf (ed.) *The Smart Princess and Other Deaf Tales*. Toronto: Second Story Press, 2007.

Cheng Fen-fen (director). *Hear Me*. Taiwan, 2009.

Cheng Yi. *Huijia de lu (The Journey to Find the Way Home)*. Shijiazhuang, China: Hebei shaonian ertong chubanshe (Hebei publishing house for children), 1998.

Ching, Stuart. "Way Back to Pālolo." *Growing Up Local: An Anthology of Poetry and Prose from Hawaii*. Eds. Erick Chock et al. Honolulu: Bamboo Ridge Press, 1998.

Cowley, Joy. *The Silent One*. Ringwood, Vic.: Puffin Books, 1986.

de Campi, Alex, and Carla Speed McNeil. *No Mercy #14*. Berkeley, CA: Image Comics, 2017.

Dogani (Crucible, aka Silenced). Directed by Hwang Dong-Hyeok. Korea: Samgeori Pictures, 2011.

Ferris, Jean. *Of Sound Mind*. New York: Farrar, Straus and Giroux, 2001.

Gino, Alex. *You Don't Know Everything Jilly P!* New York: Scholastic, 2018.

Glove. Directed by Gang Wu-Seok. Korea: Cinema Service, 2011.

Hillsbery, Kief. *War Boy*. London: Picador, 2013.

Holt, John Dominis. "The Pool." *Passages to the Dream Shore: Short Stories of Contemporary Hawaii*. Ed. Frank Stewart. Honolulu: University of Hawai'i Press, 1987. 30–38.

Jingwu, Ning (director). *Silent River*. China, 2001.

John, Antony. *Five Flavors of Dumb*. New York: Speak, 2010.

Kelly, Erin Entrada. *Hello Universe*. New York: HarperCollins Children's Books, 2017.

Kerwin, James, and Marie Kerwin (illustrator). *My Friend is Deaf*. Book and DVD set. Kanoona, NSW: Bilby Publishing, 2015.

Kirkness, Jessica. "Our Place." *Meanjin Quarterly* 77.2 (2018): 164–69. https://meanjin.com.au/memoir/our-place/

Kluger, Steve. *My Most Excellent Year*. New York: Penguin Young Readers Group, 2009.

Koe no Katachi [A Silent Voice]. Directed by Yamada Naoko. Japan: Kyoto Animation, Shochiku, 2016.

Krasinski, John. *A Quiet Place*. Hollywood, CA: Paramount Pictures, 2018.

Lakin, Patricia, illustrated by Robert G. Steele. *Dad and Me in the Morning*. Morton Grove, IL: Albert Whitman, 1994/2019.

Like for Likes (*Joahaejwo*). Directed by Park Hyeon-Jin. Korea: Liyang Film and JK Film, 2016.

Lowell, Gloria Roth, and Karen Stormer Brooks (illustrator). *Elana's Ears, Or, How I Became the Best Big Sister in the World* (K. S. Brooks, illus.). Washington, DC: Magination Press, 2000.

Matlin, Marlee. *Deaf Child Crossing*. New York: Simon and Schuster, 2002.

Matsumoto, Lisa, and Michael Furuya (illustrator). *Beyond ʻŌhiʻa Valley: Adventures in a Hawaiian Rainforest*. Honolulu: Lehua, Inc., 1996.

Matsumoto, Lisa, and Michael Furuya (illustrator). *The Christmas Gift of Aloha*. Kaneohe, Hawaii: ʻŌhiʻa Productions, Inc., 2004.

Matsumoto, Lisa, and Michael Furuya (illustrator). *How the B-52 Cockroach Learned to Fly*. Honolulu: Lehua, Inc., 1995.

Maxfield, Z. A. *St. Nacho's*. Maxfield Publishing, 2008.

McElfresh, Lynn. *Strong Deaf*. South Hampton: namelos, 2012.

Memento Mori (*Yeogo goedam 2*). Directed by Kim Tae-Yong and Min Gyu-Dong. Korea: Cinema Service, 1999.

Millman, Isaac. *Moses Goes to a Concert*. New York: Square Fish, 1998.

Moran, Edna Cabcabin. *The Sleeping Giant: A Tale from Kauaʻi*. Eva Beach: BeachHouse, 2016.

Motley, Mary L., Timy Sullivan, and Jenny Campbell (Illustrator), *Deafinitely Awesome: The Story of Acorn*. Cleveland: DEAFinitely Awesome, 2019.

Murayama, Milton. *All I Asking For Is My Body*. Honolulu: University of Hawai'i Press, 1988.

Napolean, Kawika. *ʻAiʻai: A Bilingual Hawaiian Story*. Honolulu: Kamehameha Publishing, 2010.

Napoli, Donna Jo, and Amy Bates. *Hands and Hearts: With 15 Words in American Sign Language*. New York: Harry N. Abrams, 2014.

Nelson, Jennifer L., and Kristen C. Harmon (eds.). *Deaf American Prose, 1830–1930*. Washington, DC: Gallaudet University Press, 2013.

Ness, Patrick. *Release*. London: Walker Books, 2017.

No Ordinary Hero: The SuperDeafy Movie. Directed by Troy Kotsur. Douglas Matejki and Hilari Scarl, 2013.

Oima, Yoshitoki. *A Silent Voice* (manga, seven volumes [2013]). New York: Kodansha Comics, 2015.

On, Tsui Yue (Producer) *Speech of Silence*. TV drama series, 20 episodes (Hong Kong, 2008).

Palacio, R. J. *Wonder*. New York: Knopf, 2012.

Plourde, Lynn. *Maxi's Secrets:(or What You Can Learn from a Dog)*. New York: Nancy Paulsen Books, 2016.

River of Hands: Deaf Heritage Stories. Toronto: Second Story Press, 2000.

Rorby, Ginny. *Hurt Go Happy*. New York: Tom Doherty, 2006.

Rorby, Ginny. *Sukari min vän*. Stockholm: Bonnier Carlsen, 2007.

Rosen, Roz. *Deaf Culture Fairy Tales*. Frederick, MD: Savory Words Publishing, 2017.

Satrapi, Marjane. *Persepolis: The Story of a Childhood*. New York: Pantheon Books, 2003.

Schachter, Esty. *Waiting for a Sign*. Ithaca, NY: Lewis Court Press, 2014.

Seeger, Pete, Paul DuBois Jacobs, and R. Gregory Christie. *The Deaf Musicians*. New York: G. P. Putnam's Sons, 2006.

Ségur, Sophie de. *Les malheurs de Sophie* [1858]. Paris: Hachette, 2004.

Ségur, Sophie de. *Les petites filles modèles* [1863]. Paris: Hachette BnF, 2012.

Ségur, Sophie de. *Les Vacances* [1884]. Paris: Hachette BnF, 2012.

Ségur, Sophie de. *Un bon petit diable* [1866]. Paris: Hachette BnF, 2013.

Selznick, Brian. *Wonderstruck*. New York: Scholastic, 2011.

Shenton, Rachel. *The Silent Child*. 2017. https://www.youtube.com/watch?v=YkIbPTV1NIE

Sloan, Brian. *A Really Nice Prom Mess*. New York: Simon and Schuster, 2005.

Smith, Andrew. *Stick*. New York: Feiwel and Friends, 2011.

Stryer, Andrea Stenn. *Kami and the Yaks*. Palo Alto: Bay Otter Press, 2007.

Takayama, Sandi, and Pat Hall (illustrator). *The Musubi Man: Hawai'i's Gingerbread Man*. Honolulu: Bess Press, 1996.

Takayama, Sandi, and Pat Hall (illustrator). *The Musubi Man's New Friend*. Honolulu: Bess Press, 2002.

Takayama, Sandi, and Esther Szegedy (illustrator). *The Prince and the Li Hing Mui*. Honolulu: Bess Press, 1998.

Takayama, Sandi, and and Esther Szegedy (illustrator). *Sumorella: A Hawaii Cinderella Story*. Honolulu: Bess Press, 1997.

Tan, Shaun. *The Arrival*. Melbourne, Australia: Levine Books, 1996.

Telgemeier, Raina. *Smile*. New York: Graphix, 2010.

Tildes, Phyllis Limbacher. *The Garden Wall*. Watertown, MA: Charlesbridge, 2006.

Uhlberg, Myron, and Colin Bootman. *Dad, Jackie, and Me*. Atlanta, GA: Peachtree, 2005.

Uhlberg, Myron, and Henri Sørensen (Illustrator) *The Printer*. Atlanta, GA: Peachtree, 2003.

Uhlberg, Myron, and Ted Papoulas (Illustrator). *The Sound of All Things*. Atlanta, GA: Peachtree, 2016.

Woodson, Jacqueline. *Feathers*. New York: G. P. Putnam's Sons, 2007.

Yamanaka, Lois-Ann. *Saturday Night at the Pahala Theatre*. Honolulu: Bamboo Ridge Press. 1993. 132–40.

Yolen, Jane. *The Mermaid's Three Wisdoms*. New York: Collins World, 1978.

Zhang Xini. *Jiaru woshi Hailun (If I Were Helen)*. Beijing: *Remin wenxuechubanshe* (People's literature publishing house), 2005.

Zhou, Sun (Director). *Breaking the Silence* (China, 2000).

SECONDARY SOURCES

"About Us." *National Association of the Deaf.* https://www.nad.org/about-us/. Accessed on January 15, 2018.

Agosto, Denise E., Sandra Hughes-Hassell, and Catherine Gilmore-Clough. "The All-White World of Middle-School Genre Fiction: Surveying the Field for Multicultural Protagonists." *Children's Literature in Education* 34.4 (2003): 257–75.

Alasuutari, Pertti, Leonard Bickman and Julia Brannen (eds.) *The SAGE Handbook of Social Research Methods.* California: Sage, 2008.

"Alden Charles Ravn." *ObitTree*, September 2009. https://obittree.com/obituary/us/illinois/jacksonville/williamson-funeral-home/alden-ravn/1722499/. Accessed on January 16, 2018.

"American Sign Language." Alexander Graham Bell Association for the Deaf and Hard of Hearing. 2008. https://www.agbell.org/Advocacy/American-Sign-Language. Accessed on 4 January 2019.

Andrews, Kristin. *The Animal Mind: An Introduction to the Philosophy of Animal Cognition.* New York: Routledge, 2015.

Australian Medical Association (AMA) (2017). *Report Card on Indigenous Health: A National Strategic Approach to Ending Chronic Otitis Media and Its Lifelong Impacts in Indigenous communities.* Canberra, ACT. https://ama.com.au/article/2017-ama-report-card-indigenous-health-national-strategic-approach-ending-chronic-otitis (Accessed 19 March 2021).

Bailes, Cynthia Neese. "*Mandy*: A Critical Look at the Portrayal of a Deaf Character in Children's Literature." *Multicultural Perspectives* 4.4 (2002): 3–9.

Bailes, Cynthia Neese. *A Review of Deaf Characters in Children's Picture Books.* Unpublished manuscript, 1995.

Baker, Charlotte, and Robbin Battison, eds. *Sign Language and the Deaf Community: Essays in Honor of William C. Stokoe.* Silver Spring, MD: National Association of the Deaf, 1980.

Baker-Gibbs, Ariel, and Deirdre F. Baker. "Sign in Print." *Horn Book Magazine* 89.5, September/October (2013): 28–34.

Ballin, Albert. *The Deaf Mute Howls.* Washington, DC: Gallaudet University Press, 1998.

Banks, James A., and Cherry A. McGee Banks. *Multicultural education: Issues and perspectives* (7th edition). Danvers, MA: Wiley, 2010.

Banks, James A., and Cherry A. McGee Banks, eds. *Handbook of Research on Multicultural Education.* San Francisco: Jossey-Bass, 2001.

Bauman, H-Dirksen L. "Audism: Exploring the Metaphysics of Oppression." *Journal of Deaf Studies and Deaf Education* 9:2 (2004): 239–45.

Bauman, H-Dirksen L. "Listening to Phonocentrism with Deaf Eyes: Derrida's Mute Philosophy of (Sign) Language." *Essays in Philosophy* 9.1 (2008): Article 2.

Bauman, H-Dirksen L. "Postscript: Gallaudet Protests of 2006 and the Myths of In/Exclusion." *Sign Language Studies* 10.1 (2009): 90–104.

Bauman, H-Dirksen L., and Joseph Murray. "Deaf Studies in the 21st Century: 'Deaf Gain' and the Future of Human Diversity." In Lennard J. Davis (ed.), *The Disability Studies Reader* 4th ed. New York: Routledge, 2013, 246–60.

Baynton, Douglas. "Deafness." *Keywords for Disability Studies.* Eds. Rachel Adams, Benjamin Reiss, and Davide Serlin. New York: NYU Press, 2015, 48–51.

Baynton, Douglas C. "Beyond Culture, Deaf Studies and the Deaf Body." *Open Your Eyes: Deaf Studies Talking.* Eds. H. Dirksen and L. Bauman. Minneapolis: University of Minnesota Press, 2008, 293–313.

Baynton, Douglas C. *Forbidden Signs: American Culture and the Campaign against Sign Language.* Chicago and London: University of Chicago Press, 1996.

Bell Cece. "Cece Bell: I Wanted to Show What It Felt Like to Be the Only Deaf Kid at My School." *The Guardian*, 27 April 2015. https://www.theguardian.com/childrens-books -site/2015/apr/27/cece-bell-el-deafo-newbery-medal-deafness-childrens-books. Accessed on 20 Jan. 2016.

Bélanger, Adolphe. *Le Sourd-muet devant la loi française, ses droits, ses devoirs: le sourd-muet et le Code civil, le sourd-muet et le Code d'instruction criminelle.* Paris: Atelier typographique de l'Institut National des Sourds-muets, 1906. [http://gallica.bnf.fr/ark:/12148/ bpt6k61484131/f9.image.r=sourd.langFR]

Bérubé, Michael. "Foreword: Another Word Is Possible." *Crip Theory: Cultural Signs of Queerness and Disability.* Robert McRuer. New York: NYU Press, 2006.

Bi, Lijun. "China's Patriotic Exposé: Ye Shengtao's Fairytale—Daocao ren [Scarecrow]." *Bookbird: A Journal of International Children's Literature* 51.2 (2013): 32–38.

Bi, Lijun. "Politics and Ethics in Chinese Texts for the Young: the Confucian Tradition." *The Routledge Companion to International Children's Literature.* Eds. John Stephens, Celia Abicalil Belmiro, Alice Curry, Li Lifang, and Yasmine S. Motawy. London and New York: Routledge, 2017: 39–48.

Bienvenu, M. J. "Can Deaf People Survive 'Deafness'?" In Lois Bragg (ed.), *Deaf World: A Historical Reader and Primary Source Book.* New York: NYU Press, 2001, 318–24.

Blaska, Joan K. "Children's Literature That Includes Characters with Disabilities or Illnesses." *Disability Studies Quarterly* 24.1 (2004): 1–4.

Bond, Chelsea, Murray G. Phillips, and Gary Osmond. "Crossing Lines: Sport History, Transformative Narratives, and Aboriginal Australia." *The International Journal of the History of Sport*, 32.13 (2015): 1531–45.

Bragg, Lois. *Deaf World: A Historical Reader and Primary Source Book.* New York: NYU Press, 2001.

Brenner, Robin. "Comics and Graphic Novels." In Shelby A. Wolf, Karen Coats, Patricia Enciso, and Christine A. Jenkins (eds.), *Handbook of Research on Children's and Young Adult Literature.* New York: Routledge, 2011, 256–67.

Bright, Susie. "Introduction." In Diane Noomin (ed) *Twisted Sisters 2: Drawing the Line.* Northampton, MA: Kitchen Sink Press, 1995.

Brill, Richard G. *International Congresses on Education of the Deaf—An Analytical History, 1878–1980*, Washington, DC: Gallaudet College Press, 1984.

Brittain, Isabel. "An Examination into the Portrayal of Deaf Characters and Deaf Issues in Picture Books for Children." *Disability Studies Quarterly* 24.1 (2004).

Brookover, Sophie, Elizabeth Burns, and Kelly Jensen. "What's New About New Adult?" *Horn Book Magazine* 90.1 (2014): 41–44.

Brown, Lerita Coleman. "Stigma: An Enigma Demystified." *The Disability Studies Reader* [1997]. Ed. Lennard J. Davis. London and New York: Routledge, 2013, 147–60.

Brueggemann, Brenda Jo. *Deaf Subjects: Between Identities and Places.* New York: NYU Press, 2009.

Brueggemann, Brenda Jo. "Delivering Disability, Willing Speech." In Carrie Sandahl and Philip Auslander (eds.), *Bodies in Commotion: Disability and Performance.* Ann Arbor: University of Michigan Press, 2005, 17–29.

Brueggemann, Brenda Jo. *Lend Me Your Ear: Rhetorical Constructions of Deafness.* Washington, DC: Gallaudet University Press, 1999.

Brueggemann, Brenda Jo. "Think-Between: A Deaf Studies Commonplace Book." *Signs and Voices: Deaf Culture, Identity, Language, and Arts*. Eds. Kristin A. Lindgren, Doreen DeLuca, and Donna Jo Napoli. Washington: Gallaudet University Press, 2008, 30–42.

Brueggemann, Brenda Jo. "Writing Insight: Deafness and Autobiography." *American Quarterly* 52:2 (2000): 316–21.

Buisson, Gerald J. "Using Online Glossing Lessons for Accelerated Instruction in ASL for Preservice Deaf Education Majors." *American Annals of the Deaf* 152.3 (2007): 331–43.

Burch, Susan. *Signs of Resistance: American Deaf Cultural History, 1900 to World War II*. New York: NYU Press, 2002.

Burns, Jane, and Neil Thomson. "Review of Ear Health and Hearing among Indigenous Australians." *Australian Indigenous Health Bulletin* 13.4 (2013): 1–22.

Campbell, Fiona Kumari. *Contours of Ableism: The Production of Disability and Abledness*. London: Palgrave Macmillan, 2009.

Cart, Michael. *Young Adult Literature: From Romance to Realism*, 3rd ed. Chicago: Neal-Schuman, 2016.

Cart, Michael. "Young Adult Literature: The State of a Restless Art." *SLIS Connecting* 5.1 (2016). https://doi.org/10.18785/slis.0501.07

Carter, James Bucky, ed. *Building Literacy Connections with Graphic Novels*. Urbana, IL: National Council of Teachers of English, 2007.

CCTV. "Dying Hawaiian Language Preserved by Remaining Few." *Americas Now*. YouTube. 2 September 2013. https://www.youtube.com/watch?v=gyVnDh7BQhU. Accessed on 8 February 2018.

Chapman, Madeleine. "Representation and Resistance: A Qualitative Study of Narratives of Deaf Cultural Identity." *Culture and Psychology* 27.3 (2021): 374–91.

Chen, Ge. "Influential Factors of Deaf Identity Development." *Electronic Journal for Inclusive Education* 3.2 (2014): 1–12.

Ching, Stuart. "Multicultural Children's Literature as an Instrument of Power." *Language Arts* 83.2 (2005): 128–36.

Ching, Stuart, and Jann Pataray-Ching. "The Centrality of Hawaiian Mythology in Three Genres of Hawai'i Folk Literature for Children." *Routledge Companion to International Children's Literature*. Ed. John Stephens et al. London and New York: Routledge, 2018. 289–98.

Christiansen, John B. and Irene W. Leigh. "Children With Cochlear Implants: Changing Parent and Deaf Community Perspectives." *Archives of Otolaryngology—Head & Neck Surgery* 130.5 (2004): 673–77.

Chute, Hillary. "Comics as Literature? Reading Graphic Narrative." *PMLA* 123.2 (2008): 452–65.

Chute, Hillary. "Comics Form and Narrating Lives." *Profession* 2011 (2011): 107–17.

Chute, Hillary L. *Graphic Women: Life Narrative and Contemporary Comics*. New York: Columbia University Press, 2010.

Ciocia, Stefania. "Postmodern Investigations: The Case of Christopher Boone in *The Curious Incident of the Dog in the Night-time*." *Children's Literature in Education* 40.4 (2009): 320–32.

Clark, John Lee. "The Vibrating Mouth." In *Tripping the Tale Fantastic*, ed. Christopher Jon Heuer. Handtype Press, 2017.

Coats, Karen. *The Bloomsbury Introduction to Children's and Young Adult Literature*. New York: Bloomsbury, 2017.

Council on Interracial Books for Children. "10 Quick Ways to Analyze Children's Books for Racism and Sexism." *Rethinking our Classrooms: Teaching for Equity and Justice* (Special Edition). Milwaukee, WI: Rethinking Schools, Ltd, 1994.

Couser, Thomas G. "The Empire of the 'Normal': A Forum on Disability and Self-Representation." *American Quarterly* 52.2 (2000): 305–10.

Couser, Thomas G. *Recovering Bodies: Illness, Disability and Life Writing.* Wisconsin: University of Wisconsin Press, 1997.

Couser, Thomas G. *Signifying Bodies: Disability in Contemporary Life Writing.* University of Michigan Press, 2009.

Crocker, Jennifer, and Brenda Major. "Social Stigma and Self-Esteem: The Self-Protective Properties of Stigma." *Psychological Review* 96.4 (1989): 608–30.

Curtis, James. "'Let's Go Exploring!' Illustrating Childhood Development in Calvin and Hobbes." In Michelle Ann Abate and Joe Sutcliff Sanders (eds.), *Good Grief! Children and Comics: A Collection of Companion Essays.* Columbus, Ohio: Billy Ireland Cartoon Library and Museum, 2016, 29–46.

Dadlez, E[va] M. "Truly Funny: Humor, Irony, and Satire as Moral Criticism." *Journal of Aesthetic Education* 45.1 (2011): 1–17.

Dallacqua, Ashley K., Sara Kersten, and Mindi Rhoades. "Using Shaun Tan's Work to Foster Multiliteracies in 21st-Century Classrooms." *Reading Teacher*, 69.2 (2015): 207–17.

Dallacqua, Ashley K. "Exploring Literary Devices in Graphic Novels." *Language Arts* 89.6 (2012): 365–78.

Da Pidgin Coup. "Pidgin and Education." 1999. The Charlene Junko Sato Center for Pidgin, Creole, and Dialect Studies. www.hawaii.edu/satocenter/?page_id=195. Accessed on 3 March 2018.

Darke, Paul. "No Life Away: Pathologizing Disability on Film." *The Problem Body: Projecting Disability on Film.* Eds. Sally Chivers and Nicole Markotić. Columbus: Ohio State University Press, 2010: 97–107.

Dauncey, Sarah. "Breaking the Silence? Deafness, Education and Identity in Two Post-Cultural Revolution Chinese Films." *Different Bodies: Essays on Disabilities in Film and Television.* Ed. Marja Evelyn Mogk. Jefferson and London: McFarland, 2013: 75–88.

Davis, Lennard J. "Crips Strike Back: The Rise of Disability Studies." *American Literary History* 11.3 (1999): 500–512.

Davis, Lennard J. "Deafness and Insight: The Deafened Moment as a Critical Modality." *College English* 57.8 (1995): 881–900.

Davis, Lennard J. *Disability Studies Reader.* New York: Routledge, 2013.

Davis, Lennard J. *Enforcing Normalcy: Disability, Deafness, and the Body.* London: Verso. 1995.

Davis, Lennard J. "Introduction: Normality, Power, and Culture." *The Disability Studies Reader* (4th edition). Ed. Lennard Davis. New York: Routledge, 2013: 1–14.

"Deaf People + World War II." RIT: National Technical Institute for the Deaf. https://www.rit.edu/ntid/ccs/deafww2/. Accessed on January 15, 2018.

Deng, Meng, and Genevieve Manset. "Analysis of the 'Learning in Regular Classroom' Movement in China." *Mental Retardation* 38.2 (2000): 124–30.

Deng, Meng, and Kimberly Harris. "Meeting the Needs of Students with Disabilities in General Education Classrooms in China." *Teacher Education and Special Education* 31.3 (2008): 195–207.

Dowker, Ann. "The Treatment of Disability in 19th and Early 20th Century Children's Literature." *Disability Studies Quarterly* 24. 1 (2004): 1–7.

Duggan, Jennifer. "Traumatic Origins: Orphanhood and the Superhero." In Michelle Ann Abate and Joe Sutcliff Sanders (eds.), *Good Grief! Children and Comics: A Collection of Companion Essays*. Columbus, Ohio: Billy Ireland Cartoon Library and Museum, 2016, 47–67.

Durell, Shirley "How the Social Model of Disability Evolved." *The Nursing Times* 110. 50 (2014): 20–22.

Dyches, Tina T., Mary Anne Prater, and Jennifer Jenson. "Portrayal of Disabilities in Caldecott Books." *TEACHING Exceptional Children Plus* 2.5 (2006). http://escholar ship.bc.edu/education/tecplus/ v012/iss5/art2.

Eastland, Katharine. "Deaf Meets Wonderstruck." *Humanities* 33.1 (2012).

Ehn, Billy, and Orvar Löfgren. *Kulturanalys*. Stockholm: Liber Förlag, 1982.

Elias, Norbert, and Stephen Mennell. *On the Process of Civilisation: Sociogenetic and Psychogenetic Investigations*. Dublin: University College Dublin Press, 2012.

Encrevé, Florence. "La 'famille' des sourds-muets face à l'idée de progrès au XIXe Siècle." *Revue d'histoire du XIXe siècle* 1 (2013): 145–61.

Erlich, Shoshana. "Spotlight on Deaf and Hard-of-Hearing Youth in Canada and Beyond." *Child and Youth Services* 33.1 (2012): 5–11.

Esmail, Jennifer. *Reading Victorian Deafness: Signs and Sounds in Victorian Literature and Culture*. Athens: Ohio University Press, 2013.

Eyler, Joshua R. "Disability and Prosthesis in L. Frank Baum's *The Wonderful Wizard of Oz*." *Children's Literature Association Quarterly* 38.3 (2013): 319–34.

Fairclough, Norman. *Language and Power*. New York: Longman, 1989.

Fang, Xiangshu, and Lijun Bi. "Confucianism." *Handbook of Research on Development and Religion*. Ed. Matthew Clarke. Cheltenham UK: Edward Elgar, 2013: 124–37.

Farber, Jerry. "Toward a Theoretical Framework for the Study of Humor in Literature and the Other Arts." *Journal of Aesthetic Education* 41. 4 (2007): 67–86.

Fletcher-Carter, R., and Doris Paez. "Exploring Students' Personal Cultures." In Kathee Mangan Christensen and Gilbert L. Delgado (eds.), *Deaf Plus: A Multicultural Perspective*. San Diego: Dawn Sign Press, 2000, 221–51.

Fludernik, Monika. *Towards a 'Natural' Narratology*. London: Routledge, 1996.

Foss, Katherine A. "Constructing Hearing Loss or 'Deaf Gain'? Voice, Agency, and Identity in Television's Representations of d/Deafness." *Critical Studies in Media Communication* 31.5 (2014a): 426–47.

Foss, Katherine A. "(De)stigmatizing the Silent Epidemic: Representations of Hearing Loss in Entertainment Television." *Health Communication* 29.9 (2014b): 888–900.

Foucault, Michel. *Surveiller et punir*. Paris: Gallimard, 1975.

Fouts, Roger. "My Best Friend is a Chimp." *Psychology Today* July/August (2000): 69–73.

Fouts, Roger. *Next of Kin: My Conversations with Chimpanzees*. New York: William Morrow, 1998.

Fouts, Roger S., Bill Chown, and Larry Goodin. "Transfer of Signed Responses in American Sign Language from Vocal English Stimuli to Physical Object Stimuli by a Chimpanzee (Pan)." *Learning and Motivation* 7.3 (1976): 458–75.

Fox, Dana L., and Kathy G. Short. "Complexity of Cultural Authenticity in Children's Literature: Why the Debates Really Matter." In Dana L. Fox and Kathy G. Short (eds.), *Stories Matter: The Complexity of Cultural Authenticity in Children's Literature*. Urbana, IL: National Council of Teachers of English, 2003, 3–24.

Fox, Margalit. *Talking Hands: What Sign Language Reveals about the Mind*. London: Simon and Schuster, 2007.

Frank, Arthur. "Why Study People's Stories? The Dialogical Ethics of Narrative Analysis."
    International Journal of Qualitative Methods 1:1 (2002): 109–17.
Freißmann, Stephan. "A Tale of Autistic Experience: Knowing, Living, Telling in Mark
    Haddon's *The Curious Incident of the Dog in the Night-Time.*" *Partial Answers: Journal of
    Literature and the History of Ideas* 6.2 (2008): 395–417.
Friedman, Chandler, and Greg Botelho. "Researchers Document Distinctive Hawaii Sign
    Language." *CNN*, 2 March 2013, pp. 1–4. Web. http://www.cnn.com/2013/03/02/us/hawaii
    -sign-language. Accessed on January 9, 2018.
Fujikane, Candace, and Jonathan Y. Okamura, eds. *Asian Settler Colonialism: From Local
    Governance to the Habits of Everyday Life in Hawaii.* Honolulu: University of Hawaii
    Press, 2008.
Gannon, Jack R. *Deaf heritage: A Narrative History of Deaf America.* Washington, DC:
    Gallaudet University Press, 2011.
Gardner, Jared. *Projections: Comics and the History of Twenty-First Century Storytelling.*
    Stanford, CA: Stanford University Press, 2012.
Gardner, Jared. "Storylines." *SubStance* 124.1 (2011): 53–69.
Gardner, R. Allen, and Beatrice T. Gardner. "Early Signs of Language in Child and Chimpan-
    zee." *Science* 187.4178 (1975): 752–53.
Gardner, R. Allen, and Beatrice T. Gardner. "Teaching Sign Language to a Chimpanzee."
    Science 165.3894 (1969): 664–72.
Garey, Diane, and Lawrence R. Hott. *Through Deaf Eyes.* 2007. https://www.youtube.com/
    watch?v=tJeAG8tZyf4 Accessed: June 8, 2016.
Garland-Thomson, Rosemarie. "Disability and Representation" *PMLA* 20.2 (2005): 522–27.
Garland-Thomson, Rosemarie. *Extraordinary Bodies: Figuring Physical Disability in Ameri-
    can Culture and Literature.* New York: Columbia University Press, 1997.
Garland-Thompson, Rosemarie. "The Politics of Staring: Visual Rhetorics of Disability in
    Popular Photography." *Disability Studies: Enabling the Humanities.* Eds. Sharon L. Snyder,
    Brenda Jo Brueggemann, and Rosemarie Garland Thomson. Modern Language Associa-
    tion, 2002, 56–75.
Garfield, Jay L., Candida C. Peterson, and Tricia Perry. "Social Cognition, Language Acquisi-
    tion and the Development of the Theory of Mind." *Mind & Language* 16 (2001): 494–541.
Gilbert, Ruth. "Watching the Detectives: Mark Haddon's *The Curious Incident of the Dog in
    the Night-Time* and Kevin Brooks' *Martin Pig.*" *Children's Literature in Education* 36.3
    (2005): 241–53.
Giroux, Henry A. "Rewriting the Discourse of Racial Identity: Towards a Pedagogy and
    Politics of Whiteness." *Harvard Educational Review* 67.2 (1997), 285–320.
Glickman, Neil Stephen. "Deaf Identity Development: Construction and Validation of a
    Theoretical Model." Dissertation. University of Massachusetts Amherst, 1993. http://
    scholarworks.umass.edu/dissertations_1/1201. Accessed on 5 November 2018.
Golos, Debbie, and Annie Moses. "Representations of Deaf Characters in Children's Picture
    Books." *American Annals of the Deaf* 165:3 (2011): 270–82.
Golos, Debbie B., Annie M. Moses, and Kimberly A. Wolbers. "Culture or Disability? Examining
    Deaf Characters in Children's Book Illustrations." *Early Childhood Education Journal* 40.4
    (2012): 239–49.
Goodall, Jane. *Through a Window: My Thirty Years with the Chimpanzees of Gombe.* Boston/
    New York: Mariner Books, 2010.
Goodenough, Elizabeth. *Secret Spaces of Childhood.* Ann Arbor: University of Michigan
    Press, 2003.

Gopalakrishnan, Ambika. *Multicultural Children's Literature: A Critical Issues Approach* (1st edition). Thousand Oaks, CA: SAGE Publications, 2010.

Greenwald, Brian H., and Fred S. Weiner. "Deaf President Now." https://www.gallaudet.edu/about/history-and-traditions/deaf-president-now/dpn-25th-anniversary.

Greenwald, Brian H., and John Vickrey Van Cleve. "'A Deaf Variety of The Human Race': Historical Memory, Alexander Graham Bell, and Eugenics." *Journal of the Gilded Age and Progressive Era* 14.1 (2015): 28–48.

Gregory, Susan. "The Language and Culture of Deaf People: Implications for Education." *Language and Education* 6.2–4 (1992): 183–97.

Gregory, Susan, Pamela Knight, Wendy McCracken, Stephen Powers, and Linda Watson (eds.) *Issues in Deaf Education*. Abingdon, Oxon: David Fulton, 1998.

Grieder, Jerome. *Intellectuals and the State in Modern China, A Narrative History*. New York: Free Press, 1981.

Grigely, Joseph. "Blindness and Deafness as Metaphors: An Anthological Essay." *Journal of Visual Culture* 5.2 (2006): 227–41.

Groensteen, Thierry. *Comics and Narration*. Translated by Ann Miller. Jackson: University Press of Mississippi, 2013.

Groensteen, Thierry. *The System of Comics*. Translated by Bart Beaty and Nick Nguyen. Jackson: University Press of Mississippi, 2007.

Gutierrez, Ben. "Local Deaf Community Learns about Newly-Discovered Language." *Hawaii News Now*, March 2013. http://www.hawaiinewsnow.com/story/22037075/local-deaf-community-learns-about-newly-discovered-language. Accessed on 9 January 2018.

Guizot, François. *Histoire de la civilisation en Europe* [1856]. Paris: Didier, 1870. (http://gallica.bnf.fr/ark:/12148/bpt6k432075c.r=guizot+histoire.langFR)

Hall, Alice. *Literature and Disability*. Abingdon: Routledge, 2015.

Haller, Beth, and Sue Ralph. "John Callahan's Pelswick Cartoon and a New Phase of Disability Humor." *Disability Studies Quarterly* 23. 3/4 (2003): 1–16.

Happé, Francesca G. E. "The Role of Age and Verbal Ability in the Theory of Mind Task Performance of Subjects with Autism." *Child Development* 66.3 (1995): 843–55.

Hastrup, Kirsten. "Writing Ethnography: The State of the Art." *Anthropology and Autobiography*. Eds. Judith Okely and Helen Calloway. London: Routledge, 1992.

Hartwell, Stephanie W., and Paul R. Benson. "Social Integration: A Conceptual Overview and Two Case Studies." *Mental Health, Social Mirror*. Eds. William R. Avison, Jane D. McLeod, and Bernice A. Pescosolido. London: Springer, 2007, 329–54.

Hayes, Michael T., and Rhonda S. Black. "Troubling Signs: Disability, Hollywood Movies and the Construction of a Discourse of Pity." *Disability Studies Quarterly* 23.2 (2003): 114–32.

Hazama, Dorothy Ochiai, and Jane Okamoto Komeiji. *Okage Sama De: The Japanese in Hawaii 1885–1985*. Honolulu: Bess Press, 1986.

Healy, Catherine. "Living on the Edge: Parallels between the Deaf and Gay Communities in the United States." https://www.swarthmore.edu/sites/default/files/assets/documents/linguistics/2007_healy_catherine.pdf. Accessed on 20 November 2018.

Herman, David. "Cognitive Narratology" http://wikis.sub.uni-hamburg.de/lhn/index.php/Cognitive_Narratology. Last modified: 13 March 2013. Accessed 25 August 2018.

Herman, David. "Cognitive Narratology." *Handbook of Narratology*. Eds. Peter Hühn, John Pier, Wolf Schmid, and Jörg Schönert. Berlin: de Gruyter, 2009.

Herman, David. *Story Logic: Problems and Possibilities of Narrative*. Lincoln: University of Nebraska Press, 2002.

Heuscher, Julius E. "The Role of Humor and Folklore Themes in Psychotherapy." *American Journal of Psychology* 137.12 (1980): 1546–49.

Hickey, Leo. "Introduction." In Leo Hickey (Ed.), *The Pragmatics of Translation*. Clevedon: Multilingual Matters, 1998: 1–9.

Hindhede, Anette Lykke. "Negotiating Hearing Disability and Hearing Disabled Identities." *Health: An Interdisciplinary Journal for the Social Study of Health, Illness & Medicine* 16.2 (2012): 169–85.

Holcomb, Thomas K. "Deaf Epistemology: The Deaf Way of Knowing." *American Annals of the Deaf* 154.5 (2010): 471–78.

Holcomb, Thomas. *Introduction to American Deaf Culture*. New York: Oxford University Press, 2013.

Hollos, Marida, and Philip A. Cowan. "Social Isolation and Cognitive Development: Logical Operations and Role-taking Abilities in Three Norwegian Social Settings." *Child Development* 44.3 (1973): 630–41.

Hopper, Rosemary. "What Are Teenagers Reading? Adolescent Fiction Reading Habits and Reading Choices." *Literacy* 39.3 (2005): 113–20.

Horstkotte, Silke, and Nancy Pedri. "Focalization in Graphic Narrative." *Narrative* 19.3 (2011): 330–57.

Humphries, Tom L. "Of Deaf-Mutes, the Strange, and the Modern Deaf Self." In Lois Bragg (ed.), *Deaf World: A Historical Reader and Primary Source Book*. New York: NYU Press, 2001, 348–64.

Itakura, Shoji. "A Chimpanzee with the Ability to Learn the Use of Personal Pronouns." *Psychological Record* 42.2 (1992): 157–73.

Johnston, Trevor. "W(h)ither the Deaf Community? Population, Genetics, and the Future of Australian Sign Language." *American Annals of the Deaf* 148 (2004): 358–75.

Kaland, Mary, and Kate Salvatore. "The Psychology of Hearing Loss." *ASHA Leader* 7.5 (2002): 4–5, 14–15.

Kato, Masae. "Cultural Notions of Disability in Japan: Their Influence on Prenatal Testing." M. Sleeboom-Faulkner (ed.) *Frameworks of Choice: Predictive and Genetic Testing in Asia*. Amsterdam: University of Amsterdam Press, 2010, 125–44.

Katz-Wise, Sabra L., Margaret Rosario, and Michael Tsappis. "Lesbian, Gay, Bisexual, and Transgender Youth and Family Acceptance." *Pediatric Clinics of North America* 63.6 (2016): 1011–25.

Kawamoto, Kevin. "Hegemony and Language Politics in Hawaii." *World Englishes* 12.2 (1993): 193–207.

Keen, Suzanne. "Fast Tracks to Narrative Empathy: Anthropomorphism and Dehumanization in Graphic Narratives." *SubStance* 40. 1 (2011): 135–55.

Keen, Suzanne. "A Theory of Narrative Empathy." *Narrative* 14. 3 (2006): 207–36.

Kennon, Patricia (2016). "Childhood, Power, and Travel in Salvatore Rubbino's Picture Books: A Walk in the City." *Jeunesse: Young People, Texts, Cultures* 8.1 (2016): 20–41.

Kerr, Euan. "Author Brian Selznick Takes a Unique Approach to *Wonderstruck*." 2011. https://www.mprnews.org/story/2011/10/17/selznick-wonderstruck

Kiley-Worthington, Marthe. "The Mental Homologies of Mammals. Towards an Understanding of Another Mammal's World View." *Animals* 7.12 (2017): 1–22.

Kincheloe, Pamela, J. "*A Quiet Place* Falls into A Tired Trope About Deafness." 2018. https://www.huffpost.com/entry/opinion-kincheloe-quiet-place-deaf-people_n_5ad10645e4boedca2cb9acc6

KITV. "UH Researchers Discover Hawaii Sign Language." 1 March 2013. https://www.you tube.com/watch?v=1w-WSET6HM. Accessed on 1 February 2018.

Kivel, Beth D. and D. Kleiber. "Leisure in the Identity Formation of Lesbian/Gay Youth:Personal, but Not Social." *Leisure Sciences* 22.4 (2000): 215232

Krentz, Christopher. *Writing Deafness: The Hearing Line in Nineteenth-Century American Literature*, Chapel Hill: University of North Carolina Press, 2007.

Kritzer, Jeffrey B. "Special Education in China." *Eastern Education Journal* 40.1 (2011): 57–63.

Kunze, Peter C. "What We Talk about When We Talk about Helen Keller: Disabilities in Children's Biographies." *Children's Literature Association Quarterly* 38.3 (2013): 304–18.

Kusters, Annelies, Maartje De Meulder, and Dai O'Brien. "Innovations in Deaf Studies: Critically Mapping the Field." *Innovations in Deaf Studies: The Role of Deaf Scholars*. Eds. Annelies Kusters, Maartje De Meulder, and Dai O'Brien. New York: Oxford University Press, 2017, 1–56.

Ladd, Paddy. *Understanding Deaf Culture: In Search of Deafhood*. Clevedon, England: Multilingual Matters, 2003.

Lander, Karen, and Cheryl Capek. "Investigating the Impact of Lip Visibility and Talking Style on Speechreading Performance." *Speech Communication* 55.5 (2013): 600–605.

Lane, Harlan. "Construction of Deafness." *The Disability Studies Reader*, 4th ed. Ed. Lennard J. Davis. New York: Routledge, 2013.

Lane, Harlan. "Constructions of Deafness." *Disability & Society*, 10.2 (1995): 171–190.

Lane, Harlan L. "Do Deaf People Have a Disability?" *Sign Language Studies* 2.4 (2002): 356–79.

Lane, Harlan L. *The Mask of Benevolence: Disabling the Deaf Community*. New York: Alfred Knopf, 1992.

Lane, Harlan, and Benjamin Bahan. "Ethics of Cochlear Implantation in Young Children: A Review and Reply from a DEAF-WORLD Perspective." *Otolaryngology—Head and Neck Surgery* 119.4 (1998): 297–313.

Lane, Harlan L., Robert Hoffmeister, and Ben Bahan. *A Journey into the Deaf-World*. San Diego: DawnSignPress, 1996.

Leach, Amanda. "Bulging Ear Drums and Hearing Loss: Aboriginal Kids have the Highest Otitis Media Rates in the World." *The Conversation*. September 16, 2016. https://thecon versation.com/bulging-ear-drums-and-405 hearing-loss-aboriginal-kids-have-the -highest-otitis-media-rates-in-the-world-64165 (Accessed 19 March 2021).

Leininger, Melissa, Tina Taylor Dyches, Mary Anne Prater, and Melissa Allen Heath. "Newbery Award Winning Books 1975–2009: How Do They Portray Disabilities?" *Education and Training in Autism and Developmental Disabilities* 45.4 (2010): 583–96.

Lerner, Miriam Nathan. "Narrative Function of Deafness and Deaf Characters in Film." *M/C Journal* 13.3 (2010). https://doi.org/10.5204/mcj.260

Levesque, Jack. "CBS Hurt Deaf Children with 'Caitlin's Story.'" In Lois Bragg (ed.), *Deaf World: A Historical Reader and Primary Source Book*. New York: New York University Press, 2001, 40–42.

LeZotte, Ann Clare. "Review: *Wonderstruck* by Brian Selznick." 2016. http://disabilityinkidlit .com/2016/12/02/review-wonderstruck-by-brian-selznick/

Li Yongle. "*Dangqian longsheng sixiangdaode zhuangkuang ji jiaoyu duice*" (The current moral state of deaf students and educational strategies). *The Science Education Article Collects* 2, 2011. http://www.cnki.com.cn/Article/CJFDTOTAL-KJWZ201102016.htm. Accessed on 15 December 2017.

Lindgren, Kristin A., Doreen DeLuca, and Donna Jo Napoli. *Signs and Voices: Deaf Culture, Identity, Language, and Arts.* Washington, DC: Gallaudet University Press, 2008.

Linton, Simi. *Claiming Disability: Knowledge and Identity: Cultural Front.* New York: NYU Press, 1998.

Luczak, Raymond. *Assembly Required: Notes from a Deaf Gay Life.* Alexandria, VA: RID Press, 2009.

Luczak, Raymond. *The Last Deaf Club in America.* Handtype Press, 2018.

Lukens, Rebecca J. *A Critical Handbook of Children's Literature* (5th ed.). New York: Harper Collins, 1995.

MacCann, Donnarae. "Editor's Introduction: Racism and Antiracism: Forty Years of Theories and Debates." *The Lion and the Unicorn* 25.3 (2001): 337–52.

Maher, John C. "'I'm Deaf. This is Sign. Get Used to It.' Sign Language in Japan: The Vision and the Struggle." *Civic Engagement in Contemporary Japan: Established and Emerging Repertoires.* New York: Springer-Verlag, 2010, 139–52.

Maples, Joellen, Katrina Arndt, and Julia M. White. "Re-Seeing *The Mighty*: Critically Examining One Film's Representations of Disability in the English Classroom." *The English Journal* 100.2 (2010): 77–85.

Margolin, Uri. "Cognitive Science, the Thinking Mind, and Literary Narrative" in David Herman (ed.) *Narrative Theory and the Cognitive Sciences.* Stanford: Center for the Study of Language and Information, 2003: 271–94.

Martin, Paul, and Patrick Bateson. *Measuring Behaviour: An Introductory Guide.* Cambridge: Cambridge University Press, 2007.

Matos, Angel Daniel. "'Without a Word or Sign': Enmeshing Deaf and Gay Identity." *Lessons in Disability.* Ed. Jacob Stratman. Jefferson, North Carolina: McFarland, 2016, 221–43.

McCarthey, Sarah J. and Elizabeth Birr Moje. "Identity Matters." *Reading Research Quarterly* 37.2 (2002): 228–38.

McAvoy, Audrey. "Hawaii Sign Language Found to Be Distinct Language. *U.S. News,* 1 March 2013. https://www.usnews.com/news/us/articles/2013/03/01/hawaii-sign-language-found-to-be-distinct-language. Accessed on 8 March 2018.

McDonald, Donna. *HEARSAY: How Stories about Deafness and Deaf People are Told.* PhD thesis, Griffith University, Australia, 2011.

McDonald, Donna. "Not Silent, Invisible: Literature's Chance Encounters with Deaf Heroes/Heroines." *American Annals of the Deaf* 154: 2 (2010): 463–70.

McClintock, Jonathan. "The Success of Soft Multiculturalism." *Spectator Australia.* (2017 January 2). Retrieved from https://www.spectator.com.au/2017/01/success-soft-multiculturalism/

McCloud, Scott. *Reinventing Comics: How Imagination and Technology are Revolutionizing an Art Form.* New York: HarperCollins, 2000.

McCloud, Scott. *Understanding Comics: The Invisible Art.* New York: Harper, 1993.

McGrail, Ewa, and Alicja Rieger. "Humor in Literature about Children with Disability: What Are We Seeing in Literature?" *The Educational Forum* 78.3 (2014): 291–304.

McKee, David, and Graeme Kennedy. "Lexical Comparison of Signs from American, Australian, British, and New Zealand Sign Languages." *The Signs of Language Revisited.* Eds. Karen Emmorey and Harlan L. Lane. Mahwah, NJ: Lawrence Erlbaum, 2014 [2000], 43–73.

McRuer, Robert. "Compulsory Able-Bodiedness and Queer/Disabled Experience." *The Disability Studies Reader,* 4th ed. Ed. Lennard J. Davis. New York: Routledge, 2013 [1995], 369–80.

McRuer, Robert. *Crip Theory: Cultural Signs of Queerness and Disability*. New York: NYU Press, 2006.

Mertens, Donna M. "Social Experiences of Hearing-Impaired High School Youth," *American Annals of the Deaf* 134.1 (1989): 15–19.

Micu, Patrik. "Artisternas ilska—bryter med H&M efter barnbilden." *Expressen* 12 January 2018. https://www.expressen.se/noje/artisternas-stora-ilska-mot-hochm-efter-bilden/. Accessed on 12 January 2018.

Mitchell, David T., and Sharon L. Snyder. *Narrative Prosthesis: Disability and the Dependencies of Discourse*. Ann Arbor: University of Michigan Press, 2001.

Molaro, Christian. "Education morale et éducation corporelle des jeunes des classes pauvres au XIXᵉ siècle. Entre conceptions théoriques et organisation sociale." *Revue d'histoire de l'enfance «irrégulière»*. Le Temps de l'histoire 8 (2006): 19–35.

Morales, Rodney. "Literature." *Multicultural Hawaii: The Fabric of a Multiethnic Society*. Ed. Michael Haas. New York: Garland, 1998. 107–29.

Morioka, Masahiro. "A Phenomenological Study of 'Herbivore Men.'" *The Review of Life Studies*. Life Studies Press 4 (2013): 1–20.

Morrell, Ernest, and Jodene Morell. "Multicultural Readings of Multicultural Literature and the Promotion of Social Awareness in ELA Classrooms." *New England Reading Association Journal* 47.2 (2012): 10–16.

Morris, Jenny. "A Feminist Perspective." *Framed: Interrogating Disability in the Media*. Eds. Ann Pointon and Chris Davies. London: BFI, 1997: 21–30.

Mow, Shanny. "How Do You Dance without Music?" In Sherman Wilcox (ed.), *American Deaf Culture: An Anthology*. Silver Spring, MD: Linstok, 1989, 33–44.

Muller, Vivienne. "Constituting Christopher: Disability Theory and Mark Haddon's *The Curious Incident of the Dog in the Night-Time.*" *Papers: Explorations into Children's Literature* 16.2 (2006): 118–25.

Myers, Shirley Shultz, and Jane K. Fernandes. "Deaf Studies: A Critique of the Predominant U.S Direction." *Journal of Deaf Studies and Deaf Education* 15.1 (2010): 30–49.

Nakamura, Karen. *Deaf in Japan: Signing and the Politics of Identity*. Cornell University Press, 2006.

Neithardt, Leigh A. *Disability Studies: Defining "Disability," Describing the Field, and Dismantling the "Overcoming Narrative."* Unpublished manuscript, Department of Teaching and Learning, Ohio State University, Columbus, Ohio, 2014.

Nodelman, Perry. *Alternating Narratives in Fiction for Young Readers—Twice Upon a Time* (1st ed.). New York: Palgrave Macmillan, 2017.

Norden, Martin. *The Cinema of Isolation: A History of Physical Disability in the Movies*. New Brunswick: Rutgers University Press, 1994.

NSW Education. "What Are Opportunity Classes?" 2021. https://education.nsw.gov.au/public-schools/selective-high-schools-and-opportunity-classes/year-5/what-are-opportunity-classes (Accessed 28 March 2021).

Oatley, Keith. "Theory of Mind and Theory of Mind in Literature." *Theory of Mind and Literature*. Eds. Paula Leverage, Howard Mancing, Richard Schwerckert, and William Marston. Indiana: Purdue University Press, 2014, 13–26.

Orosan-Weine, Pamela. "*The Swan*: The Fantasy of Transformation versus the Reality of Growth." *Configurations* 15.1 (2007): 17–32.

Padden, Carol. "The Deaf Community and the Culture of Deaf People." *Sign Language and the Deaf Community*. Eds. Charlotte Baker and Robbin Battison. Silver Spring, MD: National Association of the Deaf, 1980, 89–103.

Padden, Carol A. "Talking Culture: Deaf People and Disability Studies." *PMLA* 120.2 (2005): 508–13.

Padden, Carol, and Tom Humphries. *Inside Deaf Culture*. Cambridge, MA: Harvard University Press, 2005.

Padden, Carol, and Tom Humphries. *Deaf in America: Voices from a Culture*. Cambridge, MA: Harvard University Press, 1988.

Pajka, Sharon. "Deaf Characters in Adolescent Literature: A Collection of Adolescent Books with Deaf Characters, Websites, Author Interviews and Book Reviews." http://pajka.blog spot.com/

Pajka-West, Sharon. "Representations of Deafness and Deaf People in Young Adult Fiction." *M/C Journal* 13.3 (2010).

Palmer, Alan. *Fictional Minds*. Lincoln: University of Nebraska Press, 2008.

Parasnis, Ila (ed.). *Cultural and Language Diversity and the Deaf Experience*. New York: Cambridge University Press, 1996.

Pattee, Amy. "Between Youth and Adulthood: Young Adult and New Adultliterature." *Children's Literature Association Quarterly* 42.2 (2017): 218–30.

Perlin, Ross. "The Race to Save a Dying Language." *The Guardian*, 10 August 2016. https://www.theguardian.com/news/2016/aug/10/race-to-save-hawaii-sign-language. Accessed on 20 November 2017.

Peters, Cynthia. *Deaf American Literature: From Carnival to the Canon*. Washington, DC: Gallaudet University Press, 2000.

Pidgin: The Voice of Hawai'i. DVD. Marlene Booth and Kanalu Young. Harriman, New York: New Day Films, 2009.

Pollard, Scott. "Introduction: The Art of Our Art, the Quirkiness of Our Forms." *Children's Literature Association Quarterly* 38.3 (2013): 263–66.

Postema, Barbara. "Draw a Thousand Words: Signification and Narration in Comics Images." *International Journal of Comic Art* 9.1 (2007): 487–501.

Pray, Janet L., and I. King Jordan. "The Deaf Community and Culture at a Crossroads: Issues and Challenges." *Journal of Social Work in Disability & Rehabilitation*, 9.2–3 (2010): 168–93.

Propes, Richard. *The Independent Critic*. http://theindependentcritic.com/no_ordinary_hero_the_superdeafy_movie. Accessed on 4th February 2018.

Propp, Vladimir. *Morphologie du conte*: suivi de « Les transformations des contes merveilleux ». Paris: Seuil, 1970.

Rendall, Drew, and Michael J. Owren. "Communication without Meaning or Information: Abandoning Language-based and Informational Constructs in Animal Communication Theory." *Animal Communication Theory: Information and Influence*. Ed. Ulrich E. Stegman. Cambridge: Cambridge University Press, 2013, 151–88.

Resene, Michelle. "A 'Curious Incident': Representations of Autism in Children's Detective Fiction." *The Lion and the Unicorn* 40.1 (2016): 81–99.

Rice, Carla, Eliza Chandler, Elisabeth Harrison, Kirsty Liddiard, and Manuela Ferrari. "Project Re-Vision: Disability at the Edges of Representation." *Disability and Society* 30. 4 (2015): 513–27.

Rich, Adrienne. "Compulsory Heterosexuality and Lesbian Existence." *Powers of Desire: The Politics of Sexuality*. Ed. Ann Snitow, Christine Stansell, and Sharon Thompson. New York: Monthly Review Press, 1983, 177–205.

Rieger, Alicja, and Ewa McGrail. "Exploring Children's Literature with Authentic Representations of Disability." *Kappa Delta Pi Record* 51. 1 (2015): 18–23.

Robbins, Hollis. "The Emperor's New Critique." *New Literary History* 34.4 (2003): 659–75.

Romaine, Suzanne. "Hawai'i Creole English as a Literary Language." *Language in Society* 23.4 (1994): 527–54.

Rosenblum, Gianine, and Michael Lewis. "Emotional Development in Adolescence." In *Blackwell Handbook of Adolescence*. Ed. Gerald R. Adams and Michael Berzonsky. Oxford: Blackwell, 2003, 269–89.

Rubin, Ellen, and Emily Strauss Watson. "Disability Bias in Children's Literature." *The Lion and the Unicorn* 11.1 (1987): 60–67.

Rudman, Masha Kabakow. *Children's Literature: An Issues Approach* (3rd ed.). White Plains, NY: Longman, 1995.

Safran, Stephen. "Movie Images of Disability and War: Framing History and Political Ideology." *Remedial and Special Education* 22.4 (2001): 223–32.

Sakoda, Kent, and Jeff Siegel. *Pidgin Grammar: An Introduction to the Creole Language of Hawai'i*. Honolulu: Bess Press, 2003.

Salas, Rachel G., Frank Lucido, and JoAnn Canales. *Multicultural Literature: Broadening Young Children's Experiences*. (Report No. ED-468 866). Texas A&M Early Childhood Development Center, 2002.

Sanchez, Rebecca. *Deafening Modernism, Embodied Language and Visual Poetics in American Literature*. New York: NYU Press, 2015.

Sandahl, Carrie. "Queering the Crip or Cripping the Queer?: Intersections of Queer and Crip Identities in Solo Autobiographical Performance." *GLQ: A Journal of Lesbian and Gay Studies* 9.1 (2003): 25–56.

Sato, Charlene. "Language Change in a Creole Continuum: Decreolization?" *Progression and Regression in Language: Sociocultural, Neuropsychological, and Linguistic Perspectives*. Eds. Kenneth Hystenstam and Ake Viberg. New York: Cambridge University Press, 1993, 122–43.

Sato, Charlene. "Sociolinguistic Variation and Language Attitudes in Hawaii." *English Around the World: Sociolinguistic Perspectives*. Ed. Jenny Cheshire. New York: Cambridge University Press, 1991, 647–63.

Saunders, Kathy. "What Disability Studies Can Do for Children's Literature." *Disability Studies Quarterly* 24.1 (2004): 1–11.

Sava, Oliver. "*Hawkeye* #19 Uses Deafness to Help a Broken Clint Barton Find His Voice" *A.V. Club*, 1 August 2014.

Schank, Roger C., and Robert P. Abelson. *Scripts, Plans, Goals, and Understanding: An Inquiry into Human Knowledge Structures*. Hillsdale, NJ: Lawrence Erlbaum, 1977.

Searls, Susan C., and David R. Johnson. "Growing up Deaf in Deaf Families: Two Different Experiences." In Ila Parasnis (ed.), *Cultural and Language Diversity and the Deaf Experience*. New York: Cambridge University Press, 1996, 201-224.

Selleck, Morgan A., and Robert Thayer Sataloff. "The Impact of the Auditory System on Phonation: A Review." *Journal of Voice* 28.6 (2014): 688–93.

Sengas, Richard J., and Leila Monaghan. "Signs of their Times: Deaf Communities and the Culture of Language." *Annual Review of Anthropology* 3:1 (2002): 69–97.

Shen, Dan. "Unreliability," paragraph 2. In Peter Hühn et al. (eds.). *The Living Handbook of Narratology*. Hamburg: Hamburg University Press.

Shettleworth, Sara. J. *Fundamentals of Comparative Cognition*. New York: Oxford University Press, 2013.

Shioshita, Joy. "Beyond Good Intention: Selecting Multicultural Literature." *Children's Advocate* (a newsletter published by Action Alliance for Children), September/October 1997.

Reprinted at: https://www.leeandlow.com/educators/race/beyond-good-intention
-selecting-multicultural-literature

Siebers, Tobin. *Disability Theory*. Ann Arbor: University of Michigan Press, 2008.

Silva, Roberta. "Representing Adolescent Fears: Theory of Mind and Fantasy Fiction." *International Research in Children's Literature* 6.2 (2013): 161–75.

Sims Bishop, Rudine. "Mirrors, Windows, and Sliding Glass Doors." *Perspectives: Choosing and Using Books for the Classroom* 6.3 (1990): ix–xi.

Singer, Margot, and Nicole Walker. *Bending Genre: Essays on Creative Nonfiction*. New York: Bloomsbury, 2013.

Skelton, Tracey, and Gill Valentine. "'It's My Umbilical Cord to the World . . . The Internet': d/ Deaf and Hard of Hearing People's Information and Communication Practices." *Towards Enabling Geographies: 'Disabled' Bodies and Minds in Society and Space*. Eds. Vera Chouinard, Edward Hall, and Robert Wilton. New York: Ashgate, 2010, 85–106.

Sleeter, Christine E., and Carl A. Grant. *Making Choices for Multicultural Education: Five Approaches to Race, Class, and Gender* (3rd ed.). New York: Merrill, 1999.

Smith, Vivion, ed. "Laurent Clerc." *Gallaudet University*. http://www.gallaudet.edu/tutorial
-and-instructional-programs/english-center/reading-english-as-second-language/
practice-exercises/laurent-clerc. Accessed on 15 January 2018.

Sparrow, Robert. "Implants and Ethnocide: Learning from the Cochlear Implant Controversy." *Disability & Society* 25.4 (2010): 455–66.

Staff Reviews, Youth. "Window into Deaf Culture Leaves Hands Full of Reflections." *The Hawaii State Theatre Council Presents Hitting the Stage*, 19 October 2016. http://hittingth
estage.com/home/2016/10/19/window-into-deaf-culture-leaves-hands-full-of-reflections.
Accessed on 30 January 2018.

Stephens, John. "Cognitive Maps and Social Ecology in Young Adult Fiction." *International Research in Children's Literature* 8.2 (2015): 142–55.

Stephens, John. *Language and Ideology in Children's Fiction*. London and New York: Longman, 1992.

Stephens, John. "Narratology." *The Routledge Companion to Children's Literature*. Ed. David Rudd. London and New York: Routledge, 2010, 51–62.

Stephens, John. "Schemas and Scripts: Cognitive Instruments and the representation of Cultural Diversity in Children's Literature." Eds. Kerry Mallan and Clare Bradford *Contemporary Children's Literature and Film: Engaging with Theory*. London: Palgrave Macmillan, 2011, 12–35.

Stevens, Carolyn S. *Disability in Japan*. New York: Routledge, 2013.

Stibbe, Arran. "Disability, Gender and Power in Japanese Television Drama." *Japan Forum*, Volume 16.1 (2004): 21–36.

Strickland, Ashley. "A Brief History of Young Adult Literature." *CNN* 2015. https://edition
.cnn.com/2013/10/15/living/young-adult-fiction-evolution/index.html. Accessed on 5 November 2018.

Style, Emily. "Curriculum as Window and Mirror." *Listening for All Voices: Gender-Balancing the School Curriculum*. Eds. Emily Style and Peggy McIntoch. Summit, NJ: Oak Knoll School Monograph, 1988. https://nationalseedproject.org/Key-SEED-Texts/
curriculum-as-window-and-mirror.

Suh, Myung-Whan, Hyo-Jeong Lee, Jun Sic Kim, Chun Kee Chung, and Seung-Ha Oh. "Speech Experience Shapes the Speechreading Network and Subsequent Deafness Facilitates It." *Brain* 132.10 (2009): 2761–71.

Sumida, Stephen H. *And the View from the Shore: Literary Traditions of Hawaii.* Seattle: University of Washington Press, 1991.

Supalla, Samuel J., and Jody H. Cripps. "Toward Universal Design in Reading Instruction." *Bilingual Basics* 12.2 (2011): 1–13.

Supalla, Samuel J., Jody H. Cripps, and Andrew P. J. Byrne. "Why American Sign Language Gloss Must Matter." *American Annals of the Deaf* 161.5 (2017): 540–51.

Sutton-Spence, Rachel. "The Role of Sign Language Narratives in Developing Identity for Deaf Children." *Journal of Folklore Research* 47.3 (2010): 265–305.

Sutton-Spence, Rachel, and Donna West. "Negotiating the Legacy of Hearingness." *Qualitative Inquiry* 17.5 (2011): 422–32.

Tanigawa, Noe. "Hawai'i Sign Language Still Whispers." Hawai'i Public Radio. 22 November 2016. http://hawaiipublicradio.org/post/hawai-i-sign-language-still-whispers. Accessed on 8 March 2018.

Taylor-Gooby, Peter, and Edmund Waite. *From Stronger to Weaker Multi-Culturalism? How the UK Policy Community Sees the Future of Ethnic Diversity Policies.* 2014. Retrieved from https://kar.kent.ac.uk/38883/

Thoutenhooftd, Ernst. "Philosophy's Real World Consequences for Deaf People: Thoughts on Iconicity, Sign Language and Being Deaf." *Human Studies* 23:3 (2000): 261–79.

Travis, Ben, and Chris Hewitt. "Thirteen Things We Learned about *A Quiet Place* from John Krasinski." 2018. https://www.empireonline.com/movies/features/13-secrets-learned -quiet-place-john-krasinski/ Accessed: April 25, 2019.

Tribunella, Eric. "Children's Literature and the Child Flâneur." *Children's Literature* 38 (2010): 64–91.

University of Hawai'i at Mānoa. "Research Team Discovers Existence of Hawai'i Sign Language." 1 March 2013. https://manoa.hawaii.edu/news/article.php?aId=5600. Accessed on January 9, 2018.

Valentine, James. "Disabled Discourse: Hearing Accounts of Deafness Constructed through Japanese Television and Film." *Disability & Society* 16.5 (2001): 707–27.

Valet, Alexy. "About Inclusive Participation in Sport: Cultural Desirability and Technical Obstacles." *Sport in Society* 21:1 (2018): 137–51.

Van Cleve, John Vickrey, and Barry A. Crouch. *A Place of Their Own: Creating the Deaf Community in America.* Washington, D. C. : Gallaudet University Press, 1989.

Wang Cai. "*Longxiao sixiangpinde jiaoyu de hexin*" (The key to moral education in schools for the deaf). *Shanxi jiaoyu* (Shangxi Education) 63 (2010). DOI: 10.16773/j.cnki.1002 -2058.2010.z1.182. Accessed 15 December 2017.

Warhol, Robyn. "The Space Between: A Narrative Approach to Alison Bechdel's *Fun Home.*" *College Literature*, 38.3 (2011): 1–20.

Webb, Jean. "Health and Sickness." *The Edinburgh Companion to Children's Literature.* Eds. Clémentine Beauvais and Maria Nikolajeva. Edinburgh: Edinburgh University Press, 2017, 281–88.

Welch, Olga M. "Building a Multicultural Curriculum: Issues and Dilemmas." In Kathee Christensen (ed.), *Deaf Plus: A Multicultural Perspective.* San Diego: Dawn Sign Press, 2000, 1–28.

Whannel, Garry. "Winning and Losing Respect: Narratives of Identity in Sport Films." *Sport in Society* 11.2/3 (2008): 195–208.

Wheeler, Elizabeth D. A. "No Monsters in This Fairy Tale: *Wonder* and the New Children's Literature." *Children's Literature Association Quarterly* 38.3 (2013): 335–50.

Whiteman, Gail, and Nelson Phillips. "The Role of Narrative Fiction and Semi-Fiction in Organizational Studies." *The SAGE Handbook of New Approaches in Management and Organization*. Eds. Barry Daved and Hans Hansen. California: Sage, 2008, 288–300.

Wing, George. "The Associative Feature in the Education of the Deaf." In Lois Bragg (ed.), *Deaf World: A Historical Reader and Primary Source Book*. New York: NYU Press, 2001, 165–74.

Wood, Naomi. "The Ugly Duckling's Legacy: Adulteration, Contemporary Fantasy, and the Dark." *Marvels & Tales* 20.2 (2006): 193–207.

Woodward, James C. "Implications for Sociolinguistic Research among the Deaf." *Sign Language Studies* 1 (1972): 1–7.

Woolfe, Tyron, Stephen C. Want, and Michael Siegal. "Signposts to Development: Theory of Mind in Deaf Children." *Child Development* 73.3 (2002): 768–78.

Wrigley, Owen. *The Politics of Deafness*. Washington, DC: Gallaudet University Press, 1996.

Yadegarfard, Mohammadrasool, Mallika E. Meinhold-Bergmann, and Robert Ho. "Family Rejection, Social Isolation, and Loneliness as Predictors of Negative Health Outcomes (Depression, Suicidal Ideation, and Sexual Risk Behavior) among Thai Male-to-Female Transgender Adolescents." *Journal of LGBT Youth* 11 (2014): 347–63.

Yang, Hanlin, and Hongbo Wang. "Special Education in China." *Journal of Special Education* 28.1 (1994): 93–105.

Ye Shengtao (under the name of Ye Shaojun). "*Wenyi tan*" (On literature and art) [1921]. Republished in *Ye Shengtao lun chuangzuo* (Ye Shengtao on literary creation). Shanghai: Shanghai wenyi chubanshe, 1982.

Yoon, Bogum, Anne Simpson, and Claudia Haag. "Assimilation Ideology: Critically Examining Underlying Messages in Multicultural Literature." *Journal of Adolescent & Adult Literacy* 54.2 (2010): 109–18.

Young, Morris. *Minor Re/Visions: Asian American Literacy Narratives as a Rhetoric of Citizenship*. Carbondale: Southern Illinois University Press, 2004.

Zunshine, Lisa. "Theory of Mind and Fictions of Embodied Transparency." *Theory of Mind and Literature*. Eds. Paula Leverage, Howard Mancing, Richard Schwerckert, and William Marston. Indiana: Purdue University Press, 2014, 63–91.

Zunshine, Lisa. *Why We Read Fiction: Theory of Mind and the Novel*. Columbus: Ohio State University Press, 2006.

About the Contributors

Cynthia Neese Bailes is professor emerita at Gallaudet University, where she is a member of the board of trustees. She has served at Gallaudet since 1979, first as a teacher at the Model Secondary School for the Deaf, of which she was principal for five years, and later joined Gallaudet's Department of Education, which she chaired from 2007 to 2010. She has long been involved with the university's bilingual efforts, infusing ASL/English bilingualism in her teaching and research and participating in various university-wide efforts to promote the university's bilingual mission. Her publications include coauthorship of the longitudinal project *Rita: A Case Study in ASL/English Acquisition, Learning, and Literacy.*

Nina Benegas is a high-school English teacher at Alliance Marc and Eva Stern Math and Science School in East Los Angeles and a part-time lecturer in the First-Year Seminar Program at Loyola Marymount University. She earned her bachelor's degree from the College of the Holy Cross, where she studied American Sign Language, deaf studies, and rhetoric and composition under Drs. John Pirone and Patricia Bizzell. She completed her master's degree at Loyola Marymount University, where she wrote her thesis on translingual rhetorical analysis and composition pedagogy. She has presented her research at such conferences as the Italian Association of North American Studies and the National Council of Teachers of English.

Lijun Bi is a lecturer at Monash University, Australia. After early study at Nanjing Normal University, she completed a doctorate at the University of Melbourne in which she identified and documented the role of moral-political education in early modern Chinese children's literature and its link to the nationalist sentiment. A specialist in Chinese children's literature, she is the author of *Chinese*

Children's Literature in the 20th Century: Its Political and Moral Themes and has published articles on the social role of children's books in China. Lijun has also built a strong nexus between her teaching practice and her research interests in pedagogy, especially the experiential interactive and cooperative learning approach. Her other research interests include moral education in China and Chinese intellectual history.

Hélène Charderon joined Mary Immaculate College, University of Limerick, Ireland, in 2016, where she graduated with her PhD in 2020. She is interested in, has published articles on, and presented at national and international conferences about nineteenth-century French children's literature. Her publications can be found in *L'enfant dans la littérature d'expression française et francophone Études rassemblées et présentées par Anna Ledwina* (Wydawnictwo Uniwersytetu Opolskiego, Opole 2019) and *Cahiers George Sand* 2019. Her research pertains to the representations of children in nineteenth- and twentieth-century French and English literature. She is particularly interested in the relation between text and ideology, and in the implication of children's literature in contemporary social debates.

Stuart Ching is an associate professor in the English Department at Loyola Marymount University, where he serves as associate chairperson and teaches courses on children's literature, linguistics, creative writing, and rhetoric and composition. His articles on multicultural children's literature, cross-cultural issues in writing instruction, and language diversity in schools have appeared in *Language Arts*, the *New Advocate*, *English Journal*, and *International Research in Children's Literature*, as well as in collections such as *The Subject Is Story* and *Representations: Doing Asian American Rhetoric*. His fiction has appeared in the anthologies *Growing Up Local: An Anthology of Poetry and Prose from Hawaii*, *The Best of Honolulu Fiction*, and *A Voice for Earth: American Writers Respond to the Earth Charter*.

Helene Ehriander is a professor in comparative literature and research leader of the Centre for Childhood Research in Literature, Language and Learning (CHILLL) at the Linnæus University, Växjö, Sweden. She defended her thesis on *Humanism and the View on History in Kai Söderhjelm's Historical Novels for Children and Young People*, in Comparative Literature at the University of Lund in 2003. She has recently published research on Astrid Lindgren, steampunk for young adults, the historical novel for young readers and creative writing. Ehriander was the project leader of the Linnaeus University project "The Book Dog and Astrid Lindgren," 2013–2016, and she has continued research concerning book dogs since the project ended. She is a member of Linnæus University Centre for Intermedial and Multimodal Studies (IMS).

Xiangshu Fang is a senior lecturer at the School of Humanities and Social Sciences of Deakin University, Australia. He received his PhD from the University of Melbourne. A linguist by background, Xiangshu's main research interests now include Confucianism and Chinese intellectual history, focusing on the enduring legacies of the past-in-the-present. He has published on moral and political education in China.

Sara Kersten-Parrish is an assistant professor of literacy education in the Department of Education and School Psychology at John Carroll University, Cleveland, Ohio. She gained a PhD in literature for children and young adults at the Ohio State University in 2016. Her publications have appeared in journals such as *Children's Literature in Education, International Journal of Qualitative Studies in Education*, the *English Journal, Literacy Research and Instruction*, and the *Reading Teacher*. Her research centers on concepts of multiliteracies and multimodality with preservice teachers and elementary-aged children. She uses qualitative methods to explore how children and preservice teachers use multiliteracies pedagogies and multimodal texts, such as nonfiction, graphic novels, picture books, and board games to expand understandings of literacy. She also pursues autoethnographic work on deafness in research and academic spaces.

Helen Kilpatrick is senior lecturer in Japanese at the University of Wollongong, Australia. She is the author of *Miyazawa Kenji and his Illustrators* (Brill 2013) and several articles on Japanese literature and art for young people on topics such as the Fukushima triple disaster, the *shōjo*, (de-)constructions of the nation state in the fantasy of Uehashi Nahoko, and Buddhism and transculturalism in the work of Miyazawa Kenji. Awards include the 2013 Inoue Yasushi Award for Outstanding Research on Japanese Literature in Australasia and the 2016 International Prize for Outstanding Contribution to Japanese Children's Literature from the Children's Literature Association. Her research interests are in constructions of gender, interculturality, and ecology in modern Japanese literature, film, and visual art.

Jessica Kirkness holds a PhD in research and creative writing from the Department of Media, Music, Communication and Cultural Studies at Macquarie University, Australia, where she teaches nonfiction writing and cultural studies. Her current research is focused on the relationship between deafness, literature, and music. As a grandchild of two deaf adults, Jessica's lived experience and interaction with deafness significantly informs her work. As part of her creative practice PhD, Jessica wrote a memoir that explores the nuances of interactions across the "hearing line"—the invisible boundary between the deaf and the hearing. Her writing has appeared in *Meanjin Quarterly*.

Sung-Ae Lee is a lecturer in Asian studies in the Department of International Studies at Macquarie University, Sydney, Australia. Her major research focus is on fiction, film, and television drama of East Asia, with particular attention to Korea. Her research centers on relationships between cultural ideologies in Asian societies and representational strategies. She is interested in cognitive and imagological approaches to adaptation studies, Asian popular culture, Trauma Studies, fiction, and film produced in the aftermath of the Korean War, and the literature and popular media of the Korean diaspora. Her work has appeared in *Adaptation, Asian Ethnology, Children's Literature in Education, Diaspora, International Research in Children's Literature, Journal of Asian American Studies, Mosaic,* and in essay collections such as *Grimms' Tales Around the Globe, Fairy Tale Films Beyond Disney, The Fairy Tale World,* and *The Palgrave Handbook of Children's Film and Television*.

Jann Pataray-Ching joined California State Polytechnic University, Pomona, in 2001. She received her PhD from Indiana University, Bloomington, in curriculum, language, and literacy. She is interested in, has published articles on, and presented at national and international conferences on multiple-ways-of-knowing inquiry curricula, literacy education, and children's and adolescent Asian-American and Hawaii-Pacific literature. Her publications can be found in *The Routledge Companion to International Children's Literature, Language Arts Journal, Educational Forum, Early Childhood Education Journal,* and *New Advocate*. She has taught literacy education courses in the teacher-credential program and numerous master's courses in the Curriculum and Instruction Program, and she chairs master's and doctoral committees. She is the program coordinator of the Curriculum and Instruction Program and chairperson of the Education Department.

Angela Schill is an associate professor at Utah Valley University. Her research interests focus on cognitive and multicultural studies, from which she seeks to develop models for analyzing representations of disabled people. She argues that misrepresentations have greatly affected society's view of the disabled community and other alterities and is committed to further exploring this potential impact and its implications.

Josh Simpson holds a PhD from the University of Strathclyde in Scotland. His research focuses on queer voices and human rights in children's and young adult literature. He is a cofounder of Researchers Exploring Inclusive Youth Literature, a network dedicated to the study and promotion of inclusive and diverse youth literature. In 2018 he was appointed assistant executive editor of *International Research in Children's Literature*.

John Stephens is a former president of the International Research Society for Children's Literature and foundation editor of *International Research in Children's Literature* (2008–2016). In 2007 he received the 11th International Brothers Grimm Award and in 2013 the Anne Deveraux Jordan Award, both given to recognize significant contributions to the field of children's literature in scholarship and service. He is author of *Language and Ideology in Children's Fiction*; *Retelling Stories, Framing Culture* (with Robyn McCallum); and *New World Orders in Contemporary Children's Literature* (with Clare Bradford, Kerry Mallan, and Robyn McCallum). He edited *Ways of Being Male: Representing Masculinities in Children's Fiction and Film*; *Subjectivity in Asian Children's Literature and Film*; and *The Routledge Companion to International Children's Literature*. He has also authored over a hundred articles.

Corinne Walsh currently holds a postdoctoral position in the Centre for Aboriginal Economic Policy Research (CAEPR) at the Australian National University, working in a project to explore why Indigenous people with disability and their carers, families, and communities might not be accessing services. Corinne has a PhD from ANU, for which she carried out a community-based/ethnographic analysis of middle ear disease (otitis media) and hearing loss, with the Aboriginal community of Yarrabah in Far North Queensland as the case-study site. Having a mild to profound, binaural, sensorineural hearing loss herself since infancy, Corinne has very personal, lived experience with this topic. Corinne was awarded the Libby Harricks Award in July 2020 from Hearing Matters Australia, which recognizes someone with hearing loss who has managed to achieve academically and personally despite their impairment.

Nerida Wayland is an educator at the Lindfield Learning Village in Sydney, Australia. Her qualifications include a master of arts in children's literature and a PhD in English from Macquarie University, Australia. Her research explores the function of humor in texts for young people and examines the power of comedy to interrogate normative social ideologies: primarily by highlighting the ideological silences, subject matter, and subject positions that have traditionally been marginalized, absent, and considered taboo. She has previously been published in *Jeunesse: Young People, Texts and Cultures*.

Vivian Yenika-Agbaw (1959–2021) was professor of literature and literacy at the Pennsylvania State University, University Park, where she taught undergraduate and graduate courses in children's and adolescent literature. She is the author of *Representing Africa in Children's Books: Old and New Ways of Seeing*, author/coauthor of over seventy articles and book chapters, coeditor of the *Journal of Children's Literature* (2019–2021), and an IRSCL board member (2017–2019). She also coedited *African Youth in Contemporary Literature and Popular Culture: Identity Quest* (with Linda Mhando); and *Using Nonfiction for Civic Engagement in Classrooms: Critical Approaches* (with Ruth McKoy Lowery and Paul Ricks). Yenika-Agbaw also reviewed manuscripts for *Children's Literature in Education*, *Children's Literature*, the *Lion and the Unicorn*, and *Marvels & Tales: Journal of Fairy-tale Studies*.

Index

CPSIA information can be obtained
at www.ICGtesting.com
Printed in the USA
BVHW040859211122
652364BV00007B/4